Advance Praise for
Hidden Politics in the UN Sustainable Development Goals

"This book is a tremendous learning tool. Each of the seventeen SDGs is subjected to a sharp critical analysis that will spark debate and provide readers with the resources needed to begin their own research and reach their own conclusions. Highly recommended."

— CRAIG N. MURPHY, professor emeritus, Wellesley College

"With striking originality, Adam Sneyd tears down the façade of the UN Sustainable Development Goals. Who, you might ask, does not want to end poverty and hunger? Who isn't for peace, justice, and a healthy planet? Yet, as this spirited, inspiring book exposes, the Global Goals are doing more to legitimize a destructive and exploitative world order than truly advance global sustainability."

— PETER DAUVERGNE, professor of International Relations, University of British Columbia

"This is a must-read for anyone interested in understanding the limits of the UN Sustainable Development Goals. Deploying a critical political economy lens, Sneyd does a brilliant job in dispelling the myths around these powerful benchmarks in global development."

— SUSANNE SOEDERBERG, professor and Canada Research Chair, Queen's University

"Big business has long embraced the SDGs and Sneyd brilliantly lays out why that is. The SDGs do nothing to confront the structural enablers of corporate power, greed and impunity, or to put an end to tax dodging and union busting. This book puts a decisive end to the fiction that corporate-driven partnerships under the SDGs will end overconsumption and help us to realize the Brundtland Commission's vision for truly sustainable development."

— DR. MARIA HENGEVELD, Corporate Researcher, SOMO, Amsterdam

"This book is a concise, well-written, and impactful critique of the UN Sustainable Development Goals from the perspective of critical international political economy. I think a wide range of readers will enjoy it."

— JESSE OVADIA, associate professor, political science, University of Windsor

"From the very beginning, the Sustainable Development Goals were compromised. Far from reflecting the universal aspirations of the people of this planet, the non-binding character of the SDGs means that its targets were technocratic rather than being transformational. As a result, they did not confront the complex crises facing global civil society. Rather, they sought to maintain the power relations at a global, national and local level which were and are the fulcrum through which the SDGs were shaped, launched, and implemented, to a greater or lesser degree, by states since 2015. In a book that will be welcomed by academics, students, policy-makers and advocates alike, Adam Sneyd's *Hidden Politics in the Sustainable Development Goals* explains how and why this took place, and demonstrates why it is necessary to challenge the dominant social forces that shape how our planet is changing. An important and outstanding contribution."

— **A. HAROON AKRAM-LODHI**, professor of economics, global justice and development, Trent University

"In *Hidden Politics in the UN Sustainable Development Goals*, Adam Sneyd unveils the political undercurrents shaping the ambitious agenda of the Sustainable Development Goals (SDGs). This pivotal work in Critical Development Studies exposes how the SDGs, while aimed at sustainable global development, are entangled in political strategies that reinforce the existing liberal international economic order, perpetuate global capitalism, and sustain the status quo. This book stands out for placing the politics of sustainable development at its core, challenging the reader to rethink the global order and the role of the SDGs within it. By linking the goals to broader political agendas and highlighting the emerging ideological conflicts, Sneyd contributes to a more nuanced understanding of global politics. This book is not just a critique but a call to action, urging for a fundamental rethinking of the goals to achieve genuine transformative change."

— **DR. BONNY IBHAWOH**, professor of Global Human Rights, McMaster University and UN Independent Expert on the Right to Development

"The Sustainable Development Goals promised a new era of cooperation and prosperity. What happened? As the liberal order crumbles around us, Sneyd uncovers the hidden politics of UN goal-setting and shows how our institutions of global governance badly miscalculated the destabilizing effects of war, authoritarian populism and catastrophic climate collapse. This book is a must-read."

— **MARC FROESE**, professor of political science, Burman University

"This analysis is a powerful counterpunch to the feel good assumptions of the Sustainable Development Goals. Sneyd (and Schneider) stress test the goals in a way so that scholars and practitioners alike can see where further inequities and injustices will emerge, even if we succeed at achieving the Global Goals."

— **ROBERT HUISH**, professor, Dalhousie University and host of the Global Development Primer podcast

"Politicians all too often make and break ambitious targets without consequence, but seeing this phenomenon unfold with the UN's Sustainable Development Goals is especially concerning given humanity's survival depends on the realization of many of these targets. Sneyd provides a much-needed explanation for what we are doing wrong, and where we can rectify. This book will enlighten anyone who feels like they are blindly striving to implement the SDGs but deep down knows that something is fundamentally off. Many of us cannot put our finger on what 'it' is, and Sneyd has succinctly and thoughtfully shed light on the matter in a way that I hope will lead to a serious shake-up of the UN's Global Goal-setting process."

— **SOPHIA CARODENUTO**, assistant professor, department of geography, University of Victoria

"With 2030 around the corner, governments are scrambling to show progress on the SDGs. Sneyd's *Hidden Politics in the UN Sustainable Development Goals* offers a critical and timely analysis of the SDG project's shortcomings and lessons for how to avoid such pitfalls in the future."

— **MATIAS E. MARGULIS**, University of British Columbia

"While well-intentioned, the Sustainable Development Goals (SDGs) are political artifacts which collectively play a role in legitimizing a particular vision of global capitalism. In *Hidden Politics*, Adam Sneyd does the work of disarticulating happy-sounding outcomes from the political economic contestation which underlies global development in practice. I've been waiting for years for someone to write this book - and Adam Sneyd has thankfully delivered! It will be an enormously helpful text for teaching students about globalization, the political economy of development, and of course the SDGs."

— **RYAN KATZ-ROSENE**, associate professor, University of Ottawa

ALSO IN THE CRITICAL DEVELOPMENT STUDIES SERIES

Contested Global Governance Space and Transnational Agrarian Movements (2023)
by Mauro Conti

The Political Economy of Agribusiness (2023)
by Maria Luisa Mendonça

Global Fishers: The Politics of Transnational Movements (2023)
by Elyse Noble Mills

Tiny Engines of Abundance (2022)
by Jim Handy

COVID-19 *and the Future of Capitalism: Postcapitalist Horizons Beyond Neo-Liberalism* (2021)
by Efe Can Gürcan, Ömer Ersin Kahraman & Selen Yanmaz

Extractivism: Politics, Economy and Ecology (2021)
by Eduardo Gudynas

The Political Economy of Agrarian Extractivism: Lessons from Bolivia (2020)
by Ben M. McKay

Development in Latin America: Toward a New Future (2019)
by Maristella Svampa, translation by Mark Rushton

Politics Rules: Power, Globalization and Development (2019)
by Adam Sneyd

Critical Development Studies: An Introduction (2018)
by Henry Veltmeyer & Raúl Delgado Wise

Hidden Politics in the UN Sustainable Development Goals

ADAM SNEYD
foreword by James Schneider

critical development studies

FERNWOOD
PUBLISHING

Practical
ACTION
PUBLISHING

Copyediting: Erin Seatter
Cover Design: John van der Woude
Text Design: Lauren Jeanneau
Printed and bound in Canada

Published in North America by Fernwood Publishing
2970 Oxford Street, Halifax, Nova Scotia, B3L 2W4
Halifax and Winnipeg
www.fernwoodpublishing.ca

Published in the rest of the world by Practical Action Publishing
27a Albert Street, Rugby, Warwickshire CV21 2SG, UK

Fernwood Publishing Company Limited gratefully acknowledges the financial
support of the Government of Canada through the Canada Book Fund and
the Canada Council for the Arts. We acknowledge the Province of Manitoba
for support through the Manitoba Publishers Marketing Assistance Program
and the Book Publishing Tax Credit. We acknowledge the Nova Scotia
Department of Communities, Culture and Heritage for support through
the Publishers Assistance Fund.

Library and Archives Canada Cataloguing in Publication
Title: Hidden politics in the UN Sustainable Development Goals / Adam Sneyd ;
foreword by James Schneider.
Names: Sneyd, Adam, 1978- author.
Series: Critical development studies ; 11.
Description: Series statement: Critical development studies ; 11 | Includes
bibliographical references and index.
Identifiers: Canadiana 2024038041X | ISBN 9781773636900 (softcover)
Subjects: LCSH: Sustainable Development Goals. | LCSH: Sustainable
development—Political aspects.
Classification: LCC HC79.E5 S64 2024 | DDC 338.9/27—dc23

MIX
Paper | Supporting
responsible forestry
FSC
www.fsc.org   FSC® C013916

Contents

Critical Development Studies Series..viii

Series Editors ix

Foreword.. 1

Introduction 5

Goal 1: No Poverty...12

Goal 2: Zero Hunger...20

Goal 3: Good Health and Well-Being..29

Goal 4: Quality Education..38

Goal 5: Gender Equality 47

Goal 6: Clean Water and Sanitation 55

Goal 7: Affordable and Clean Energy 64

Goal 8: Decent Work and Economic Growth...72

Goal 9: Industry, Innovation, and Infrastructure 81

Goal 10: Reduced Inequalities...90

Goal 11: Sustainable Cities and Communities 99

Goal 12: Responsible Consumption and Production 108

Goal 13: Climate Action..117

Goal 14: Life below Water...125

Goal 15: Life on Land 134

Goal 16: Peace, Justice, and Strong Institutions....................................143

Goal 17: Partnerships for the Goals 153

Conclusions...168

Acknowledgements 176

Index 177

Critical Development Studies Series

Three decades of uneven capitalist development and neoliberal globalization have devastated the economies, societies, livelihoods and lives of people around the world, especially those in societies of the Global South. Now more than ever, there is a need for a more critical, proactive approach to the study of global and development studies. The challenge of advancing and disseminating such an approach — to provide global and development studies with a critical edge — is on the agenda of scholars and activists from across Canada and the world and those who share the concern and interest in effecting progressive change for a better world.

This series provides a forum for the publication of small books in the interdisciplinary field of critical development studies — to generate knowledge and ideas about transformative change and alternative development. The editors of the series welcome the submission of original manuscripts that focus on issues of concern to the growing worldwide community of activist scholars in this field. Critical development studies (CDS) encompasses a broad array of issues ranging from the sustainability of the environment and livelihoods, the political economy and sociology of social inequality, alternative models of local and community-based development, the land and resource-grabbing dynamics of extractive capital, the subnational and global dynamics of political and economic power, and the forces of social change and resistance, as well as the contours of contemporary struggles against the destructive operations and ravages of capitalism and imperialism in the twenty-first century.

The books in the series are designed to be accessible to an activist readership as well as the academic community. The intent is to publish a series of small books (54,000 words, including bibliography, endnotes, index and front matter) on some of the biggest issues in the interdisciplinary field of critical development studies. To this end, activist scholars from across the world in the field of development studies and related academic disciplines are invited to submit a proposal or the draft of a book that conforms to the stated aim of the series. The editors will consider the submission of complete manuscripts within the 54,000-word limit. Potential authors are encouraged to submit a proposal that includes a rationale and short synopsis of the book, an outline of proposed chapters, one or two sample chapters, and a brief biography of the author(s).

Series Editors

HENRY VELTMEYER is a research professor at Universidad Autónoma de Zacatecas (Mexico) and professor emeritus of International Development Studies at Saint Mary's University (Canada), with a specialized interest in Latin American development. He is also co-chair of the Critical Development Studies Network and a co-editor of Fernwood's Agrarian Change and Peasant Studies series. The CDS *Handbook: Tools for Change* (Fernwood, 2011) was published in French by University of Ottawa Press as *Des outils pour le changement : Une approche critique en études du développement* and in Spanish as *Herramientas para el Cambio*, with funding from Oxfam UK by CIDES, Universidad Mayor de San Andrés, La Paz, Bolivia.

ANNETTE AURÉLIE DESMARAIS is the Canada Research Chair in Human Rights, Social Justice and Food Sovereignty at the University of Manitoba (Canada). She is the author of *La Vía Campesina: Globalization and the Power of Peasants* (Fernwood, 2007), which has been republished in French, Spanish, Korean, Italian and Portuguese, and *Frontline Farmers: How the National Farmers Union Resists Agribusiness and Creates our New Food Future* (Fernwood, 2019). She is co-editor of *Food Sovereignty: Reconnecting Food, Nature and Community* (Fernwood, 2010); *Food Sovereignty in Canada: Creating Just and Sustainable Food Systems* (Fernwood, 2011); and *Public Policies for Food Sovereignty: Social Movements and the State* (Routledge, 2017).

RAÚL DELGADO WISE is a research professor and director of the PhD program in Development Studies at the Universidad Autónoma de Zacatecas (Mexico). He holds the prestigious UNESCO Chair on Migration and Development and is executive director of the International Migration and Development Network, as well as author and editor of some twenty books and more than a hundred essays. He is a member of the Mexican Academy of Sciences and editor of the book series, Latin America and the New World Order, for Miguel Angel Porrúa publishers and chief editor of the journal *Migración y Desarrollo*. He is also a member of the international working group, People's Global Action on Migration Development and Human Rights.

Foreword

Crises abound. Global living standards are falling. One in ten people on Earth goes to bed hungry. More humans are displaced than at any time in history. Life expectancy is falling in nine out of ten countries. The past twelve months have seen temperatures more than 1.5°C above preindustrial levels. Today, as I write, temperatures are more than 2° above those levels. Major, irreversible changes to our environment will turbocharge existing crises that are almost certainly baked in already.

Human history is speeding up. Seismic events that mark a before and an after in the world system occur with unprecedented regularity — the COVID-19 pandemic, the war in Ukraine, and the genocide of Gaza, all in the past few years. In much of the world, politics has become more volatile and, at times, more violent. We know we live in a time of historical flux.

But geologic time, our planet's deep history, is also speeding up — and alarmingly so. For about the past twelve thousand years — pretty much all of known human history — humanity has lived in the Holocene geological era. It provided an unusually stable climate in which human society expanded dramatically. It gave us our assumptions about nature: the pattern of the seasons, the migration of animals, and the temperature. But that era is over, and we are moving to something else rapidly.

We've known this for sixteen years now. In 2008, the august Stratigraphy Commission of the Geological Society of London published a report presenting evidence that the Holocene was over and we were now in an era "without close parallel" in the previous many millions of years. A key factor in bringing on these tremendous, literally epochal, shifts is the concentration of carbon dioxide in the atmosphere, leading to warmer air and water temperatures. For almost all of the Holocene, the concentration was around 260–280 parts per million. That's the preindustrial level. In 2008, human activity had already pushed it to 385. The forecast for 2024 is 424. Up and up it goes.

1

Geological history is moving at an unprecedented pace. Human history sits on top of that underlying planetary history. Humanity, we might say, makes its own history, but not in circumstances of its own choosing.

It wasn't supposed to be this way. Just nine short years ago, to great fanfare, world leaders announced the Sustainable Development Goals (SDGs). They claimed to chart a course to resolve many of the crises that haunt hundreds of millions if not billions of humans: poverty, hunger, ill health, violence, inequality, and so on. The SDGs set seventeen targets to be hit by 2030. At present rates, two, maybe three, will be. Eight are going in the wrong direction entirely. In short, the SDGs have already failed, badly.

How are we to understand this overabundance of crises and our collective failure to address them? What can be done to improve the conditions of life on Earth for humanity? To engage with these huge questions, let us analytically triage the crises into three categories, which interact with each other: those *within*, *of*, and *beneath* the world system. From there we can see why the SDGs have failed and an outline of how we could change course.

Crises *within* the world system are those crises produced by the system operating perfectly normally. Many things that are devastating for millions are either irrelevant or integral to the smooth reproduction of the global system. Hunger, poverty, conflict, deprivation, and even genocide create sorrow for large portions of humanity but the accumulation of capital and the maintenance of systems of power is generally unaffected.

However, these crises *within* the system still threaten to undermine it. They generate responses, resistance, and organizing from people and communities that, from time to time, cohere into a broader crisis *of* the system. If sufficient counterpower builds up, or some great failure from rulers strips away consent to their governance, then the system's social settlement struggles to reproduce itself. This process is what Italian revolutionary theorist Antonio Gramsci called an "organic crisis," which can be thought of as a crisis of the social settlement or a crisis *of* the system. We saw such a crisis *of* the system in the 1970s as the workers, women, and the excluded of the Global North and the nations and peoples of the Global South made claims on a fairer share of global power and resources, a new social settlement.

We are also living in such a crisis *of* the system today where the system of rule struggles to reproduce itself. But in our case, the social settlement is not so much being challenged from below as much as it is falling apart from above. The effects are clear in many countries around the world: political volatility, low levels of trust in institutions, and declining living standards for the majority.

Our world system, with its methods of rule, its social settlements, and its challenges for people, sits atop a physical world. Should our physical world be radically transformed — by an asteroid collision, nuclear war, or climate breakdown — our social systems would also be radically transformed. Here we meet crises *beneath* the world system. Our changing climate, caused by our existing world system and its distribution of power, is creating a crisis *beneath* that system that will bring disruption like nothing we've ever known.

The latest science suggests that at 1.5° of warming, major tipping points — thresholds that trigger large, accelerating, and likely irreversible changes, like the melting of the Greenland ice sheet — become likely. Our climate, nature, the environment, or whatever we call it, is set to change significantly, disrupting harvests, supply chains, political systems, and our assumptions about the world.

The SDGs were announced the same year that world leaders agreed in Paris that they would limit global warming to below 1.5°, under the mantra "1.5 to stay alive." Aiming only at crises *within* the system, the SDGs, in essence, do not engage with or even head off crises *of* the system while ignoring crises *beneath* the system. They are an elite project to maintain the system, not transform it, as this book you are holding shows in meticulous detail, goal by goal. That's their hidden politics.

But, as it turns out, crises *of* and *beneath* the system are too great for the crises *within* the system to even be substantially ameliorated, let alone resolved. Both the crisis *beneath* the system and the distribution of power *of* the system must be addressed.

Fifty years ago, in another moment of multiplying crises, the peoples of the Global South sought to resolve crises *within* the system by creating and winning a crisis *of* the system. They strove for a new, more favourable, more equal distribution of power. In 1974, through the United Nations General Assembly, the global majority declared a New International Economic Order (NIEO) to form a new base "of economic relations between all peoples and all nations." They sought to improve the system by fundamentally changing the system. The NIEO included concrete measures to do so, such as technology transfer to the South, institutions to coordinate research, nationalization of natural resources, condition-free finance for development, cancellation of debts, access to fertilizers, and much more besides.

The architects of the NIEO had the ideas to change the world — and they had enough power to get it firmly on the global agenda. But ultimately, they did not have enough power to see it through. The global ruling class — predominantly in the banks, boardrooms, and government ministries of the Global North — fought back hard and won. Today, we live among the ashes of the dream of the NIEO.

The SDGs are a project from above to keep things fundamentally the same, whereas the NIEO was a project from below to change things fundamentally. Both failed, and we have to learn the lessons. That means we build a project of counterpower that unites those struggling against the crises *within* the system. Then we direct that unity onto the struggle to transform the social settlement, creating and then winning a crisis *of* the system. From there, we use that victory to act against and adapt to the rapidly developing crises *beneath* the system that are set to turbocharge the crises *within* the system.

If we are serious, we need a strategy to engage all three levels of crisis. After all, they interact and metastasize each other. That requires exposing attempts by our rulers to hide their real politics as they pretend to change the system while buttressing it. The Tancredis of this world are not our leaders but our enemies.

The end isn't nigh; it has already happened. We have left one epoch and a new one is being established. Dramatic change is coming, and people, agriculture, and cities will move. But one important truth will ring out: the system of rule that puts the wealth and power of a tiny few ahead of the material comfort and dignity of the vast majority and the very planetary systems on which we all rely cannot continue. It must be overthrown and replaced.

Humanity is on a bumpy road, and it will get bumpier still. But however dangerous and frightening that road becomes, we can navigate it — and even enjoy the ride — if popular, democratic forces forcibly take the driving seat. That project for counterpower is inherently conflictual. If it is successful, some corporations, states, and institutions will have far less wealth and power and the people will have more. The rich and powerful will fight, and fight hard, to stop that happening.

Our task is huge, larger than any humanity has collectively faced before. But we have no choice other than to give it a shot by exposing the hidden politics of our current failing system and building the collective will and capacity to construct another.

— James Schneider, St. Vincent
March 2024

Introduction

The Sustainable Development Goals (SDGs), also known as the Global Goals, were adopted by the United Nations (UN) in 2015 and heralded as a universal call to action to end poverty, protect the planet, and ensure that by 2030 all people would enjoy peace and prosperity (UN 2015). This book is about the politics of the SDGs. It shows how each of the seventeen SDGs endorsed by the UN is fundamentally political. Taken together, the SDGs constitute a political project that necessitates careful political analysis. While states are not legally bound to implement their commitments to the goals, the UN expects governments to take ownership of this project and to establish national implementation frameworks (UN 2016). The UN's nonbinding call to action has nevertheless stimulated a massive and highly political global outpouring of interest in sustainable development and the Global Goals. Yet behind all the SDG cheerleading and feelgoodery lies a much darker reality. To put it bluntly, the package of ambitions contained in *Transforming Our World: The 2030 Agenda for Sustainable Development* (UN 2015) is anything but transformative. In fact, the 2030 Agenda advances a set of minimalist reforms, which, if implemented, would bolster the legitimacy of the current liberal international economic order and entrench global capitalism. The chapters that follow show how this political orientation infuses the targets and indicators that accompany each of the SDGs. They also document, goal by goal, the political inadequacies of the metrics being used to measure progress.

More broadly, in this book I focus on the emergence of perspectives that challenge the liberal orientation of the SDGs and advance alternative viewpoints on global ordering. The ideas proposed to countervail the 2030 Agenda or to correct its deficiencies are growing in influence. As even the UN itself now admits, many of the goals will not be achieved (UN 2022). During these increasingly turbulent times, information about the problems and faltering progress of the SDGs can be used to further political agendas of various types. By putting politics at the centre of the analysis, this contribution directly engages with the profusion of new and conflicting notions on what needs to be done to build a better world.

The claim that the Global Goals serve to reinforce the legitimacy of the liberal international economic order requires some initial elaboration. The goals aim to align international cooperation and global capitalism with a business-friendly vision for development that can be considered more inclusive and sustainable than the status quo. The subsequent chapters of this book demonstrate how this approach buttresses the present mix of international organizations and governance frameworks. They document the ways that the 2030 Agenda is congruent with the globalization of possessive individualism and designed to strengthen the world trading system and fortify the global financial and investment architecture. At best, this agenda advances exceedingly minor and dated ambitions to reform the institutions of global economic governance. Put another way, the SDGs were ostensibly designed to build a more democratic, effective, moral, and inclusive order (Scholte 2002). As such, they can be considered an attempt to salvage or sustain the legitimacy of the contemporary international order. Many well-intentioned governments, businesses, civil society organizations, and global citizens have made considerable investments in the success of this system maintenance project.

Unfortunately, those responsible for drafting the 2030 Agenda were not forthright about the politics of their ambitions. They portrayed their aspirations as universal, and simply failed to anticipate or articulate the possibility that the SDGs could generate sustained political pushback. This lack of foresight is curious, as efforts to govern the world are always political and tend to be subject to political contestation (Mazower 2013). We do not even have to go that far back in history to find a serious example of this global politics. In the 1970s, political contests over the failings of the interstate, international order and the global capitalist system were fraught. As Robert W. Cox (1979) painstakingly detailed, many views on what needed to be done to the world order came into conflict at that time. Some voices sought to maintain the liberal international economic order at all costs. Others pushed for reforms that would advance the interests of developing countries or were committed to transforming the system entirely. These debates crystallized around the calls made by developing countries for a New International Economic Order (NIEO) within and beyond the UN system. Over the course of forty-six pages, Cox detailed the perspectives that mercantilists, liberals, social democrats, Third World liberationists, and Marxists articulated on the matter. He showed that the push for a NIEO did not start or stop with the UN Declaration and Programme of Action on the topic. The many conflicting ideological viewpoints on the NIEO animated a prolonged political contest over the institutions of global economic governance. This disorder over how to order the world economy persisted until the early 1980s. At that time, in the context of the Third World debt crisis, Western views in favour of maintaining the liberal international economic order won the day. The transformative demands that developing countries had articulated were relegated to the dustbin for decades.

Today, perspectives on global ordering have reached a similar inflection point. Since 2015, the liberal consensus on the international order and global financialized capitalism has broken down. A range of nationalist voices now fight back against any global guidance related to national policies, legislation, economic activities, and perceived ways of life (Drache and Froese 2022). Around the world, populist politicians stoke fear about nebulous "globalist" agendas and portray the SDGs as an elitist or "socialist" project contrary to "freedom" and the interests of "the people." At the other end of the political spectrum, progressives have endeavoured to resuscitate the NIEO (Progressive International 2024). Under the guidance of the Progressive International, a transnational nongovernmental organization, political activists and socially concerned researchers have mobilized proposals to radically transform the world political and economic order. These change-oriented viewpoints contrast sharply with the 2030 Agenda's efforts to reinforce a kinder and cleaner version of business as usual. Over the past several years, another cluster of opinion has emerged that forcefully challenges the idea of infinite economic growth. Many political ecologists and green supporters of environmental and climate justice have embraced calls to radically reduce global consumption and production. They seek to relocalize economies, bolster communities, enshrine the commons, and build a world order that unhooks the global economic system from planetary despoliation (Kallis et al. 2020).

Collectively, these emerging perspectives on the global order are at odds with the assertion that the 2030 Agenda reflects universal ambitions. The limitations of the SDGs cannot be understood in isolation from this resurgent global politics. However, many scholarly analyses of the SDGs have set this broader politics to the side and have focused solely on functional challenges related to implementing the goals. Numerous contributions to the literature have also understated or overlooked the politics that underpins and animates the SDG project. For instance, a recent edited volume on the interlinkages between the seventeen goals focused exclusively on the governance mechanisms and policy instruments necessary to implement the goals in diverse contexts (Breuer et al. 2023). This contribution simply assumed the beneficence and necessity of the SDGs and glossed over the emerging political challenges. Numerous other works published in dedicated book series or as one-off contributions to the literature, including those that are cited in the following chapters, reflect these shortcomings. By and large, many experts have failed to substantively engage with both the politics of the SDGs and the rise of political conflict over how the world should be ordered. Even the analyses of staunch critics of the 2030 Agenda, such as the Japanese philosopher Kohei Saito, have not been rigorously attentive to politics. Saito's (2024) characterization of the SDGs as the new "opiate of the masses" drew popular attention to the fact that the goals bolster status quo interests and practices. His depiction nonetheless obscured the rise of right-wing politicians across the world who now prominently, routinely, and inaccurately portray the goals to be against "the people."

Of the more enlightening academic analyses of SDG politics, Lars Niklasson's (2019) keen political insights largely predate the global emergence of reactionary populist movements. Magdalena Bexell and Kristina Jönsson (2021) have also authored a rigorous and authoritative book on SDG-related political challenges. While Bexell and Jönsson apply their discourse analysis primarily to SDG implementation issues, their approach sheds needed light on the politics of the goals. It can also serve as a useful aid for those who seek to develop more comprehensive accounts of the politics of ordering the world at a time of heightened global political conflict. Similarly, a comprehensive edited volume that assesses the impact of the SDGs on major institutions and political processes also comes very close to engaging with the new political reality (Biermann et al. 2022). There, too, however, the contributors focus mostly on the political impact of the SDGs, and not on the ramifications of an increasingly divisive politics for people and the planet. In sum, despite the vast global outpouring of analytical literature on the Global Goals, little has been written about the overall politics of the 2030 Agenda.

This book takes this gap as its point of departure. It focuses directly on the political assumptions and orientations that have been built into each goal. The analysis presented in the ensuing chapters primarily foregrounds the hidden politics of the targets and indicators associated with the SDGs. In pursuing this emphasis, I identify many troubling disconnections between goals that sound great (e.g., "No Poverty") and the indicators that allegedly measure progress towards these noble-sounding ends. Moreover, to contribute to correcting the gap identified above, the book also speaks briefly to the new political discord over the content of each goal. Conflicting perspectives are increasingly consequential, and future researchers must embrace the challenge of comprehensively mapping the ideologies that contend to shape the twenty-first-century global "disorder."

How the Book Proceeds

Each chapter focuses on one of the seventeen SDGs. I draw upon an organizational strategy and style of argumentation first employed by Ha-Joon Chang and Ilene Grabel (2004). At the outset of each chapter, I uncritically summarize the UN goals and their mission statements in a section entitled "What They Tell Us." These brief sections refer to recent UN progress assessments and introduce and restate UN calls for action on each goal. They also include a two-column textbox that presents the relevant SDG targets and indicators in full. These sections draw upon and reproduce UN language to serve as a point of reference for readers. They are not intended to be analytical and do not include any of my original language or thinking beyond the occasional paraphrase or coherence connection.

Subsequently, the overviews of what the UN tells us about the 2030 Agenda are juxtaposed with a deeper critical analysis of the hidden politics. In these longer analytical sections, I articulate how the SDG targets and indicators are inattentive to highly consequential political factors, ideas, conflicts, and power relations. Thus, I highlight the limits of the goals in relation to the issues that they seek to address and underscore the paths that have not been taken. These sections typically showcase a sharp disjuncture between SDG ambitions and the means employed to move forward the 2030 Agenda. They also raise difficult questions about the ways that progress is measured in relation to the goals. To close each chapter, a brief final paragraph reiterates the gloomy findings of the UN secretary-general's 2023 SDG midpoint review and points to some of the broader political challenges that are teased out more fully in the book's concluding chapter.

In the conclusion, I reiterate the book's conceptual framework and findings. I also speak to some of the political headwinds constraining the realization of progressive social change and a greener future. Progressives and ecologists who seek to build a better world now confront goals that are heavily skewed towards the maintenance of the liberal international economic order. They also face a surge of right-wing populist and nationalist sentiment that often conflates the UN goals with the machinations or agenda of a so-called global elite. The book's concluding summary cuts through the ideological cacophony to reinforce the point that the goals are political and ultimately subject to political interpretation, engagement, and implementation. In other words, I debunk the notion that SDG ambitions are universal. This aspect of the book's conclusion aims to give students, scholars, practitioners, and global citizens entry points to think more deeply about the relevant ideological perspectives at a critical juncture on the road to 2030 (UN 2023). Put another way, it helps readers identify key aspects of the political debates that now set the limits of the possible for the realization of transformative change. This short provocation can also be considered a point of departure for future analyses of sustainable development politics. The concluding chapter then articulates how the analytical approach of the book contributes to development studies scholarship on the goals. Ultimately, I call for a global effort to fundamentally rethink and redesign the goals.

This book can be read in several ways. For those seeking to immerse themselves in the politics of the Global Goals and the book's argument, a cover-to-cover reading could be instructive. On the other hand, some development practitioners may find it useful to treat this work as a reference text and focus primarily on the chapters that intersect with their areas of interest. The fact that there are seventeen SDGs also poses a challenge for course instructors intending to assign this book. If students will read this book over a twelve-week course of study, focusing on a subset of the goals that intersects with economic, social, and environmental themes could make sense. For instance, asking students to read about Goals 1, 2, 5, 6, 7, 8, 9, 12, 13, 14, 16, and 17 would cover a lot of ground. Instructors could also squeeze this content into a twelve-week format by presenting options to students — for example, asking students to decide between reading about Goal 1 or 10, Goal 3 or 4, Goal 6 or 11, and Goal 14 or 15. For readers who can design their own strategies of engagement with what follows, it is also possible for the seventeen body chapters to be read as stand-alone pieces and in any order whatsoever.

References

Bexell, M., and K. Jönsson. 2021. *The Politics of the Sustainable Development Goals: Legitimacy, Responsibility, and Accountability*. London: Routledge.

Biermann, F., T. Hickmann, and C-A Senit. (eds.). 2022. *The Political Impact of the Sustainable Development Goals: Transforming Governance through the Goals?* Cambridge: Cambridge University Press.

Breuer, A., D. Malerba, and S. Srigiri, P. Balasubramanian (eds.). 2023. *Governing the Interlinkages between the SDGs: Approaches, Opportunities, and Challenges*. London and New York: Routledge.

Chang, H.-J., and I. Grabel. 2004. *Reclaiming Development: An Alternative Economic Policy Manual*. London: Zed Books.

Cox, R.W. 1979. "Ideologies and the New International Economic Order: Reflections on Some Recent Literature." *International Organization* 33, 2.

Drache, D., and M. Froese. 2022. *Has Populism Won? The War on Liberal Democracy.* Toronto: ECW Press.

Kallis, G., S. Paulson, G. D'Alisa, and F. Demaria. 2020. *The Case for Degrowth.* Cambridge: Polity Press.

Niklasson, L. 2019. *Improving the Sustainable Development Goals: Strategies and the Governance Challenge.* London: Routledge.

Mazower, M. 2013. *Governing the World: The History of an Idea, 1815 to the Present.* New York: Penguin Books.

Progressive International. 2024. *The New International Economic Order.* progressive.international/blueprint/collection/7e22256c4-1bb2-49a3-bf78-a3e0bc6160d2-new-international-economic-order/en.

Saito, K. 2024. *Slow Down: The Degrowth Manifesto.* New York: Astra House.

Scholte, J.A. 2002. "Civil Society and Governance in the Global Polity." In *Towards a Global Polity: Future Trends and Prospects,* edited by R. Higgott and M. Ougaard. London: Routledge.

UN (United Nations). 2015. *Transforming Our World: The 2030 Agenda for Sustainable Development.* New York: UN. sdgs.un.org/2030agenda.

———. 2016. *Academic Impact.* New York: UN. un.org/en/academic-impact/page/sustainable-development-goals.

———. 2022. *The Sustainable Development Goals Report 2022.* New York: UN.

———. 2023. *Global Sustainable Development Report: Times of Crisis, Times of Change.* New York: UN.

Goal ①
No Poverty

What They Tell Us

Mission statement: End poverty in all its forms everywhere.

Together we can finish the job of eradicating global poverty in all its dimensions. This goal is well within our reach as the world has made real progress on poverty reduction over time. The root causes of poverty can be found in the factors that prevent people from being productive (UN 2023). These can include unemployment, social exclusion, high vulnerability to disasters, diseases, and other phenomena that work against productive participation in the economy. To advance this goal, individuals must engage with policymaking processes to ensure that they address poverty, and governments must create enabling environments for poverty reduction (UN 2023). However, as "things stand, the world is not on track to end poverty by 2030, with poorer countries now needing unprecedented levels of pro-poor growth to achieve this goal" (UN 2022, 26). In 2022, COVID-19, inflation, and the war in Ukraine pushed an additional seventy-five million to ninety-five million people into extreme poverty compared with prepandemic projections. Low-income countries have been hardest hit, and poverty reduction has been set back by years (UN 2023).

	Poverty Targets		Indicators
1.1	By 2030, eradicate extreme poverty for all people everywhere, currently measured as people living on less than $1.25 a day	1.1.1	Proportion of the population living below the international poverty line by sex, age, employment status, and geographic location (urban/rural)
1.2	By 2030, reduce at least by half the proportion of men, women and children of all ages living in poverty in all its dimensions according to national definitions	1.2.1	Proportion of the population living below the national poverty line, by sex and age
		1.2.2	Proportion of men, women, and children of all ages living in poverty in all its dimensions according to national definitions

Poverty Targets	Indicators
1.3 Implement nationally appropriate social protection systems and measures for all, including floors, and by 2030 achieve substantial coverage of the poor and the vulnerable	1.3.1 Proportion of population covered by social protection floors/systems, by sex, distinguishing children, unemployed persons, older persons, persons with disabilities, pregnant women, newborns, work-injury victims, and the poor and the vulnerable
1.4 By 2030, ensure that all men and women, in particular the poor and the vulnerable, have equal rights to economic resources, as well as access to basic services, ownership and control over land and other forms of property, inheritance, natural resources, appropriate new technology and financial services, including microfinance	1.4.1 Proportion of population living in households with access to basic services 1.4.2 Proportion of total adult population with secure tenure rights to land, (a) with legally recognized documentation, and (b) who perceive their rights to land as secure, by sex and type of tenure
1.5 By 2030, build the resilience of the poor and those in vulnerable situations and reduce their exposure and vulnerability to climate-related extreme events and other economic, social, and environmental shocks and disasters	1.5.1 Number of deaths, missing persons, and directly affected persons attributed to disasters per 100000 population 1.5.2 Direct economic loss attributed to disasters in relation to global gross domestic product (GDP) 1.5.3 Number of countries that adopt and implement national disaster risk reduction strategies in line with the Sendai Framework for Disaster Risk Reduction 2015–2030 1.5.4 Proportion of local governments that adopt and implement local disaster risk reduction strategies in line with national disaster risk reduction strategies
1.a Ensure significant mobilization of resources from a variety of sources, including through enhanced development cooperation, in order to provide adequate and predictable means for developing countries, in particular least developed countries, to implement programmes and policies to end poverty in all its dimensions	1.a.1 Total official development assistance grants from all donors that focus on poverty reduction as a share of the recipient country's gross national income 1.a.2 Proportion of total government spending on essential services (education, health, and social protection)
1.b Create sound policy frameworks at the national, regional, and international levels, based on pro-poor and gender-sensitive development strategies, to support accelerated investment in poverty eradication actions	1.b.1 Pro-poor public social spending

The Hidden Politics

Quantifying poverty by ascribing a dollar value to it is a fundamentally political act. This approach to identifying and acting on poverty is rooted in the controversial idea that poverty is a condition that entails a state of absolute deprivation. While no one would argue that destitution should persist or remain unaddressed, defining where exactly poverty starts and stops does not occur in a political vacuum. Political consensus is required on where specifically to draw the line, and in the case of the dollar-per-day metric, a consensus has been forged and continues to be driven by academic economists and the World Bank. The quantitative viewpoint that poverty can be eliminated by raising incomes that fall below a certain threshold has come to dominate global responses to poverty. Whether intentionally or not, the overemphasis on the absolute poverty of income continues to serve a clear political end. Governments and international organizations have consistently drawn on evidence of positive trends in dollar-per-day poverty to legitimize their economic agendas and political priorities. Consequently, the poor do not stand alone in having a vested interest in efforts to eradicate income poverty. Focusing on the proportion of people that fall below the global poverty line is also a ready-made source of political capital where and when the data exist to support the notion that the war on want is being "won."

Given the evident overemphasis on the income dimension of poverty, it might seem refreshing that SDG 1 also prioritizes poverty reduction in relation to other dimensions of poverty and national definitions. That said, the goal's first target (1.1) leaves the "other" dimensions of poverty to be addressed solely up to national discretion. Definitions of poverty at the country level continue to be shaped and constrained by the powerful global consensus on income poverty that development finance institutions have maintained for decades. In an attempt to influence national perspectives, other viewpoints have emphasized capability deprivation, inadequate meeting of basic needs, and a lack of happiness. Similarly, much rigorous scholarship frames poverty as a historic and global process of disempowerment, and not simply as an individual economic outcome. However, these academic approaches have in many cases lacked the political influence or financial backing necessary to meaningfully alter policy. Put another way, a considerable volume of social science research has focused on the other dimensions of poverty in particular places, but the translation from knowledge to political will and policy action has been lacking.

Political ideas about what kind of poverty matters for policy persist. Their lingering influence is evident in the circumscribed approach that SDG 1 takes to the broader dimensions of poverty and to national definitions. While income poverty must be eradicated to meet this goal, the second target (1.2) endeavours only to halve the number of people that live in other dimensions of poverty. Moreover, this restrained-by-design effort is conditional on the integration of other dimensions of poverty into national definitions. Consequently, if a national definition excludes the viewpoint that poverty also involves a lack of happiness, no efforts are required to address that dimension. Governments are in the driver's seat when it comes to defining what, if any, of the other dimensions of poverty they seek to ameliorate.

The third (1.3) target's call for the implementation of social protection systems and measures for all is also subject to the political clause of national appropriateness. States that do not wish to develop universal social benefits can simply assert these grounds to justify their inaction, and they can remain in technical compliance with the goal while doing so. The capacity to make sovereign decisions and enjoy the space necessary to pursue autonomous policies remains inviolable under the goals.

Interestingly, the national appropriateness stipulation is not mentioned explicitly in the catch-all fourth target (1.4), which seeks to ensure equal rights to economic resources and access to basic services, control over land and property, and new technologies and financial services. Nonetheless, the politics associated with this empowerment wish list are not promising. Only two indicators for tracking progress were agreed to, and they do not cover all aspects of the target. The first indicator (1.4.1) focuses on the proportion of households with access to basic services. Many of the households that lack access to basic services the world over can be found in informal settlements where inhabitants do not have formal legal rights to the land or housing that they occupy. It remains exceedingly difficult to render residents of informal rental housing or "illegal" slums legible to authorities in resource-constrained contexts. Measuring access to basic services can also prove highly contentious when the failure of development policies brings stark financial consequences. In an instance that I witnessed years ago, several nongovernmental organizations walked out of a multistakeholder meeting on water services access convened by an international financial institution. Supporters of the walkout aimed to protest a presentation on the proportion of households with water access that they believed was riddled with wildly inaccurate data to paper over policy failure and secure additional financial support.

Turning to the politics of the second indicator (1.4.2), governments in countries where statutory land tenure systems coexist with customary or traditional land tenure systems might also consider this topic to be politically sensitive. Rules around land tenure define how property rights are allocated within societies and govern how access is granted to rights to use, control, and transfer land (FAO 2002). Improving the proportion of the adult population with land-use rights that are legal or perceived to be secure by sex and type of land tenure can absolutely advance this goal. That said, many authoritarian regimes seek to attract more foreign investors to their agrifood and natural resource sectors. From their perspective, greater numbers of residents with legal land titles could complicate or undercut government intentions to open up more land for resource extraction and commodity production. Beyond the indicators, the politics of this target's call for greater access to financial services stands out. The thrust to bank the poor — to encourage savings and debt-based financial products — as a path out of poverty has been widely and devastatingly critiqued (Soederberg 2017). Even without a relevant measure of progress, the liberal belief that financial inclusion can deliver antipoverty result shines through.

The fifth target (1.5) seeks to build resilience and reduce the vulnerability of the poor to climate change. It also includes indicators that do not address an overarching political problem. The first indicator (1.5.1) laudably directs governments to produce data that accurately capture the numbers of affected, missing, and dead people attributable to natural disasters. However, it fails to stipulate a level for reducing the human impact of adverse and extreme events. As such, this indicator simply encourages better disaster accounting. Likewise, the next indicator (1.5.2) calls for better accounting of economic losses that are directly attributable to natural disasters. The hope underlying this approach seems to be that greater knowledge of the human and economic costs could encourage policymakers to take disasters more seriously. Knowing trends in the proportion of governments at all levels that adopt and implement disaster risk reduction strategies, and how those trends relate to human and economic costs, could enable better outcomes for the poor (1.5.3). Targets under SDG 11 (Sustainable Cities and Communities) reiterate this focus with more emphasis on the need for reducing human and economic costs. Whether or not enhanced knowledge builds resilience and reduces the vulnerability of the poor will consequently depend on the success of efforts to achieve SDG 11, and on the effectiveness of disaster and climate-related assistance, finance, investment, and strategy more broadly. The 2030 Agenda implicitly acknowledges the scale of the political challenge facing progress on each of the latter fronts. Nearly every goal contains implementation-related targets that include language on the need for better strategy and more robust assistance, finance, and investment. Notwithstanding government commitments to the SDGs, political will remains the elephant in the room.

On SDG 1 specifically, the first implementation target (1.a) calls for governments to track the proportion of domestic resources allocated to poverty reduction programs, essential services, and pro-poor public spending. No levels for these antipoverty expenditures are stipulated. Moreover, what exactly constitutes "pro-poor" public spending is left undefined. Governments are consequently free to develop their own interpretations of the term, and to utilize these in relation to their interventions at their own discretion. The second implementation target (1.b) calls for policy at all levels to be informed by pro-poor and gender-sensitive strategies. This target's associated indicator (1.b.1) is so broadly defined that it is open to all varieties of use and abuse. Governments that are genuinely committed to these ends can highlight their successes with reference to their specific policies. On the other hand, those that are merely interested in gaining better access to poverty reduction funding can employ the appropriate language in the hope of scoring bigger payouts.

Taken together, the sweeping scope of this goal and its political inconsistencies, assumptions, and ramifications will not bring about the end of poverty in all its forms everywhere. Even countries that were formerly held to be poverty-reduction "success" stories, such as India, will fail to eradicate poverty (Subramanian et al. 2023). While multiple overlapping global crises have complicated progress on poverty, the goal's overemphasis on low income as the primary source of poverty downplays some of the biggest sources of disempowerment in the global economy. Modern slavery, child labour, sex and human trafficking, and all forms of employment and entrepreneurship that serve informal and illicit markets recreate relationships that disempower and impoverish people each day. Although SDG 1 does explicitly call for the eradication of many of these poverty-creating practices, these ends are not linked directly to the goal. Furthermore, the idea that tracking progress on an arbitrary measure of absolute deprivation will somehow eradicate poverty is itself problematic. Simply put, all people everywhere would need to be banked and employed in the formal sector for governments to verify that the income dimension of poverty had been fully eradicated. UN estimates currently suggest that billions of people around the world remain informally employed and unbanked.

Efforts to achieve SDG 1 have also been driven by the perspective that poverty prevents people from being productive. From this biased point of view, sustenance farmers and gatherers who have limited connections to the money economy and global markets could be considered unproductive. This wrongheaded notion finds its worst expression in the culturally inappropriate and often racist stereotype that underemployed rural people are prone to sitting around and waiting for the fruit to drop. The supposed connection between productivity gains and poverty reduction is ultimately a remnant of discredited ideas about how to modernize "traditional" economies. A discussion on the politics of productivity ensues in the next chapter, but for now, it is important to note that insights on this topic can always be found by answering two simple questions. First, productivity of what? And second, productivity for whom? Sustenance farmers produce food and reproduce social relationships. Their lifeways, and their bartering and sharing strategies, can be productive for their families, kin, and communities. Empowered people with an interest in making sustenance farmers more productive in a different sense, and who are committed to improving the productivity of sustenance farmers for distant others, should at least have the courage to state the politics of their positions and agendas more explicitly. Where and when elites consider the poor to be potential drivers of growth, cultures are assuredly under threat. If the quest to eradicate poverty ultimately fuels a reduction in cultural diversity, we would all lose, and the poor would still be with us. As the World Bank admitted in October 2022, SDG 1 will not be achieved (Kharas and McArthur 2023). Moreover, even though the 2030 Agenda frames this goal as the greatest global challenge, it contains no mechanisms that enable the poor to hold the agents of poverty eradication accountable for their actions.

Other known political impediments to this goal include the lack of a dedicated global funding instrument, and the dearth of effective frameworks to manage resource revenues in many developing countries (Tiba 2023). The coherence of the 2030 Agenda's emphasis on poverty with the African Union's Agenda 2063 for sustainable transformation, and with similar action plans spearheaded by the European Union and the Organisation for Economic Co-operation and Development (OECD), is also a political problem. Competing policy priorities could frustrate progress, especially where initiatives that put a lower emphasis on poverty prevail (Cichos and Lange Salvia 2019). The politics that fuel the persistence of poverty also threaten the implementation of the other sixteen SDGs (Leal Filho el al. 2021). Each of the other goals contain at least one target associated with poverty, and a recent survey of development experts found that most are concerned that the consequences of climate change will undermine antipoverty work. Only a few experts have disregarded the climate challenge while continuing to argue that SDG 1 is achievable. Hoy and Sumner (2021), for instance, assert that activist governments pursuing redistribution with growth can potentially deliver results that fight poverty. Rose-tinted glasses can of course be quite blinding. The climate emergency poses the ultimate political problem facing efforts to end poverty.

According to the UN secretary-general's midpoint review of the SDGs, as many as 575 million people could remain in extreme poverty in 2030, and around two-thirds of all UN members are not on course to halve their national rates of poverty by that date (UNSG 2023). While the secretary-general's report was forthright about these challenges, it did not detail a key source of real and potential political pushback against SDG 1. The liberal interpretation of the causes and consequences of poverty that animates SDG 1 is increasingly contested domestically and internationally.

References

Cichos, K. and A. Lange Salvia. 2019. *SDG 1 No Poverty: Making the Dream a Reality.* Dubai: Emerald Publishing.

FAO (Food and Agriculture Organization). 2002. "3. What Is Land Tenure." Rome: FAO. fao.org/3/y4307e/y4307e05.htm.

Hoy, C., and A. Sumner. 2021. "The End of Global Poverty: Is the UN Sustainable Development Goal 1 (Still) Achieveable?" *Global Policy* 12, 4.

Kharas, H., and J.W. McArthur. 2023. "A Purpose-Driven Fund to End Extreme Poverty by 2030." Washington, DC: Brookings Institution.

Leal Filho, W., V.O. Lovren, M. Will, et al. 2021. "Poverty: A Central Barrier to the Implementation of the Sustainable Development Goals." *Environmental Science and Policy* 125.

Soederberg, S. 2017. "Universal Access to Affordable Housing? Interrogating an Elusive Development Goal." In *The Politics of Destination in the 2030 Sustainable Development Goals: Leaving No-One Behind?*, edited by C. Gabay and S. Ilcan. London: Routledge.

Subramanian, S.V., M. Ambade, A. Kumar, et al. 2023. "Progress on Sustainable Development Goal indicators in 707 districts of India: A Quantitative Mid-line Assessment Using the National Family Health Surveys, 2016 and 2021." *The Lancet: Regional Health Southeast Asia* 13.

Tiba, S. 2023. "Unlocking the Poverty and Hunger Puzzle: Toward Democratizing the Natural Resource for Accomplishing SDGs 1&2." *Resources Policy* 82.

UN (United Nations). 2022. *The Sustainable Development Goals Report 2022.* New York: UN.

———. 2023. "Goal 1: End Poverty in All Its Forms Everywhere." un.org/sustainabledevelopment/poverty.

UNSG (United Nations Secretary-General). 2023. *Progress towards the Sustainable Development Goals: Towards a Rescue Plan for People and Planet. Report of the Secretary-General (Special Edition).* New York: United Nations General Assembly and Economic and Social Council.

Goal ❷
Zero Hunger

What They Tell Us

> **Mission statement:** End hunger, achieve food security and improved nutrition, and promote sustainable agriculture.

We can end hunger together by ensuring that all people everywhere have reliable access to safe, nutritious, and sufficient food by 2030 (UN 2023). Even today, more than enough food is produced to feed everyone on Earth sufficiently (FAO 2023). There are many root causes of hunger and food insecurity, so we must make certain that our approach to building a more food-secure world targets all dimensions of the problem. Individuals around the world can and must make decisions to support local farmers or markets. Ultimately, people everywhere must make more sustainable food choices as consumers and as voters to make zero hunger a reality. Hunger and malnutrition undermine individual productivity and consequently are an impediment to better livelihoods. Even before COVID-19, hunger was on the rise (UN 2023). Roughly 30 per cent of the world's population remains food insecure. Food supply systems "have been partially undermined by a cascading combination of growing conflicts, climate-related shocks, and widening inequalities" (UN 2022, 28). The scale of the global food crisis is enormous but zero hunger is within our grasp (World Food Programme n.d.).

Hunger Targets		Indicators	
2.1	By 2030, end hunger and ensure access by all people, in particular the poor and people in vulnerable situations, including infants, to safe, nutritious, and sufficient food all year round	2.1.1	Prevalence of undernourishment
		2.1.2	Prevalence of moderate or severe food insecurity in the population, based on the Food Insecurity Experience Scale (FIES)
2.2	By 2030, end all forms of malnutrition, including achieving, by 2025, the internationally agreed targets on stunting and wasting in children under 5 years of age, and address the nutritional needs of adolescent girls, pregnant and lactating women, and older persons	2.2.1	Prevalence of stunting among children under 5 years of age
		2.2.2	Prevalence of malnutrition among children under 5 years of age, by type (wasting and overweight)

Hunger Targets	Indicators
2.2 (continued)	2.2.3 Prevalence of anaemia in women aged 15 to 49 years, by pregnancy status (percentage)
2.3 By 2030, double the agricultural productivity and incomes of small-scale food producers, in particular women, Indigenous Peoples, family farmers, pastoralists, and fishers, including through secure and equal access to land, other productive resources and inputs, knowledge, financial services, markets, and opportunities for value addition and non-farm employment	2.3.1 Volume of production per labour unit by classes of farming/pastoral/forestry enterprise size 2.3.2 Average income of small-scale food producers, by sex and Indigenous status
2.4 By 2030, ensure sustainable food production systems and implement resilient agricultural practices that increase productivity and production, that help maintain ecosystems, that strengthen capacity for adaptation to climate change, extreme weather, drought, flooding, and other disasters and that progressively improve land and soil quality	2.4.1 Proportion of agricultural area under productive and sustainable agriculture
2.5 By 2020, maintain the genetic diversity of seeds, cultivated plants, and farmed and domesticated animals and their related wild species, including through soundly managed and diversified seed and plant banks at the national, regional, and international levels, and promote access to and fair and equitable sharing of benefits arising from the utilization of genetic resources and associated traditional knowledge, as internationally agreed	2.5.1 Number of (a) plant and (b) animal genetic resources for food and agriculture secured in either medium- or long-term conservation facilities 2.5.2 Proportion of local breeds classified as being at risk, not at risk or at unknown level of risk of extinction
2.a Increase investment, including through enhanced international cooperation, in rural infrastructure, agricultural research and extension services, technology development, and plant and livestock gene banks in order to enhance agricultural productive capacity in developing countries, in particular least developed countries	2.a.1 The agriculture orientation index for government expenditures 2.a.2 Total official flows (official development assistance plus other official flows) to the agriculture sector
2.b Correct and prevent trade restrictions and distortions in world agricultural markets, including through the parallel elimination of all forms of agricultural export subsidies and all export measures with equivalent effect, in accordance with the mandate of the Doha Development Round	2.b.1 Agricultural export subsidies
2.c Adopt measures to ensure the proper functioning of food commodity markets and their derivatives and facilitate timely access to market information, including on food reserves, in order to help limit extreme food price volatility	2.c.1 Indicator of food price anomalies

The Hidden Politics

At first glance, SDG 2's call for a multidimensional approach to food security can seem comprehensive. The goal also conveys the impression of a shared commitment to transforming food systems and achieving a more inclusive and sustainable world (UN 2020). Nonetheless, the goal is in fact far from comprehensive and is more notable for the politics and practices that it does not address. Acting on food system challenges will assuredly have an impact on global development (Blay-Palmer and Young 2019). As it stands, this goal fails to provide guidance that will guarantee net positive outcomes over the coming decades. The analysis presented below suggests that its political oversights and internal inconsistencies could ultimately yield greater corporate control over food production, distribution, and retailing, and frustrate efforts to achieve truly sustainable food systems.

The limitations of this goal's intentions and outcomes are evident from the first target (2.1) and associated indicators (2.1.1 and 2.1.2). Ensuring year-round access to safe, nutritious, and sufficient food for all people is obviously a laudable objective. Yet serious politics are found even in the rather innocuous language of safety, nutrition, and sufficiency. Discussions of food safety, for instance, are often limited to the science of handling, preparation, and storage. But is it safe to provide food-insecure populations with foods that have been produced through conventional methods that degrade soils and water quality and amplify the climate emergency? Who or what is rendered safe by business as usual in the global system of emergency food provision? And what happens in conflict situations when distribution systems on the ground render people physically unsafe? Similarly, for the purposes of this target, should the emergency provision of nutraceutical or therapeutic food products developed in labs by university spin-off ventures be counted as a "win"? Put another way, at what level of reliance does the provision of corporate ready-to-use products such as Plumpy'Nut peanut paste — a therapeutic nutritional product designed for use in emergencies — preclude the development of longer-term food security solutions? Likewise, at what point does it become unviable to ensure the delivery of sufficient food through the global distribution of surplus agricultural production? Alternatively, in what ways, if any, does the emergency provisioning system impede the development of local systems that could ensure better year-round food access?

Collectively, the rhetorical questions above suggest that we must be attentive to the politics of the terminology employed in the SDG 2 targets. A focus on the prevalence of undernourishment and food insecurity might seem a clear way to measure progress towards this goal. Even so, the two indicators are far too narrow to capture the broader contextual challenges facing efforts to ensure access to safe, nutritious, and sufficient food. We now know, for example, that the prevalence of undernourishment across the African continent is expected to increase significantly by 2030 due to poor governance, state fragility, war and conflict, inequality, the climate emergency, and other factors (Atukunda et al. 2021). While some causes of this setback are covered by other Global Goals, many unanswered questions remain about the political blind spots and internal inconsistencies of this target.

The second target's (2.2) drive to end all forms of malnutrition is similarly circumscribed. The indicators (2.2.1 and 2.2.2) on this target commendably emphasize the need to end stunting, wasting, and overweight for all children under five. Progress on these serious challenges and on anaemia (2.2.3) has to date been sluggish at best. Still, these indicators offer a very limited story if the aim truly is to end all types of malnutrition. No indicator was developed to capture annual per capita consumption of leafy green vegetables purchased within a certain radius of production. Data on the per capita consumption of pseudo foods, which are high in fat, sugar, and salt and notably low in nutrients, are also not being collected (Winson 2013). Knowing the year-round availability and accessibility of a basket of nutrient-dense foods would also be rather helpful, but globally comparable statistics on this front are regrettably unavailable. Efforts to track the rollout of taxes on sweetened beverages or consumer subsidies for nutrient-dense local foods by jurisdiction are also not being made. Overall, the absence of these and other possible indicators of progress on malnutrition is troubling. This highly ambitious target may fail to deliver on its promise, and there is little doubt that politics played a big part in what is currently being counted. Taking even the most limited conventional definition of malnutrition, a wider range of diet-related indicators related to obesity would reasonably have been expected. In sum, data under this target are dangerously thin.

The third target (2.3) seeks to double the productivity and incomes of small-scale food producers, and this emphasis is highly political. First and foremost, these aspirations are presented prior to and separately from the subsequent target's (2.4) considerations of sustainable agriculture and the climate emergency. Carving out the drive to raise productivity and incomes from the broader sustainability challenge of agriculture is hugely problematic. Doing so reflects a failure of the 2030 Agenda to acknowledge that the definition of productive agriculture is now a moving target. Dynamic new approaches to sustainable agriculture have unsettled the static twentieth-century understanding of agricultural productivity as the volume of production per labour unit on a daily or seasonal basis. Many twenty-first-century production systems consider productivity over a much longer time horizon and create many new productive and income-generating relationships with the land. Their productivity and income-bolstering potential cannot be adequately grasped using dated methods that focus on the output of individual crops per labour unit. Intercropping systems for organic cotton, for example, can produce value-added food products and generate demand for organic fertilizers and pesticides while enhancing soil and ecosystem health and raising production volumes (Sneyd 2011). Sustainable rice intensification approaches have also been shown to improve rice production and increase farmer incomes with fewer inputs and many environmental benefits (Thakur et al. 2022). The local demonstration effects, knowledge spillovers, and innovations that these and similar systems can induce over time will have significant consequences for productivity and incomes.

However, the indicators (2.3.1 and 2.3.2) for the third target are not disaggregated by the type of production system or sustainability approach that small-scale producers adhere to. They simply draw attention to production volumes per labour day and to annual income. This limitation effectively excludes recent developments in agricultural productivity and income from data that are supposed to yield insights on trends in productivity and income. This data gap is even more unsettling given that the global food system generates up to one-third of all human-caused greenhouse gas emissions (Blay-Palmer and Young 2019). The technologies and practices that are now referred to as climate-smart agriculture remain far from a universal cure-all. In some cases, they may underperform relative to the climate mitigation and adaptation successes associated with farmer adherence to control systems for global standards and certifications. Consequently, data that have been comprehensively disaggregated by production type could yield real insight on the future of small-scale farming. They could also do so in relation to this target's emphasis on equal access to land, inputs, financial services, markets, value-added opportunities, and nonfarm employment. Not all types of small-scale farming have the same potential to empower women and Indigenous Peoples and ensure their equal access to farming essentials. As both indicators on this target fail to integrate this aspiration, data collection on this target is unserious.

The subsequent target (2.4) for sustainable food production systems and resilient agricultural practices also exhibits a yawning gap between ambition and progress tracking. At present, no data are available on the proportion of agricultural areas under productive and sustainable agriculture (2.4.1)

(Our World in Data team 2023). Moreover, no efforts have been made to disaggregate this missing-in-action data by sustainability approach. This oversight is troubling insofar as it increases the difficulty of ascertaining the uptake of specific approaches to sustainability. Some types of climate-smart agriculture enjoy the support of transnational agribusiness, whereas other approaches, including agroecology, are backed by less powerful place-based and farmer organizations. Research now suggests that the application of ecological concepts and principles to farming could expedite efforts to achieve all dimensions of food security (Blay-Palmer and Young 2019). That said, inattention to the growth of land under specific types of sustainable agriculture obscures the politics of achieving a more sustainable global food system. Aspirations for agroecology and the right of peoples to healthy and culturally appropriate foods produced by systems that they control have fuelled a global movement for food sovereignty (Childs 2021). Supporters of this position face an uphill political battle as they attempt to relocalize food production for sustainability and challenge business narratives on the topic. The failure of this target to recognize that the science of sustainable agriculture is highly contested and subject to political interpretations that advance identifiable interests is rather shocking. Some might term it an "epic fail." Even the indicators associated with the next target (2.5) on the maintenance of genetic diversity do better on politics. They focus on the numbers of genetic resources in conservation facilities (2.5.1) and on the extinction risk classification of local breeds (2.5.2). Implicit in both indicators is an acknowledgement of the seriousness of the political threat, and the data can be readily used to inform efforts to address it directly.

Turning to SDG 2's first implementation target (2.a), the call for increased investments in rural infrastructure, agricultural research, and new technologies to enhance agricultural productive capacity in developing countries is open to serious political abuse. At the most general level, rural infrastructure projects can enrich well-connected urban elites and dispossess rural people of their lands and lifeways. Agricultural research can similarly be driven by transnational corporate greed rather than local need. Investments earmarked for the purchase of imported proprietary seed technologies can also have a fundamentally different impact than finance that enables local technological innovators and green start-ups. Put another way, the success of efforts to mobilize finance in support of SDG 2 bears no necessary relation to the achievement of global food security. More financial resources can assuredly recentre agriculture in national policy, and fund programs and projects that will expedite this goal. But massive cash injections can also be used to grease the wheels of patron-client relations. Donors and investors clearly have their own distinct sets of interests. Their priorities can divert government attention from genuine food security priorities or pervert their interpretations of such priorities. With data collection efforts focused only on the prominence of agriculture in government expenditures (2.a.1) and on total official flows to agriculture (2.a.2), this implementation target is an open invitation to unchecked growth of agricultural expenditures. To say the least, giving investors with cash to burn such a green light to advance their interests may not be congruent with the focus of SDG 16 on uniting people around the world in a drive to reduce corruption and build effective and accountable institutions. This target's emphasis on scaling up financial resources also seems to rule out the idea of doing more to end hunger with less reliance on big projects and big agriculture (Mendonça 2023). To date, a wide range of small-scale, low-cost, and collaborative bottom-up initiatives have durably improved food security and the sustainability of food systems (Vivero-Pol et al. 2019). A money-driven big push could put many of these local innovations at risk.

The focus of the second implementation target (2.b) on international trade in world agricultural markets is also telling as regards corporate interests. This target emphasizes government measures, including the correction and prevention of trade restrictions and distortions, and the elimination of agricultural export subsidies. Its sole indicator of success is the value of agricultural export subsidies over time (2.b.1). This exceedingly narrow focus on trade politics completely disregards the control that corporations exercise over three strategic segments of the world food economy: the provision of inputs, the agricultural commodity trade and food processing, and food retailing (McKeon 2017). Taken together, these aspects of the food system are at the heart of world trade in food. Yet this target is entirely silent on the politics of the trade that these firms maintain and increasingly govern (Clapp and Fuchs 2009). As companies assume more governance functions that go beyond purely economic and managerial considerations in relation to their global supply chains, the political challenges that this target neglects will only continue to grow.

The final implementation target's (2.c) emphasis on ensuring the proper functioning of food commodity markets is also inattentive to corporate control and interests. Nonetheless, its focus on tracking the volatility of food prices (2.c.1) should be lauded. To ensure food access, it is an absolute must for governments to be attentive to these data and to take corrective actions as needed (Margulis 2023). But are food commodity markets truly functioning "properly" when a small handful of companies dominate world trade in agricultural commodities, food processing, and food retailing? Managing the short-term political risk of food price anomalies is not the only essential metric in this space. As we all saw during the COVID-19 pandemic, corporate restrictive practices, commodity market speculation, and profiteering fuelled wild swings in food commodity prices. Yet this target does not mandate efforts to assess corporate contributions to the volatility of global prices. It also fails to acknowledge that there is no universal or one-size-fits-all approach to governing food commodity markets. Governance approaches remain subject to political interpretations and contestation, so here, too, inattention to a core dynamic could undercut the success of this SDG.

The UN secretary-general's report at the midpoint to 2030 was crystal clear about the underperformance of work to address the global hunger challenge. If present trends continue, over 670 million people worldwide could be hungry in 2030 (UNSG 2023). While the secretary-general's report noted that the recent spike in global hunger has been exacerbated by factors including the COVID-19 pandemic, the emergence of new political conflicts, climate change, and growing inequalities, it remained silent on other political deficiencies linked to the 2030 Agenda itself. SDG 2 promotes a strikingly liberal standpoint on food system change that is assuredly not apolitical. Nationalists have stoked fear about the possible ways that the "globalist" food agenda could undercut rural culture and lifeways. Social progressives and greens counter nationalist talking points *and* critique this goal's overt strategy to advance corporate interests in perpetuating global food supply chains and entrenching the use of proprietary agricultural technologies.

References

Atukunda, P. W.B. Eide, K.R. Kardel, P.O. Iversen, and A.C Westerberg. 2021. "Unlocking the Potential for Achievement of the UN Sustainable Development Goal — 'Zero Hunger' — in Africa: Targets, Strategies, Synergies and Challenges." *Food & Nutrition Research* 65, 7686.

Blay-Palmer, A., and L. Young. 2019. "Food System Lessons from the SDGs." In *Achieving the Sustainable Development Goals: Global Governance Challenges*, edited by S. Dalby, S. Horton, R. Mahon, and D. Thomaz. London: Routledge.

Childs, C. 2021. "Food Sovereignty: Returning Power to Those Who Produce." *Medium*, January 27. medium.com/una-nca-snapshots/food-sovereignty-returning-power-to-those-who-produce-1815210f44ff.

Clapp, J., and D. Fuchs (eds.). 2009. *Corporate Power in Global Agrifood Governance*. Cambridge, MA: The MIT Press.

FAO (Food and Agriculture Organization). 2023. "Sustainable Development Goals." Rome: United Nations. fao.org/sustainable-development-goals-helpdesk/overview/agrifood-systems-and-the-2030-agenda/en.

Margulis, M. 2023. *Shadow Negotiators: How UN Organizations Shape the Rules of World Trade for Food Security*. Stanford: Stanford University Press.

McKeon, N. 2017. "Are Equity and Sustainability a Likely Outcome When Foxes and Chickens Share the Same Coop? Critiquing the Concept of Multistakeholder Governance of Food Security." In *The Politics of Destination in the 2030 Sustainable Development Goals: Leaving No-One Behind?*, edited by C. Gabay and S. Ilcan. London: Routledge.

Mendonça, M. L. 2023. *The Political Economy of Agribusiness: A Critical Development Perspective.* Halifax: Fernwood Publishing.

Our World in Data team. 2023. "End Hunger, Achieve Food Security and Improved Nutrition and Promote Sustainable Agriculture." ourworldindata.org/sdgs/zero-hunger.

Sneyd, A. 2011. *Governing Cotton: Globalization and Poverty in Africa.* Basingstoke, UK: Palgrave Macmillan.

Thakur, A.K., K.G. Mandal, R.K. Mohanty, and N. Uphoff. 2022. "How Agroecological Rice Intensification Can Assist in Reaching the Sustainable Development Goals." *International Journal of Agricultural Sustainability* 20, 2.

UN (United Nations). 2020. *Zero Hunger: Why It Matters.* un.org/sustainabledevelopment/wp-content/uploads/2018/09/Goal-2.pdf.

———. 2022. *The Sustainable Development Goals Report 2022.* New York: UN.

———. 2023. "Goal 2: Zero Hunger." un.org/sustainabledevelopment/hunger.

UNSG (United Nations Secretary-General). 2023. *Progress towards the Sustainable Development Goals: Towards a Rescue Plan for People and Planet. Report of the Secretary-General (Special Edition).* New York: United Nations General Assembly and Economic and Social Council.

Vivero-Pol, J.A., T. Ferrando, O. De Schutter, and U. Mattei (eds.). 2019. *Routledge Handbook of Food as Commons.* London: Routledge.

Winson, T. 2013. *The Industrial Diet: The Degradation of Food and the Struggle for Healthy Eating.* Vancouver: University of British Columbia Press.

World Food Programme n.d. *A Global Food Crisis.* wfp.org/global-hunger-crisis.

Goal ③
Good Health and Well-Being

What They Tell Us

Mission statement: Ensure healthy lives and promote well-being for all at all ages.

Deep collaborations to improve the resilience of health systems and ensure improved well-being for all are urgently required. The COVID-19 pandemic demonstrated that when demand for health care surges, most countries do not have adequate health facilities, medical supplies, or numbers of health care workers (UN 2020). To address this challenge and improve health and well-being during more normal times, there must be a big push for sustainable investments in health systems. Care and coverage must be made more accessible, and the burden of zoonotic and noncommunicable diseases must be better addressed. If we pursue these ends expeditiously, better well-being will be within our grasp. Prior to the pandemic, gains "were evident in many areas of health" (UN 2022, 30). Robust action is required to put us back on the path towards achieving this goal. Individuals can raise awareness about the importance of good health and hold people to account for their commitments to improve health care access (UN 2020). Only about one half of the global population will be covered by essential health services in 2030 if current trends continue (UN 2023).

Health Targets	Indicators
3.1 By 2030, reduce the global maternal mortality ratio to less than 70 per 100,000 live births	3.1.1 Maternal mortality ratio 3.1.2 Proportion of births attended by skilled health personnel
3.2 By 2030, end preventable deaths of newborns and children under 5 years of age, with all countries aiming to reduce neonatal mortality to at least as low as 12 per 1,000 live births and under-5 mortality to at least as low as 25 per 1,000 live births	3.2.1 Under-5 mortality rate 3.2.2 Neonatal mortality rate

Health Targets	Indicators
3.3 By 2030, end the epidemics of AIDS, tuberculosis, malaria and neglected tropical diseases and combat hepatitis, water-borne diseases, and other communicable diseases	3.3.1 Number of new HIV infections per 1,000 uninfected population, by sex, age, and key populations 3.3.2 Tuberculosis incidence per 100,000 population 3.3.3 Malaria incidence per 1,000 population 3.3.4 Hepatitis B incidence per 100,000 population 3.3.5 Number of people requiring interventions against neglected tropical diseases
3.4 By 2030, reduce by one third premature mortality from non-communicable diseases through prevention and treatment and promote mental health and well-being	3.4.1 Mortality rate attributed to cardiovascular disease, cancer, diabetes, or chronic respiratory disease 3.4.2 Suicide mortality rate
3.5 Strengthen the prevention and treatment of substance abuse, including narcotic drug abuse and harmful use of alcohol	3.5.1 Coverage of treatment interventions (pharmacological, psychosocial, and rehabilitation and aftercare services) for substance use disorders 3.5.2 Harmful use of alcohol, defined according to the national context as alcohol per capita consumption (aged 15 years and older) within a calendar year in litres of pure alcohol
3.6 By 2020, halve the number of global deaths and injuries from road traffic accidents	3.6.1 Death rate due to road traffic injuries
3.7 By 2030, ensure universal access to sexual and reproductive health-care services, including for family planning, information and education, and the integration of reproductive health into national strategies and programmes	3.7.1 Proportion of women of reproductive age (aged 15–49 years) who have their need for family planning satisfied with modern methods 3.7.2 Adolescent birth rate (aged 10–14 years; aged 15–19 years) per 1,000 women in that age group
3.8 Achieve universal health coverage, including financial risk protection, access to quality essential health-care services and access to safe, effective, quality, and affordable essential medicines and vaccines for all	3.8.1 Coverage of essential health services 3.8.2 Proportion of population with large household expenditures on health as a share of total household expenditure or income
3.9 By 2030, substantially reduce the number of deaths and illnesses from hazardous chemicals and air, water and soil pollution and contamination	3.9.1 Mortality rate attributed to household and ambient air pollution 3.9.2 Mortality rate attributed to unsafe water, unsafe sanitation, and lack of hygiene 3.9.3 Mortality rate attributed to unintentional poisoning
3.a Strengthen the implementation of the World Health Organization Framework Convention on Tobacco Control in all countries, as appropriate	3.a.1 Age-standardized prevalence of current tobacco use among persons aged 15 years and older

Health Targets	Indicators
3.b Support the research and development of vaccines and medicines for the communicable and noncommunicable diseases that primarily affect developing countries, provide access to affordable essential medicines and vaccines, in accordance with the Doha Declaration on the TRIPS Agreement and Public Health, which affirms the right of developing countries to use to the full the provisions in the Agreement on Trade-Related Aspects of Intellectual Property Rights regarding flexibilities to protect public health, and, in particular, provide access to medicines for all	**3.b.1** Proportion of the target population covered by all vaccines included in their national programme **3.b.2** Total net official development assistance (ODA) to medical research and basic health sectors **3.b.3** Proportion of health facilities that have a core set of relevant essential medicines available and affordable on a sustainable basis
3.c Substantially increase health financing and the recruitment, development, training, and retention of the health workforce in developing countries, especially in least developed countries and small island developing States	**3.c.1** Health worker density and distribution
3.d Strengthen the capacity of all countries, in particular developing countries, for early warning, risk reduction and management of national and global health risks	**3.d.1** International Health Regulations (IHR) capacity and health emergency preparedness **3.d.2** Percentage of bloodstream infections due to selected antimicrobial-resistant organisms

The Hidden Politics

During and after the COVID-19 pandemic, the global, national, and local politics that can undermine good health and well-being became all too familiar. Governments in some countries attempted to politicize the responses of international public institutions and foreign powers. National and subnational authorities that took the emerging scientific consensus and public health guidance seriously introduced strict measures to curb the spread of the virus and faced enduring political pushback for doing so. As the disease strained universal and public health care systems, advocates of private, for-profit health care worked to secure political gains. Simultaneously, avaricious health entrepreneurs sought to corner markets for personal protective equipment and essential health products, compounding the challenge many governments faced to procure and ensure supplies. International cooperation to develop a vaccine then faced severe coordination and funding gaps. Transnational pharmaceutical corporations were ultimately given the green light to fill this void. They raced to fund, develop, or acquire the rights to viable vaccines while lobbying for the relaxation of established regulatory procedures. Funding mechanisms to enable developing and least developed countries to acquire effective vaccines fell so far short of ambitions that UN experts were compelled to call for an end to "vaccine apartheid" (OHCHR 2022; Stein 2021). Populist politicians parroted antivaccine talking points and politicized inoculation campaigns. Rules related to mask wearing became a political flash point, and public health authorities in some cases faced political threats. In the end, right-wing politicians underscored and inflated the negative impacts that health measures had on economies and spuriously lambasted the effectiveness of social protection programs that had been put in place to mitigate the fallout. Taking these and other challenges into account, it is not a stretch to assert that in this case, a serious pandemic fuelled a sustained political circus.

Practical and relevant targets under SDG 3 are unfortunately not immune to the forces and factors that can politicize good health and well-being. While they can be employed to encourage the pursuit of needed interventions, these targets tend to gloss over the extent of underlying political challenges. For example, the first target's (3.1) call to reduce global and national maternal mortality ratios directly addresses a persistent and consequential problem. However, the sole focus of the associated indicators (3.1.1 and 3.1.2) on the maternal mortality ratio and the percentage of births attended by trained personnel is disturbing. No numerical objective has been established for the latter indicator. Its language is also broad enough to facilitate the inclusion of skilled birth attendants that are not trained physicians or nurse practitioners. While this expansive definition tacitly acknowledges the realities of childbirth in many developing countries, it facilitates the statistical inclusion of low- and lower-skilled birth attendants. Reducing maternal mortality ratios is also about much more than the presence or absence of essential support workers. Prenatal education, including education and training related to nutrition and physical fitness for healthy pregnancies, can be impactful. However, this target does not include any indicators related to the existence of related laws or policies, or on the coverage rates of programs on these topics. The second target (3.2) on reducing preventable under-five (3.2.1) and neonatal (3.2.2) deaths is similarly inattentive to contextual factors. It does not include any indicators to monitor trends in the regularity of contact with medical practitioners, or in the coverage of parental education for child health. This gap is curious, as many other goals under the 2030 Agenda do encourage governments to take notice of trends in coverage rates.

The third target's (3.3) push to end and combat communicable diseases remains subject to the global to local politics that we are by now all too familiar with. This target recognizes that ongoing efforts to bring an end to the epidemics of AIDS, tuberculosis, malaria, and other neglected tropical diseases, and to combat hepatitis, water-borne, and other communicable diseases, are not achieving progress equally or at the same pace. Thus, the indicators under this target (3.3.1–3.3.5) draw attention to the number of new HIV infections and to incidence rates or numbers of interventions required against other diseases. Over time, data on infections, incidence rates, and interventions that are disaggregated by sex, age, and key populations can be used to identify problem areas and successes. At best, governments could employ this data to pursue reforms to their disease eradication programs. That said, the direction of trends in new infections, incidence rates, and numbers of interventions is not solely determined in national or domestic contexts. Fights against communicable diseases are often shaped and constrained by international and global factors. These can include funding levels and priorities, research and development incentives, and cooperation or the lack thereof to build consensus on needed approaches, interventions, and programming. The 2030 Agenda's overarching emphasis on the domestic level of analysis, national outcomes, and local ownership is, in this instance, rather unhelpful. It has precluded the inclusion of indicators under this target that would enable funding laggards to be called out. Measures related to the financial performance or impact of disease-related global funds have also been excluded. While information on these topics continues to be produced, this target does not oblige governments to be attentive to it. If data everywhere were to show the relative underperformance of work on a specific disease, perhaps the spotlight would fall on possible international or global sources of the shortcoming. As it stands, the official data omit the impacts that international or global political forces can have on the progress of the fight to end communicable disease.

The fourth (3.4), fifth (3.5), and sixth (3.6) targets articulate strong ambitions related to noncommunicable diseases, mental health, substance abuse, and road injuries and deaths. They stand as a global call to action to arrest some of the leading global sources of ill health and causes of death. Nonetheless, the indicators associated with each target are at best imperfect, and their wide variations showcase a glaring inconsistency in the approach to data collection under the SDGs. To advance the fourth target's aspiration to curb premature mortality by one-third, governments are encouraged to be vigilant regarding trends in the mortality rates attributed to cardiovascular disease, cancer, diabetes, and chronic respiratory disease (3.4.1). To promote mental health and well-being, they are also implored to pay attention to the suicide mortality rate (3.4.2). While both indicators spotlight statistics on death, this emphasis is insufficient. It can be employed to assess the effectiveness of public health initiatives, programming, and clinical development. But the stress on mortality could also obscure the importance of the parallel need to improve disease and mental health interventions for those living with disease burdens. For diseases that currently lack cures, efforts to enhance patient quality of life enhance well-being. The exclusion of an indicator on coverage rates of programs in this area is troubling. The next target on the prevention and treatment of substance and alcohol abuse includes a robust indicator related to the coverage of pharmacological, psychosocial, rehabilitation, and aftercare services (3.5.1). Yet the sixth target on road injuries and deaths once again features an indicator that focuses only on reducing death rates from road traffic (3.6.1). It includes no language on the coverage of public education programs related to impaired driving. Why the coverage of programming in some areas of health and well-being "counts," but does not count in others, remains a mystery. At the very least, a more internally consistent approach to tracking the coverage of programs that address the primary causes of ill health and death would have been helpful.

Beyond the politics of inconsistent data collection priorities, the seventh and eighth targets have been framed in ways that could limit their impacts. The target (3.7) on universal access to sexual and reproductive care includes no language on the affordability of family planning services or products (3.7.1). Without due regard to the cost implications, how exactly universal access to sexual and reproductive care and family planning are to be ensured under this target remains unclear, to say the least. The next target (3.8) on universal health coverage does include language on financial risk protection, access to quality essential services, and the affordability of essential medicines. However, it does not challenge private, profit-driven health care services. It says nothing about the persistence of practices that thwart the realization of universal coverage in systems of private and mixed provision. And it elides any language that could be taken to imply support for the public provision of universal health care. Arguably, the emphasis of the two associated indicators (3.8.1 and 3.8.2) on health coverage rates and on household health expenditures will produce data that could be used to challenge private interests in health care. That said, statistical trends on these matters are subject to political interpretation. Corporations in this sector could readily employ them to lobby for corporate welfare or to call for more competition and regulatory reform. Bypassing any direct mention of the politics of health care provision in the writing of this target may have helped to garner support for it. But this exclusion is itself political. As it stands, aspirations for universal access under this target remain conditional on the capacity of markets to deliver it.

The ninth target's (3.9) ambition to reduce illness and death from hazardous chemicals and pollution in the air, water, and soil has also been framed in a way that is exceedingly friendly to corporations. It seeks only to spotlight mortality rates that are attributable to (i) household and ambient air pollution (3.9.1); (ii) unsafe water, sanitation, and a lack of hygiene (3.9.2); and (iii) unintentional poisoning and exposure (3.9.3). Mortality rates can be used to evaluate the effectiveness of environmental regulations, and to identify areas for sensitization campaigns and legal development. Despite this usefulness, they offer an insufficient lens on the ways that hazardous chemicals and pollution undermine good health. Corporations tend to be the source of the dirty products, by-products, unmitigated externalities, and fallout that kill people and undermine health and well-being over time. Privately held and publicly traded companies also contribute to shaping and constraining the regulation of questionable environmental practices. To ward off costly reforms, or to keep their dirty and dangerous products on the shelves, polluters can deploy complex legal strategies or rely on the persuasive power of industry associations or lobbying groups. Thus, progress on this target could be expedited if trends in corporate expenditures on lobbying related to environmental regulations were known. If efforts were also made to track corporate contributions to regulatory language, and to measure rates of corporate compliance with existing regulations, data under this target would be much more comprehensive. The omission of any diligence whatsoever related to corporations speaks to the existence of a grim contradiction under the 2030 Agenda. It belies the notion that progress on the Global Goals is a shared responsibility. Data that could be used to name and shame specific governments for failing to rein in corporate practices that drive mortality in this area have been ruled out a priori. The failure to include appropriate metrics shows that it is at best misguided to believe that that we are all united in support of the SDGs. Governments excluded inconvenient data, and as consequence, we all remain in the dark about greedy polluters that continue to do the minimum for people and the planet.

Many of the political challenges noted above also work against SDG 3's four sensible and needed implementation targets. The target (3.a) related to tobacco control focuses only on the prevalence of current tobacco use, and not on the coverage rates of associated programs. The subsequent target's (3.b) call for the research and development of vaccines and medicines for communicable and noncommunicable diseases that primarily affect developing countries also faces an uphill battle. It puts needed emphasis on the affordability of essential vaccines and medicines and reaffirms the right of developing countries to prioritize public health over patents (Hira 2009; Horner 2022). Even so, the indicators (3.b.1–3.b.3) associated with this ambition are inattentive to the many ways that pharmaceutical firms can expedite or hold back progress in this area. We are only too aware that drug prices can have a significant impact on vaccine coverage rates and on the uses to which official development assistance flows are put. The third (3.c) implementation target's push for substantial increases in health financing and the recruitment, development, training, and retention of health workforces is also conducive to corporate interests. The drive to grow the relative economic share of the health sector in developing countries will of necessity increase the opportunities that legitimate entrepreneurs have to make profits. But as the case of the bogus blood-testing start-up Theranos demonstrates, this sector is not immune to fraud. The "bezzle," defined as the stock of undiscovered fraud in any sector, tends to rise in lockstep with the growth of that sector (Galbraith 1955). Up to now, no official indicators related to the specific impact of the bezzle on good health and well-being have been established. In an ideal world, the crucial final target (3.d) on building capacity for early warning, risk reduction, and management of national and global health risks would also stand above political contestation or abuse. However, the pandemic should have disabused us of such fanciful thinking. Each of the crucial implementation targets under SDG 3 faces serious political roadblocks.

While the UN secretary-general's report at the SDG midpoint acknowledged that progress was evident on HIV and hepatitis, it underscored how the COVID-19 pandemic negatively impacted many other areas of global public health (UNSG 2023). However, the secretary-general's "rescue plan" for the goals failed to recognize the extent of the looming political challenge. Simply put, SDG 3 advances an approach to health that reinforces the liberal international economic order, and this orientation has become a political lightning rod. In the aftermath of the pandemic, many right-wing populists forcefully reject the idea of global health leadership. Progressive and green voices challenge these populist reactions *and* hotly contest SDG 3's liberal intentions and political limitations.

References

Galbraith, J.K. 1955. *The Great Crash: 1929*. Boston: Houghton Mifflin.

Hira, A. 2009. "The Political Economy of the Global Pharmaceutical Industry: Why the Poor Lack Access to Medicine and What Might be Done About it." *International Journal of Development Issues* 8, 2.

Horner, R. 2022. "Global Value Chains, Import Orientation, and the State: South Africa's Pharmaceutical Industry." *Journal of International Business Policy* 5.

OHCHR (United Nations Office of the High Commissioner on Human Rights). 2022. "UN Expert Urges States to End 'Vaccine Apartheid.'" Press release, June 14. ohchr.org/en/press-releases/2022/06/un-expert-urges-states-end-vaccine-apartheid.

Our Work in Data team. 2023. "Ensure Healthy Lives and Promote Well-being for All at All Ages." ourworldindata.org/sdgs/good-health-wellbeing.

Stein, F. 2021. "Risky Business: COVAX and the Financialization of Global Vaccine Equity." *Globalization and Health* 17, 112.

UN (United Nations). 2020. *Good Health and Well-Being: Why It Matters.* un.org/sustainabledevelopment/wp-content/uploads/2017/03/3_Why-It-Matters-2020.pdf.

———. 2022. *The Sustainable Development Goals Report 2022.* New York: UN.

———. 2023. "Goal 3: Ensure Healthy Lives and Promote Well-being for All at All Ages." un.org/sustainabledevelopment/health.

UNSG (United Nations Secretary-General). 2023. *Progress towards the Sustainable Development Goals: Towards a Rescue Plan for People and Planet. Report of the Secretary-General (Special Edition).* New York: United Nations General Assembly and Economic and Social Council.

Goal 4

Quality Education

What They Tell Us

> **Mission statement:** Ensure inclusive and equitable quality education and promote lifelong learning opportunities for all.

There is a clear need for education to move up the list of global priorities. Quality education can help people fight poverty and thrive (UN 2020). An emphasis on education will also help reduce economic and gender inequality. Moreover, education makes significant and growing contributions to peacebuilding and global prosperity (UN 2023). In the interest of enabling young people to acquire the knowledge and skills they need to live healthy, tolerant, and gainful lives, the world needs to unite behind this important goal. Unfortunately, the "COVID-19 pandemic came at a time when the world was already struggling with a crisis in learning: too many children lacked the fundamentals of reading and numeracy" (UN 2022, 34). In 2018, at least 773 million adults were functionally illiterate, and the proportion of children with minimum proficiency in reading fell below 60 per cent in all middle- and low-income countries. Given these realities, individuals must lobby their governments to make firm commitments to education for all, including vulnerable and marginalized groups. COVID-19 caused a global education crisis, and governments must be convinced to pursue this goal with urgency (UN 2020).

Education Targets		Indicators	
4.1	By 2030, ensure that all girls and boys complete free, equitable and quality primary and secondary education leading to relevant and Goal-4 effective learning outcomes	4.1.1	Proportion of children and young people (a) in grades 2/3; (b) at the end of primary; and (c) at the end of lower secondary achieving at least a minimum proficiency level in (i) reading and (ii) mathematics, by sex
		4.1.2	Completion rate (primary education, lower secondary education, upper secondary education)

Education Targets	Indicators
4.2 By 2030, ensure that all girls and boys have access to quality early childhood development, care, and pre-primary education so that they are ready for primary education	4.2.1 Proportion of children aged 24–59 months (2-5 years) who are developmentally on track in health, learning and psychosocial well-being, by sex 4.2.2 Participation rate in organized learning (one year before the official primary entry age), by sex
4.3 By 2030, ensure equal access for all women and men to affordable and quality technical, vocational, and tertiary education, including university	4.3.1 Participation rate of youth and adults in formal and non-formal education and training in the previous 12 months, by sex
4.4 By 2030, substantially increase the number of youth and adults who have relevant skills, including technical and vocational skills, for employment, decent jobs, and entrepreneurship	4.4.1 Proportion of youth and adults with information and communications technology (ICT) skills, by type of skill
4.5 By 2030, eliminate gender disparities in education and ensure equal access to all levels of education and vocational training for the vulnerable, including persons with disabilities, Indigenous Peoples, and children in vulnerable situations	4.5.1 Parity indices (female/male, rural/urban, bottom/top wealth quintile and others such as disability status, Indigenous Peoples, and conflict-affected, as data become available) for all education indicators on this list that can be disaggregated
4.6 By 2030, ensure that all youth and a substantial proportion of adults, both men and women, achieve literacy and numeracy	4.6.1 Proportion of population in a given age group achieving at least a fixed level of proficiency in functional (a) literacy and (b) numeracy skills, by sex
4.7 By 2030, ensure that all learners acquire the knowledge and skills needed to promote sustainable development, including, among others, through education for sustainable development and sustainable lifestyles, human rights, gender equality, promotion of a culture of peace and non-violence, global citizenship, and appreciation of cultural diversity and of culture's contribution to sustainable development	4.7.1 Extent to which (i) global citizenship education and (ii) education for sustainable development are mainstreamed in (a) national education policies; (b) curricula; (c) teacher education; and (d) student assessment
4.a Build and upgrade education facilities that are child, disability, and gender sensitive and provide safe, nonviolent, inclusive, and effective learning environments for all	4.a.1 Proportion of schools offering basic services, by type of service
4.b By 2020, substantially expand globally the number of scholarships available to developing countries, in particular least developed countries, small island developing states, and African countries, for enrolment in higher education, including vocational training and information and communications technology, technical, engineering and scientific programmes, in developed countries and other developing countries	4.b.1 Volume of official development assistance flows for scholarships by sector and type of study
4.c By 2030, substantially increase the supply of qualified teachers, including through international cooperation for teacher training in developing countries, especially least developed countries and small island developing states	4.c.1 Proportion of teachers with the minimum required qualifications, by education level

The Hidden Politics

The first enthusiastic target (4.1) under SDG 4 sounds the right note. It aims to ensure that all girls and boys complete free, equitable, and quality primary and secondary education leading to relevant and effective learning outcomes. That said, this call for global action on education for all is circumscribed by inordinately weak indicators (4.1.1 and 4.1.2) and by its inattention to the political forces that impede the delivery of effective education. Headway on this target has been defined exclusively in relation to minimum proficiencies in reading and mathematics, and to completion rates. These indicators simply encourage governments to assess student progress towards basic literacy and numeracy at various stages of educational development. Delineating the quality of education for all only in relation to these topics and to rates of formal completion is hardly aspirational. Quality education under this target could have been defined much more boldly to include an emphasis on additional language training and immersion, arts education, community engagement, and a range of other essentials. Beyond its minimalist ambitions, this target is not associated with any indicators to assess progress towards free and equitable education for all. On the former, it includes no language whatsoever related to prioritizing public education systems over the private delivery of educational services. Consequently, efforts under this target are inattentive to the ways that the corporate provision of education or the development of voucher systems can undermine public education systems. Language related to the outsourcing of schooling to transnational educational providers and its potential cost and equity ramifications is similarly absent (Williams 2016). Beyond cost and delivery considerations, the target also fails to speak to the socioeconomic and political inequities that erode completion rates. These remain particularly problematic at the secondary level, and can be fuelled by poverty, inequality, religion, gender, and identity-related factors (Friedman et al. 2020). As SDGs on those topics face their own unique political obstacles and limitations, the idea that the "integrated" nature of the goals will expedite the delivery of free and equitable education is dubious at best.

A political emphasis on individual participation and performance also infuses the second target (4.2), which aims to ensure that all girls and boys have access to quality early childhood development, care, and pre-primary education. The two indicators (4.2.1 and 4.2.2) associated with this objective reflect an overarching concern with the readiness of children under five years of age for primary schooling. They encourage governments to pay close attention to the proportion of children who are developmentally on track, and to participation rates in organized learning in the year before the official primary entrance age. While sex-disaggregated data on these topics can yield actionable insights, the exclusive emphasis of both indicators on the individual development, participation, and performance of children under five is concerning. The indicators do not consider the development of pre-primary education systems, or their costs or affordability, or equity-oriented programs or subsidies. This stress on individuals seemingly downloads responsibility onto the shoulders of parents and families. Unlike many other SDG targets, pre-primary aspirations are not linked to an effort to track the existence of related laws or policies. Instead, the emphasis implicitly falls on how parents are doing to prepare their kids for the primary system. Attention to the systemic factors that can impede the performance of children under five, and to how well governments are doing to address those challenges, has been excluded a priori. Thus, the timing of the readiness of children for primary education is treated with more importance than the development of conditions that can enable pre-primary success. This is another telling example of how the orientation of many SDGs around individual performance can inadvertently or directly contribute to the individualization and atomization of society (Boeren 2019).

The third target (4.3) exemplifies the incredibly weak language and political timidity that has restricted the scope and potential impact of education for all. The utopian idea of ensuring equal access for all women and men to affordable and quality technical, vocational, and tertiary education, including university, enjoys near universal support. That said, this target does not endorse a comprehensive global push for more data on affordability and quality in further and higher education. Rather, it narrowly encourages attention to the participation rate of youth and adults in formal and nonformal education and training over the previous year (4.3.1). According to the Our World in Data team (2023), it is not clear how governments are supposed to track "nonformal" further training. Should this category include so-called third-age learning programs that primarily serve retirees? Does enrolment in unofficial certificate programs developed by individual entrepreneurs or social media influencers "count" as nonformal training? And what of those that aim to further their education through participation in the global essay and assignment resale market without formally registering for vocational or university-based courses? The inclusion of nonformal further training in the indicator detracts from efforts to produce better and more comparable data on the barriers to inclusive and effective higher education. It also stretches the definition of further and higher education in a way that is conducive to individual entrepreneurs that seek to sell proprietary educational innovations and technologies.

This orientation is consequential, as the subsequent target (4.4) directly advances the interests of so-called disrupters and innovators in the provision of further and tertiary education. The fourth target aims to substantially increase the number of people with relevant skills, including technical and vocational skills, for employment, decent jobs, and entrepreneurship. At first glance, this ambition seems to be congruent with the paths that many musicians, painters, dancers, artisans, comics, curators, writers, actors, designers, and support personnel take to finding work and building careers in the creative and cultural industries. Nonetheless, the underlying indicator (4.4.1) simply encourages governments to be attentive to the proportion of youth and adults with information and communication technology (ICT) skills, by type of skill. Being able to access and navigate Internet search engines, and to maintain a virtual presence, can be essential for success in many artistic, creative, and cultural professions. But these skills clearly are not the linchpin of many prosperous careers. They are just one of several essential means that can be employed to develop underlying talent and link it up with others. If governments everywhere were to exclusively prioritize the development of ICT skills under this target, society would be the poorer for it. While that eventuality might seem far-fetched, the overemphasis on building technological skills could encourage poorer governments to copy ICT policies that are not appropriate to their level of development (Boeren 2019). This direction is also rooted in a functionalist understanding of education. Functionalist viewpoints deprioritize the contributions that education makes to social creativity and are overly attentive to the ways that education can expedite economic growth (Enns 2015). Thus, resource-constrained governments in search of quick "wins" under the education goal might gravitate towards this target. It offers guidance that may seem more practical and measurable than the intensive work required to build accessible, affordable, and quality systems of further and higher education. In sum, the inclusion of only one seemingly practical indicator under this target could inadvertently unleash forces that impede progress on education for all.

The fifth (4.5) and sixth (4.6) targets under SDG 4 seek to redress unequal educational outcomes related to discrimination, and to promote universal literacy and numeracy. They inject a needed emphasis on reducing inequality into efforts to achieve education for all. That said, both targets are less than ambitious. The fifth target does include ostensibly strong language on the need to eliminate gender disparities in education. Yet it does not aim to eradicate unbalanced educational outcomes associated with other identities and vulnerabilities. Instead, it simply asserts that access to all levels of education and vocational training for other vulnerable groups should be ensured. This discrepancy is consequential, as the associated indicator (4.5.1) calls for governments to pay particular attention to parity indices. While gender-related parity indices for enrolment, school life expectancy, and completion rates exist, globally comparable data on parity for other vulnerable groups is unavailable (Our World in Data team 2023). This data gap could encourage some governments to develop indices related to disability, Indigenous Peoples, or conflict-affected groups. But realistically, the ready availability of gender-related data, and the apparent prioritization of gender under this target, could embolden resource-constrained governments to treat other identities and vulnerabilities as secondary considerations. Speaking of derivative concerns, the goal's sixth target very clearly delineates the bounds of its push for universal literacy and numeracy. The language of the target openly prioritizes efforts to ensure that all youth achieve basic or functional literacy and numeracy. Adult achievements in this area matter only to the extent that substantial proportions around the world can meet basic standards (4.6.1). What exactly constitutes a "substantial" proportion of functionally literate and numerate adults has not been defined. In this way, the 2030 Agenda considers the plight of mature adults who cannot read and write to be of less importance than youth education. This highly political guidance flies in the face of strong evidence suggesting that basic adult education can have significant and positive socioeconomic impacts (Hickey and Hossain 2019).

The seventh target (4.7) stands out for focusing on curriculum content and building connections between education and efforts to achieve the Global Goals. The idea that all learners should acquire the knowledge and skills needed to promote sustainable development and act as global citizens is praiseworthy. Having taught many courses on these topics at the University of Guelph over the years, this objective is music to my ears. Even so, its feasibility remains in question. Calls to mainstream global citizenship education and education for sustainable development at all levels directly challenge the persistence and rise of nationalist and nativist politics. Populist politicians can readily and inaccurately characterize these ends as a socialist threat to school systems. After all, mainstreaming this emphasis in national education policies, curricula, teacher education, and student assessments could significantly reduce the number of uneducated flag-waving jingoists over time.

Beyond this political barrier, the push to mainstream education in this area faces other high hurdles. Its effectiveness depends on simultaneous action to scale up the capacity of citizens the world over to think critically.

Helping students in higher education to become more open-minded and skeptical, and to learn how to respect and evaluate research, evidence, reasoning, and diverse points of view, is always a tall order. It is also difficult for teachers at other levels to practise these skills, let alone impart them. Evidence from research on teacher training suggests that the capacity for teachers to set aside their assumptions and think more critically about global development needs to be scaled up considerably (Varadharajan and Buchanan 2017). Sustainable development and global citizenship are also incredibly vast fields of study. Students can earn related bachelor's, master's, and doctoral degrees and still lack comprehensive knowledge about certain research approaches or specific topics. Unfortunately, the indicator (4.7.1) associated with this target narrows its scope considerably. It does include specific language on gender equality and human rights education, but it leaves out other aspirations, including education for sustainable lifestyles and cultural appreciation. More broadly, the target also fails to call for education on a range of critical contemporary topics, including colonialism and the need to decolonize understandings of development and global citizenship.

The implementation-related targets under this goal also face considerable political obstacles. Of these, the call to build and upgrade education facilities to ensure more inclusive, safe, and effective learning environments could not be more inoffensive (4.a). Yet the politics of building and maintaining schools has become much more complex as student safety and gender inclusivity have continued to garner headline-grabbing attention. The contributions that so-called voluntourists make to school building in developing countries also raise serious political concerns (Sneyd 2019). Moreover, language under this target emphasizes drinking water and sanitation facilities (4.a.1), but conspicuously excludes school feeding programs and the development of related infrastructure. There is no doubt that politics has in this case constrained ambitions and necessitated the use of minimalist language.

The next target (4.b) on expanding higher education scholarships for developing countries is also permeated with politics and openly invites political conflict. The idea of making more scholarships available to young people from least developed, small island, and African countries to pursue higher education opportunities in developed and other developing countries is at best very dated. Many initiatives to build higher education capacity in poorer countries have been ongoing for decades. Some of these have aimed to reduce the so-called brain drain and create new opportunities for students and researchers to gainfully apply their skills to development challenges in their home countries. Thus, the exclusive focus of this target on scaling up the volume of official development assistance flows for scholarships seems to be a relic from a bygone era (4.b.1). It entirely disregards the demonstrated potential for multistakeholder partnerships and collaborations to develop higher education capacities in poorer countries. At worst, the foreign training priority is rooted in antiquated thinking that could easily reinforce global knowledge hierarchies and colonial mindsets (Stein et al. 2019).

The final implementation target's (4.c) call to increase the supply of qualified teachers in developing countries is appropriate. Even so, efforts to increase the proportion of teachers who have received at least the minimum organized teacher training relevant for their level (4.c.1) are subject to serious domestic and international constraints. A range of other indicators could be used to inform progress towards this target — for instance, trends in the proportion of domestic education budgets allocated to teacher training subsidies, or, for that matter, trends in the proportion of education budgets not spent directly on teacher training systems and schools of education. As it stands, progress on this implementation target ultimately depends on the presence or absence of political will, and upon the existence of favourable political conditions.

The UN secretary-general's report at the SDG midpoint recognized and lamented that the world was already off-track to achieve the education targets before the post-COVID surge of interlinked global crises (UNSG 2023). While the report was informative about the shortfalls, it was much less open about how the Quality Education goal is infused with an increasingly controversial liberal perspective that aims to bolster the current international economic order.

SDG 4 is permeated with an emphasis on individual achievement that is fully aligned with the greater participation of private sector players in the delivery of education at all levels. Moreover, its minimalist priorities exude the view that education is ultimately a means to enhance economic growth. Its push to include more people in education systems in order prepare them to make larger economic contributions can be accurately described as a functional approach to education that will not liberate learners from systems of dominance and exploitation. Liberal viewpoints even circumscribe its ambitions related to the education of global citizens. As detailed above, right-wing nationalists and populists strongly oppose these aspirations and portray the goal more generally to be a telling example of international overreach into sovereign domestic affairs. For their part, green and progressive critics rail against the limitations of this goal *and* resist the surge of nationalist discontent with the liberal global agenda for education.

References

Boeren, E. 2019. "Understanding Sustainable Development Goal (SDG) 4 on 'Quality Education' From Micro, Meso and Macro Perspectives." *International Review of Education* 65.

Enns, C. 2015. "Transformation or Continuation? A Critical Analysis of the Making of the Post-2015 Education Agenda." *Globalisation, Societies and Education* 13, 3.

Friedman, J., H. York, N. Graetz, et al. 2020. "Measuring and Forecasting Progress Towards the Education-Related SDG Targets." *Nature* 580.

Hickey, S., and N. Hossain. 2019. "Researching the Politics of Education Quality in Developing Countries: Towards a New Conceptual and Methodological Approach." In *The Politics of Education in Developing Countries: From Schooling to Learning*, edited by S. Hickey and N. Hossain. Oxford: Oxford University Press.

Our World in Data team.2023. "Ensure Inclusive and Quality Education for All and Promote Lifelong Learning." ourworldindata.org/sdgs/quality-education.

Sneyd, A. 2019. *Politics Rules: Power, Globalization and Development*. Black Point, NS: Fernwood Publishing and Practical Action Publishing.

Stein, S., V. Andreotti, and R. Susa. " 'Beyond 2015', Within the Modern/Colonial Global Imaginary? Global Development and Higher Education." *Critical Studies in Education* 60, 3.

UN (United Nations). 2020. *Quality Education: Why It Matters*. un.org/sustainabledevelopment/wp-content/uploads/2018/09/Goal-4.pdf.

———. 2022. *The Sustainable Development Goals Report 2022*. New York: UN.

———. 2023. "Goal 4: Quality Education." un.org/sustainabledevelopment/education.

UNSG (United Nations Secretary-General). 2023. *Progress towards the Sustainable Development Goals: Towards a Rescue Plan for People and Planet. Report of the Secretary-General (Special Edition)*. New York: United Nations General Assembly and Economic and Social Council.

Varadharajan, M., and J. Buchanan. 2017. "Any Small Change?: Teacher Education, Compassion, Understandings and Perspectives on Global Development Education." *International Journal of Development Education and Global Learning* 9, 1.

Williams, J. 2016. "Liberia Is Outsourcing Primary Schools to a Start-Up Backed by Mark Zuckerberg." *Vox*, April 8. vox.com/2016/4/8/11347796/liberia-outsourcing-schools.

Goal ⑤
Gender Equality

What They Tell Us

> **Mission statement:** Achieve gender equality and empower all women and girls.

Gender empowerment is needed to reduce the disproportionate share of unpaid domestic work done by women and girls (UN 2020). Women also face serious disadvantages in education that reduce their labour market success. Moreover, they remain disproportionately subject to violence and discrimination. Consequently, we need gender equality now. This is not only a fundamental human right, but an essential building block for a more peaceful, prosperous, and sustainable world (UN 2023). Governments must boldly pursue a range of legal and policy actions to support the achievement of this ambitious goal. Regrettably, the "world is not on track to achieve gender equality by 2030, and the social and economic fallout from the pandemic has made the situation even bleaker" (UN 2022, 36). Progress on this goal has faltered and, in some cases, reversed due to the ongoing climate emergency and rising political and economic insecurity (UN 2023). Moreover, less than half the data required to monitor this goal are currently available (UN Women 2022). Legal reforms to advance gender have also stalled. In this context, if you are a girl, the most important thing that you can do is to stay in school (UN 2020).

Gender Targets		Indicators	
5.1	End all forms of discrimination against all women and girls everywhere	5.1.1	Whether or not legal frameworks are in place to promote, enforce and monitor equality and non-discrimination on the basis of sex
5.2	Eliminate all forms of violence against all women and girls in the public and private spheres, including trafficking and sexual and other types of exploitation	5.2.1	Proportion of ever-partnered women and girls aged 15 years and older subjected to physical, sexual, or psychological violence by a current or former intimate partner in the previous 12 months, by form of violence and by age

Gender Targets	Indicators
5.2 (continued)	5.2.2 Proportion of women and girls aged 15 years and older subjected to sexual violence by persons other than an intimate partner in the previous 12 months, by age and place of occurrence
5.3 Eliminate all harmful practices, such as child, early, and forced marriage, and female genital mutilation	5.3.1 Proportion of women aged 20–24 years who were married or in a union before age 15 and before age 18 5.3.2 Proportion of girls and women aged 15–49 years who have undergone female genital mutilation/cutting, by age
5.4 Recognize and value unpaid care and domestic work through the provision of public services, infrastructure, and social protection policies and the promotion of shared responsibility within the household and the family as nationally appropriate	5.4.1 Proportion of time spent on unpaid domestic and care work, by sex, age and location
5.5 Ensure women's full and effective participation and equal opportunities for leadership at all levels of decision-making in political, economic, and public life	5.5.1 Proportion of seats held by women in (a) national parliaments and (b) local governments 5.5.2 Proportion of women in managerial positions
5.6 Ensure universal access to sexual and reproductive health and reproductive rights as agreed in accordance with the Programme of Action of the International Conference on Population and Development and the Beijing Platform for Action and the outcome documents of their review conferences	5.6.1 Proportion of women aged 15–49 years who make their own informed decisions regarding sexual relations, contraceptive use and reproductive health care 5.6.2 Number of countries with laws and regulations that guarantee full and equal access to women and men aged 15 years and older to sexual and reproductive health care, information, and education
5.a Undertake reforms to give women equal rights to economic resources, as well as access to ownership and control over land and other forms of property, financial services, inheritance, and natural resources, in accordance with national laws	5.a.1 (a) Proportion of total agricultural population with ownership or secure rights over agricultural land, by sex; and (b) Share of women among owners or rights-bearers of agricultural land, by type of tenure 5.a.2 Proportion of countries where the legal framework (including customary law) guarantees women's equal rights to land ownership and/or control
5.b Enhance the use of enabling technology, in particular information and communications technology, to promote the empowerment of women	5.b.1 Proportion of individuals who own a mobile telephone, by sex
5.c Adopt and strengthen sound policies and enforceable legislation for the promotion of gender equality and the empowerment of all women and girls at all levels	5.c.1 Proportion of countries with systems to track and make public allocations for gender equality and women's empowerment

The Hidden Politics

Efforts to advance gender equality frameworks through development cooperation have been ongoing for decades. While much work has been done, this top-down push has underperformed (Novovic 2023). In many country contexts, gender-related initiatives have not been adequately mainstreamed into broader policies or laws. Gender equality advocates have also faced significant barriers when seeking to make their voices heard or to participate as equals in decision-making processes. According to Gloria Novovic (2023), while commitments under the Global Goals are less ambitious than other frameworks, the 2030 Agenda has upended the status quo. Its integrated and bottom-up approach to advancing the goals has enhanced the potential for gender campaigners to impact many other areas of policy. Nonetheless, the political obstacles facing aspirations for gender equality have not simply disappeared. Like all other targets under the SDGs, gender-related objectives remain subject to the obstacles that local politics can create. Even well-formulated goals such as SDG 5 are inescapably political and subject to real political constraints.

The first ambitious target (5.1) under this goal seeks to sidestep the politics that holds gender equality back. Aiming to end all forms of discrimination against women and girls everywhere, the associated indicator (5.1.1) mandates a concerted effort to assess whether countries have relevant legal frameworks in place. The good news associated with this emphasis is that data on the existence of laws that promote, enforce, and monitor equality and nondiscrimination are readily available. The Our World in Data team (2023) provides numerous charts that can be used to track whether specific countries have established laws related to equal pay, equal rights, paid or unpaid maternity leave, employment discrimination, and other aspects of discrimination. A quick scan of these data, for example, can reveal the list of countries that do not currently prohibit employment discrimination based on gender. While the emphasis on statutes can be used to call out countries that now lack such prohibitions, such as Sudan, Nigeria, Iran, and Yemen, it does have serious limits. Many other countries may have laws on the books that technically prohibit gender-based workplace discrimination, but these laws may not be fully implemented. The indicator's focus on the existence of legal frameworks to promote, enforce, and monitor equality and nondiscrimination does not directly address the political challenges associated with effective implementation. In countries where police lack the capacity or willingness to engage, or where other impediments to the pursuit of legal remedies exist, such as high legal fees or court backlogs, laws will fail to perform. In other words, the politics that holds gender equality back can persist long after governments make formal legal commitments. But this target does not call for an effort to track and reduce the barriers to legal implementation and effectiveness. It simply seeks to bypass the implementation issue entirely.

The second target (5.2) is also not immune to local politics and legal ineffectiveness. Eliminating all forms of violence against women and girls in public and private spheres remains a very tall order. At present, data on this topic are woefully deficient. Rates of physical, sexual, or psychological violence against women perpetrated by intimate partners or other persons are notoriously difficult to track. Violence against women often goes unreported, and police and prosecutorial inaction on reports that are made can reinforce this discouraging reality. Considerations related to personal safety, family and livelihood security, and cultural appropriateness often further impede reporting. It is consequently quite unsettling that the indicators (5.2.1 and 5.2.2) associated with this target encourage governments to collect data only on violent acts that have been committed against women and girls over the past year. A concerted attempt to produce more year-on-year data could ultimately establish the direction of trends in violence committed by intimate partners and other persons. However, it might not do so reliably or ethically in many contexts where women and girls do not feel safe enough to inform authorities or outsiders about violence they have experienced. Moreover, better year-on-year evidence about the perpetration of violence against women and girls is not the sole actionable route to eliminating violence. Considering the data challenges, this target could have been associated with efforts to track the implementation of programs or policies that can contribute to reducing violence against women and girls. For instance, it could have called for data on the implementation of mandatory antiviolence and antioppression training in schools and workplaces. Instead of encouraging the use of proxy indicators, this target reinforces the need for data that have tended to be unethical, unreliable, or unavailable. This emphasis is disquieting as gender experts around the world pursue new collaborations to advance evidence-based policy on SDG 5 (Eden and Wagstaff 2021). It detracts from efforts to develop good evidence related to the factors that maintain or counteract violence against women and girls.

Turning to the third target (5.3), the politics of eliminating harmful practices such as female genital mutilation and child, early, and forced marriage, has become more complex under the 2030 Agenda. In the handful of countries where these harmful practices remain commonplace, governments that seek to honour their commitments to SDG 5 can choose to develop and implement national strategies and plans that address the issue. They can also conduct voluntary national reviews that document any progress they make on the indicators (5.3.1 and 5.3.2). SDG commitments and reviews nonetheless remain nonbinding, and political authorities do not face any legal obligation to act in support of specific targets. Governments now have more autonomy over their national and subnational priorities and actions, and they have full editorial and narrative control over SDG reporting. In resource-constrained contexts, the latter development could exacerbate an already wide gap between government commitments to eradicating harmful practices, and realities on the ground. For instance, child and early marriages remain prevalent in Niger and the Central African Republic, two countries that have ratified the UN Convention on the Rights of the Child. In the SDG era, watchdogs and whistleblowers can continue to call out government failures and inaction that enable harmful practices to persist. That said, governments now have much stronger capacities to frame their development actions for interstate and global audiences. In countries where female genital mutilation rates remain ruinously high, this newfound discursive power could be employed to obscure the persistence of practices that should have been eliminated. Unfortunately, not one of the Global Goals aims to reduce the production of development-oriented public relations materials, or to address the consequences of SDG-related propaganda. Under the 2030 Agenda, countries with poor track records are simply trusted to honour their SDG commitments.

The subsequent target (5.4), which aims to recognize and value unpaid care and domestic work, is also subject to serious political limitations. The only indicator (5.4.1) associated with this aspiration focuses on the proportion of time spent on unpaid domestic and care work by sex, age, and location. Despite nearly forty years of serious scholarship on the challenge of valuing and making care and domestic work "count," data on this topic remain thin and very hard to compare (Waring 1988). Strong language on "national appropriateness" has also been inserted directly into this target. This proviso or limiting clause gives governments wide discretion to engage seriously with the need for better data and policies in this area, or to deprioritize these ambitions entirely. Furthermore, the goals on decent work and economic growth, and on reduced inequalities, do not include any language whatsoever on the need to recognize or value care and domestic work. The absence of integrated treatment is in this instance quite telling. It represents the failure of the SDGs themselves to recognize and value a burden that falls primarily on women. Under the SDGs, governments are not striving to place real values on care work or work in the home. They are not developing programs to pay caregivers for the lunches that they prepare or the clothes that they wash for family members and others in their care. Changes to the system of national accounts to enable this work to count economically are also not being pursued. The ways that unpaid care and domestic work continue to subsidize the functioning of the real economy could easily be integrated into national accounting systems. The political will to do so remains missing in action.

Furthermore, priorities for women's empowerment in leadership and decision-making under the fifth target (5.5) are disturbingly limited. Here, too, the indicators offer a telling political tale. These focus only on the proportion of seats held by women in national parliaments and local governments (5.5.1), and on the proportion of women in managerial positions (5.5.2). Calls to increase the share of women participating in and leading decision-making in political, economic, and public life are easy to make. Support for this agenda will clearly bolster the position of women in society. However, this stance will not empower all women equally. Where and when some women become empowered participants and leaders, they will enjoy advanced career prospects and improved socioeconomic status. Whether or not privileged and elite women will make contributions and decisions that reflect and advance the interests of all women remains an open question. After all, political and economic decisions are often made in highly exclusionary circumstances. History is replete with examples where women in leadership positions made decisions that undermined the status of other women. This target's inattention to the inequalities that can be generated when empowered women become entitled and are sheltered from the real challenges women face every day is notable. It showcases how the intersection of gender and inequality has eluded fully integrated treatment under the SDGs.

This omission is also evident in the ensuing target (5.6) on universal access to sexual and reproductive health and reproductive rights. Under the sixth target, data on women who make their own informed decisions regarding sex, contraceptives, and related health care are not disaggregated by socioeconomic status (5.6.1). Consequently, statistics on this issue shine light only on the proportion of women who can make their own decisions, and not on the impact that factors such as income, wealth, or job status can have on their decision-making power. The language of the second indicator (5.6.2) under this target is similarly inattentive to unequal realities. It spotlights the number of countries with laws and regulations that guarantee full and equal access to sexual and reproductive health care, information, and education. But it does not aim to assess the impact that inequalities not directly associated with laws or regulations can have on access to maternity care, contraception services, sexuality education, and disease support. Factors such as income, religion, education, and distance to health services providers can and do undermine universal access even in countries with strong legal and regulatory guarantees. This indicator's sole emphasis on the legal and regulatory level of analysis unnecessarily obscures the root causes of unequal access.

The strong and ambitious language of SDG 5's three implementation targets is also circumscribed by weak indicators. Calls for reforms that would give women equal rights to economic resources, access to ownership and control over land, financial services, inheritance, and natural resources sound comprehensive (5.a). Nonetheless, few of these wish list items can be found in the two associated indicators, which direct attention only to female ownership and rights to agricultural land (5.a.1), and to the proportion of countries where legal rights frameworks guarantee women's equal rights to land ownership and control (5.a.2). Similarly, the second implementation target (5.b) aims to promote the empowerment of women through technology. This aspiration should conjure images of farm equipment, mobility aids, household appliances, distributed electricity generation, and other technologies that can ease domestic and care work burdens. Instead, the indicator (5.b.1) solely emphasizes tracking the proportion of individuals who own a mobile telephone, by sex. Women who control smartphones can make use of many apps to empower themselves at home and in society. Yet the technologies that might make the most difference in their daily lives are not necessarily mobile or digital. The third implementation target's (5.c) emphasis on the development of sound policies and enforceable legislation suffers from a similar disconnect. Efforts to take this desire seriously could have a big impact on the political barriers facing gender equality and women's empowerment discussed above. That said, the indicator (5.c.1) puts the spotlight on the number of countries with systems in place to track and make public allocations for gender equality and women's empowerment. It does not encourage governments to measure their progress towards eliminating known obstacles to equality and empowerment. The failure to translate SDG 5's ambitious implementation targets into the associated indicators has been termed policy "shrinkage" (Novovic 2021). This worrying and highly political phenomenon could ultimately derail efforts to achieve gender equality and women's empowerment under this goal.

The UN secretary-general's report at the SDG midpoint was straightforward regarding global failures on gender equality. According to the UN's own analysis, none of SDG 5's indicators had "met or almost met" the targets by

2023 (UNSG 2023). The report endeavoured to link this poor performance to the profusion of global crises and the challenges that these have posed for health and education systems. But it did not note its own political orientation and failed to recognize that the goal itself — like each of the other SDGs — is subject to increasing political contestation. The fact remains that SDG 5 is saturated with an overemphasis on the empowerment of individual women and entirely inattentive to some of the most consequential systemic and structural sources of gender-based discrimination. Despite the clear limitations of this orientation, right-wing populists reliably politicize this approach and make forcefully deceptive arguments about an outpouring of global concern related to identity-based empowerment. For their part, social progressives and greens champion a more robust approach to gender equality than SDG 5 *and* push back against reactionary and duplicitous views on gender empowerment.

References

Eden, L., and M.F. Wagstaff. 2021. "Evidence-Based Policymaking and the Wicked Problem of SDG 5 Gender Equality." *Journal of International Business Policy* 4.

Novovic, G. 2021. "Are SDGs Counting What Counts? Feminist Analysis of Agenda 2030 Policy Shrinking. *Global Governance* 27.

———. 2023. "Gender Mainstreaming 2.0: Emergent Gender Equality Agendas Under Sustainable Development Goals." *Third World Quarterly* 44, 5.

Our World in Data team. 2023. "Achieve Gender Equality and Empower All Women and Girls." ourworldindata.org/sdgs/gender-equality.

UN (United Nations). 2020. *Gender Equality: Why It Matters*. un.org/sustainabledevelopment/wp-content/uploads/2016/08/5_Why-It-Matters-2020.pdf.

———. 2022. *The Sustainable Development Goals Report 2022*. New York: UN.

———. 2023. "Goal 5: Achieve Gender Equality and Empower All Women and Girls." un.org/sustainabledevelopment/gender-equality.

UNSG (United Nations Secretary-General). 2023. *Progress towards the Sustainable Development Goals: Towards a Rescue Plan for People and Planet. Report of the Secretary-General (Special Edition)*. New York: United Nations General Assembly and Economic and Social Council.

UN Women. 2022. "In Focus: Sustainable Development Goal 5." August 23. unwomen.org/en/news-stories/in-focus/2022/08/in-focus-sustainable-development-goal-5.

Waring, M. 1988. *If Women Counted: A New Feminist Economics*. New York: Harper and Row.

Goal 6

Clean Water and Sanitation

What They Tell Us

Mission statement: Ensure the availability and sustainable management of water and sanitation for all.

We must also strive to guarantee the human right to safe water and sanitation. For decades, humans have created water stress through misuse and mismanagement, overextracting groundwater and contaminating freshwater (UN 2023a). Distressingly, "unless progress picks up speed — dramatically — billions of people will still lack" water, sanitation, and hygiene services in 2030 (UN 2022, 38). UN-Water's integrated monitoring initiative reported in 2021 that the world must quadruple current rates of progress to have even a chance of achieving this goal by 2030 (UN-Water Integrated Monitoring Initiative for SDG 6 Steering Committee 2023). Better serving the billions who continue to survive without safely managed drinking water services or sanitation is a crucial climate change mitigation strategy (UN 2023a). Realizing the human right to water access will also be crucial for achieving many of the other Global Goals. In this context, civil society organizations should continue their work to keep governments accountable for their water, sanitation, and hygiene commitments (UN 2020).

Water and Sanitation Targets		Indicators	
6.1	By 2030, achieve universal and equitable access to safe and affordable drinking water for all	6.1.1	Proportion of population using safely managed drinking water services
6.2	By 2030, achieve access to adequate and equitable sanitation and hygiene for all and end open defecation, paying special attention to the needs of women and girls and those in vulnerable situations	6.2.1	Proportion of population using (a) safely managed sanitation services and (b) a hand-washing facility with soap and water

Water and Sanitation Targets	Indicators
6.3 By 2030, improve water quality by reducing pollution, eliminating dumping, and minimizing release of hazardous chemicals and materials, halving the proportion of untreated wastewater, and substantially increasing recycling and safe reuse globally	6.3.1 Proportion of domestic and industrial waste-water flows safely treated 6.3.2 Proportion of bodies of water with good ambient water quality
6.4 By 2030, substantially increase water-use efficiency across all sectors and ensure sustainable withdrawals and supply of freshwater to address water scarcity and substantially reduce the number of people suffering from water scarcity	6.4.1 Change in water-use efficiency over time 6.4.2 Level of water stress: freshwater withdrawal as a proportion of available freshwater resources
6.5 By 2030, implement integrated water resources management at all levels, including through transboundary cooperation as appropriate	6.5.1 Degree of integrated water resources management 6.5.2 Proportion of transboundary basin area with an operational arrangement for water cooperation
6.6 By 2020, protect and restore water-related ecosystems, including mountains, forests, wetlands, rivers, aquifers, and lakes	6.6.1 Change in the extent of water-related ecosystems over time
6.a By 2030, expand international cooperation and capacity-building support to developing countries in water- and sanitation-related activities and programmes, including water harvesting, desalination, water efficiency, wastewater treatment, recycling, and reuse technologies	6.a.1 Amount of water- and sanitation-related official development assistance that is part of a government coordinated spending plan
6.b Support and strengthen the participation of local communities in improving water and sanitation management	6.b.1 Proportion of local administrative units with established and operational policies and procedures for participation of local communities in water and sanitation management

The Hidden Politics

The challenge of achieving universal and equitable access to safe and affordable drinking water for all (6.1) is daunting, to say the least. Hundreds of millions of people continue to live without basic access to water (Bayu et al. 2020). Moreover, the Joint Monitoring Programme of the World Health Organization and the UN Children's Fund (UNICEF) for water supply, sanitation, and hygiene has found that over two billion people do not have access to safely managed drinking water services (WHO 2019). In other words, one in three people globally do not have reliable access to uncontaminated water in their homes when they need it. The indicator (6.1.1) currently associated with this target focuses needed attention on the proportion of populations that use safely managed drinking water services.

But it does not include any language related to assessing whether consumers and citizens find safe water to be affordable. This exclusion poses a very big political problem. National and local authorities, and public and private water companies, have their own context-specific ideas about the meaning of affordable water, but they cannot simply assume that their definitions are the only definitions that matter.

Take, for example, Canada's horrendous record related to the provision of safe water in many Indigenous communities (Phare 2009). Systemic mismanagement, underinvestment, and cost cutting linked to provider or government considerations of affordability have sustained a safe water crisis. In other contexts where for-profit entities fully control user fees or where public resources for safe water provision have remained deficient, affordability has also become a political lightning rod. Volume-based charges and rates for delivery and connections remain key determinants of access to safely managed services. Fee-paying local populations and those that lack the means to pay any price whatsoever for the water they consume can and do fight back against unaffordable water tariffs. The blatant omission of affordability from efforts to monitor progress towards this target will be consequential where and when water prices persistently impede universal access. While UNICEF and the WHO (2021) have authored a report on this "missing element," their recommendations are nonbinding, and water affordability remains a glaring SDG 6 oversight.

Beyond affordability, the political challenges associated with monitoring trends in water access are also significant. Numerous studies have concluded that data produced by the Joint Monitoring Programme have several notable weaknesses. For example, data collection has to date overemphasized the type of water service that people enjoy access to, and downplayed considerations related to quality (Hutton and Chase 2016). It has been effective in drawing attention to the percentage of populations that report access to water but has also obscured other types of service failure (Herrera 2019). Likewise, while compelling statistics on household water access have been produced, these have failed to capture intrahousehold inequalities and variations in access (Hutton and Chase 2016). Academic studies have also illuminated similar inequalities that are not well captured by the official data, such as rural-urban divides in water access (Anthonj et al. 2020). Addressing these and other gaps in the data will be a very tall political order. The decentralization of water services to local public and private utilities, alongside the advent of innovative decentralized water management approaches involving rainwater harvesting, water reclamation, and reuse, adds serious complications. Considering these developments, the Joint Monitoring Programme's ongoing reliance on national-level collaborators in the production of data is concerning (Herrera 2019). In this dynamic context, gatekeepers at the national level may not have the most up-to-date or accurate information on the local realities of water access. In sum, approaches to knowing about access to safe water have been deficient, and accurately monitoring trends has become much more politically complicated.

Unfortunately, efforts to end open defecation and provide equitable and adequate access to sanitation and hygiene under SDG 6's second target (6.2) suffer from similar political complications. The indicator (6.2.1) on this target rightly directs attention to monitoring the proportion of populations that use safely managed sanitation services and handwashing facilities with soap and water. To be considered "safe," excreta must be disposed of in situ or treated off-site, and a basic handwashing device to contain, transport, or regulate the flow of water to facilitate handwashing must be evident. While this definition is clear enough, the indicator includes no language on the affordability of safe sanitation services or handwashing facilities. Thus, this target's purported focus on equity and on vulnerable populations will not be monitored. This omission is disconcerting, as well over two billion people continue to lack the means necessary to access basic sanitation services and handwashing facilities (Bayu et al. 2020). In many urban and informal contexts where users must pay high fees to access community toilets, vulnerable slum dwellers continue to opt for unsafe alternatives. Research suggests that even in communities where sanitation coverage rates are supposedly high, children still commonly defecate in the open (Hutton and Chase 2016).

Moreover, concerns have been raised that the second target's definition of safely managed sanitation services is so broad that it can enable the production of politically convenient statistics. For instance, under this target the "in situ" treatment of excreta and connections to a piped sewer system are taken to be equivalent. Similarly, reused plastic containers and porcelain sinks with taps are seemingly comparable handwashing devices. Where and when these false equivalencies are baked into data collection and analyses, the inequitable realities of safely managed sanitation will be obscured (Herrera 2019). As this target lacks an indicator related to equitable access, governments can simply opt to trumpet any headline aggregate successes. If stark facts about unbalanced access nonetheless emerge, they are also free to reiterate their commitments to growth and the reduction of inequality under the related SDGs. Gross domestic product (GDP) growth has in some cases been found to have positive impacts on sanitation-related indicators (Roy and Pramanick 2019). Even so, any government that fails to embrace the equity dimension of this target, and that directs attention to other goals to deliver outcomes directly related to sanitation and hygiene, could be accused of playing politics and not taking SDG 6 seriously.

Data issues could also undercut the subsequent targets on water quality, wastewater treatment, and safe reuse (6.3) and on water-use efficiency and freshwater supplies (6.4). On the former, efforts to halve the proportion of untreated wastewater and to substantially increase recycling and safe reuse remain subject to a weak monitoring regime (Herrera 2019). Estimates of ambient water quality produced by the Joint Monitoring Programme and by independent researchers have diverged significantly in the past. Academic researchers have also raised pointed questions about the capacity of the official monitoring regime to capture the true extent of microbial contamination. Turning to the target on improving water-use efficiency and ensuring sustainable freshwater withdrawals and supply, these objectives are also notoriously difficult to monitor. The rise of decentralized water treatment systems and unofficial connections complicate efforts to monitor changes in water-use efficiency over time (6.4.1). As it stands, the best available statistics on water-use efficiency trends do not adequately capture the persistence of inefficient water-use practices (Our World in Data team 2023). Furthermore, the measurement of freshwater withdrawals as a proportion of available freshwater resources (6.4.2) has become more difficult in many countries. As rainfall patterns in many vulnerable countries have become increasingly irregular, and the availability of freshwater resources has become more variable due to climate change, freshwater stress has become more difficult to monitor (Gheuens et al. 2019). Data on water-use efficiency and freshwater supply under this target will also omit inefficiencies and stresses caused by bulk water withdrawals. The official data remain imperceptive to the inefficient and stress-inducing withdrawals that purveyors of bottled water continue to make day in, day out.

Moving beyond a focus on data and monitoring, domestic and international politics will impede efforts to achieve the next target. The fifth target's (6.5) call for enhanced transboundary water management cooperation seeks to encourage and rejuvenate planning, agreements, commissions, and authorities in this area (UN 2023b). While many international organizations are committed to helping states improve the cooperative management of transboundary lakes and rivers, the development of effective agreements remains elusive (UNECE 2021). Numerous long-standing agreements have simply failed to deliver on their potential. In basins where coups d'état have been prominent, and where political authorities have either disregarded the rule of law or sidelined cooperative structures in decision-making, transboundary agreements have underperformed. Development challenges and constraints have persisted in those contexts (Namara et al. 2011). Even if an enhanced operational arrangement for water cooperation were to be established in the Nile basin, for example, domestic political interests in Egypt, Ethiopia, and Sudan would not automatically fall into alignment. Local priorities have undermined the development of functional transboundary cooperation for the integrated management of this river basin for decades. In other resource-constrained contexts, a yawning gap persists between agreements that are operational and transboundary cooperation that is effective.

The sixth target's (6.6) call to protect and restore water-related ecosystems also faces significant political headwinds. The idea of protecting and restoring mountains, forests, wetlands, rivers, aquifers, and lakes stands in stark contrast to the overall thrust of SDG 8 and SDG 9. Those goals prioritize economic growth and the development of resource extraction infrastructure. Work to achieve SDG 6 could serve as a corrective through the tracking of changes in the extent of water-related ecosystems over time (6.6.1). Compelling graphical data on this topic will showcase the degree of ecosystem losses. That said, any research efforts that empirically link these losses to the pursuit of economic growth opportunities will be subject to politics. This politics will play out within and between ministries of the environment, natural resources, infrastructure, industry, development, and finance. It will be prominent in national legislatures and in lobby and advocacy group campaign materials targeting policymakers and the public. Governments have committed to this target *and* to the growth-related targets, and this contradictory stance can only be resolved in the political realm. Economic activities can and do destroy ecosystems, but the global public relations industry stands at the ready to produce materials for its corporate clients that downplay this reality and highlight the benefits of growth and the development of infrastructure. This target does not seek to eradicate the production of spurious arguments on the economic benefits that could flow from ecosystem loss. At best, in the context of the commitments that governments have made under SDGs 8 and 9, the target reflects naive ambitions. While the data on ecosystem loss might look serious and compelling, it does not exist in a political vacuum.

The first implementation target (6.a) under SDG 6 also faces big political hurdles. It aims to scale up international cooperation and support for water- and sanitation-related activities and programs. The associated indicator (6.a.1) focuses attention only on increasing the amount of official development assistance for such activities in government budgets. The idea that more aid for water harvesting, wastewater treatment, and associated technologies is the sole route to enhancing international cooperation in this area is simplistic and possibly erroneous. Aid flows had at best an unclear impact on water and sanitation objectives during the era of the Millennium Development Goals, the aspirational regime for development that preceded the SDGs (Herrera 2019). Today, the effectiveness of official disbursements for water and sanitation remains in question. Persistent problems have included operational delays, performance issues, transparency challenges, and blatant corruption (Bayu et al. 2020). While a lack of funding continues to impede the efforts that vulnerable governments make to implement their water and sanitation policies, research suggests that capacity development should be a higher priority (Gheuens et al. 2019). Furthermore, the exclusive emphasis on increasing aid for water and sanitation problems does nothing to address the root causes of inequalities in this area. Many studies have concluded that the economic aspects of water governance persistently generate unequal outcomes. Private sector contracts have done little to improve services for the poor in low-income and politically unstable contexts (Herrera 2019). The implementation target's silence on for-profit utilities and water tariffs is telling. Encouraging governments to throw more money at the problem might avoid muddying the waters, but it offers little hope for success.

The second implementation (6.b) target's banal call to strengthen the participation of local communities in the management of water and sanitation services is similarly problematic. Efforts to encourage the development of policies and procedures that facilitate public participation can open the door for responsive improvements to service delivery. However, formal systems of public participation have not been the main means through which regular people have participated in water and sanitation governance to date. Rather, they have often expressed themselves through campaigns and protests targeting privatizations, tariff increases, the installation of prepaid meters, disconnections, and service extension failures (Herrera 2019). Efforts to ramp up public participation in decision-making structures could help to avert future political conflicts. But without the simultaneous rollout of mechanisms to hold managers accountable to the public, any new systems of public participation could easily be sidelined or marginalized. Political conflict over water and sanitation failures cannot simply be "formalized" away. This target's silence on accountability and the veritable ways that citizens participate in water and sanitation governance ensure that it is not fit for purpose.

At the SDG midpoint, the UN secretary-general reported that billions of people continued to lack access to safe water, sanitation, and hygiene (UNSG 2023). The report decried the sheer scale of the required course correction but did not speak at all to SDG 6's political orientation and the associated limitations. This goal entails reforms that are fully aligned with maintaining and bolstering the liberal international economic order. It does not question the rise of transnational corporate control over water and sanitation systems. The goal's growth-oriented treatment of water, sanitation, and hygiene challenges is congruent with the maintenance of financial and corporate practices that may be at odds with other SDGs related to inequality and ecosystem preservation. Moreover, SDG 6 problematically assumes that greater policy attention to challenges at the individual level, alongside efforts to facilitate more individual participation in the governance of water, will unblock barriers to progress. These political assumptions are troubling at a time of surging right-wing nationalism. For their part, social progressives and greens challenge this goal's system maintenance orientation *and* the reactionary forces that oppose efforts to make the human right to water a universal reality.

References

Anthonj, C., J. Wren Tracy, L. Fleming, et al. 2020. "Geographical Inequalities in Drinking Water in the Solomon Islands." *Science of the Total Environment* 712.

Bayu, T., H. Kim, and T. Oki. 2020. "Water Governance Contribution to Water and Sanitation Access Equality in Developing Countries." *Water Resources Research* 56, 4.

Gheuens, J., N. Nagabhatla, and E.D.P. Perera. 2019. "Disaster-Risk, Water Security Challenges and Strategies in Small Island Developing States (SIDS). *Water* 11, 637.

Herrera, V. 2019. "Reconciling Global Aspirations and Local Realities: Challenges Facing the Sustainable Development Goals for Water and Sanitation." *World Development* 118.

Hutton, G., and C. Chase. 2016. "The Knowledge Base for Achieving the Sustainable Development Goal Targets on Water Supply, Sanitation and Hygiene." *International Journal of Environmental Research and Public Health* 13, 536.

Namara, R.E., B. Barry, E.S. Owusu, and A. Ogilvie. 2011. *An Overview of the Development Challenges and Constraints of the Niger Basin and Possible Intervention Strategies*. Colombo: International Water Management Institute.

Our World in Data team. 2023. "Ensure Access to Water and Sanitation for All." ourworldindata.org/sdgs/clean-water-sanitation.

Phare, M.-A. S. 2009. *Denying the Source: The Crisis of First Nations Water Rights*. Victoria, BC: Rocky Mountain Books.

Roy, A., and K. Pramanick. 2019. "Analysing Progress of Sustainable Development Goal 6 in India: Past, Present, and Future." *Journal of Environmental Management* 232.

UN (United Nations). 2020. *Clean Water and Sanitation: Why It Matters*. un.org/
    sustainabledevelopment/wp-content/uploads/2016/08/6_Why-It-Matters-2020.
    pdf.

———. 2022. *The Sustainable Development Goals Report 2022*. New York: UN.

———. 2023a. "Goal 6: Ensure Access to Water and Sanitation for All." un.org/
    sustainabledevelopment/water-and-sanitation.

———. 2023b. "Transboundary Water Management Crucial for Sustainable
    Development." News release ENV/DEV/2056, March 23. press.un.org/en/2023/
    envdev2056.doc.htm.

UNECE (United Nations Economic Commission for Europe). 2021. *Practical Guide
    for the Development of Agreements or Other Arrangements for Transboundary Water
    Cooperation*. Geneva: UN Economic Commission for Europe.

UNICEF and the WHO (United Nations Children's Fund and World Health
    Organization). 2021. "The Measurement and Monitoring of Water Supply,
    Sanitation, and Hygiene Affordability: A Missing Element of Monitoring SDG
    Targets 6.1 and 6.2." New York: UNICEF and the WHO.

UNSG (United Nations Secretary-General). 2023. *Progress towards the Sustainable
    Development Goals: Towards a Rescue Plan for People and Planet. Report of the
    Secretary-General (Special Edition)*. New York: United Nations General Assembly
    and Economic and Social Council.

UN-Water Integrated Monitoring Initiative for SDG 6 Steering Committee. 2023.
    "SDG 6 Data for All." *SDG Knowledge Hub*, March 22. sdg.iisd.org/commentary/
    guest-articles/sdg-6-data-for-all.

WHO (World Health Organization). 2019. "1 in 3 People Globally Do Not Have
    Access to Safe Drinking Water — UNICEF, WHO." News release, June 18. who.
    int/news/item/18-06-2019-1-in-3-people-globally-do-not-have-access-to-safe-
    drinking-water-unicef-who.

Goal 7
Affordable and Clean Energy

What They Tell Us

> **Mission statement:** Ensure access to affordable, reliable, sustainable, and modern energy for all.

Reliable electricity supplies are needed to ensure that countries can keep their economies growing (UN 2020). When electricity is rationed or unreliable, progress on the other Global Goals becomes much more difficult. Energy system failures undermine women's empowerment and negatively impact health care operations and educational success. Consequently, we are committed to accelerating the transition to a sustainable energy system. We must prioritize energy efficiency, adopt clean energy technology and infrastructure, and ensure access to clean and affordable energy for all (UN 2023). The world is making strides towards the targets associated with this goal. Nevertheless, "rising commodity, energy, and shipping prices have increased the costs of producing and transporting solar photovoltaics modules, wind turbines, and biofuels worldwide," adding uncertainty to the current trajectory, which is far below our ambitions (UN 2022, 40). The current pace of progress is simply insufficient to achieve SDG 7. While over 90 per cent of the global population will have access to electricity by 2030, billions will still depend on inefficient and polluting systems for cooking and power (UN 2023). The prepandemic decline in public international financial flows for clean energy is of serious concern and must be reversed (UN 2020).

Energy Targets		Indicators	
7.1	By 2030, ensure universal access to affordable, reliable, and modern energy services	7.1.1	Proportion of population with access to electricity
		7.1.2	Proportion of population with primary reliance on clean fuels and technology
7.2	By 2030, increase substantially the share of renewable energy in the global energy mix	7.2.1	Renewable energy share in the total final energy consumption

Energy Targets		Indicators	
7.3	By 2030, double the global rate of improvement in energy efficiency	7.3.1	Energy intensity measured in terms of primary energy and GDP
7.a	By 2030, enhance international cooperation to facilitate access to clean energy research and technology, including renewable energy, energy efficiency, and advanced and cleaner fossil-fuel technology, and promote investment in energy infrastructure and clean energy technology	7.a.1	International financial flows to developing countries in support of clean energy research and development and renewable energy production, including in hybrid systems
7.b	By 2030, expand infrastructure and upgrade technology for supplying modern and sustainable energy services for all in developing countries, in particular Least Developed Countries, Small Island Developing States, and land-locked developing countries, in accordance with their respective programmes of support	7.b.1	Installed renewable energy-generating capacity in developing countries (in watts per capita)

The Hidden Politics

The first target (7.1) under SDG 7 includes poorly defined terminology. This target's push to achieve universal access to affordable, reliable, and modern energy services clearly addresses a significant global challenge. But the failure to include any guidance whatsoever related to the meaning of "affordable," "reliable," and "modern" is troubling. Stakeholders within and beyond the energy sector who link their daily work and political advocacy to advancing this target could benefit from much clearer direction. At present, organizations that claim to be committed to this target might hold widely divergent views regarding what exactly constitutes "affordable" energy for households. Some with stakes in the sector certainly have a financial interest in making price per kilowatt-hour the sole consideration that matters. Others, including community-based organizations, might express concerns about prices in relation to the proportion of income that households spend on energy services. Climate activists, for their part, could highlight affordability over time and focus on criteria other than the prices that consumers incur directly, such as household carbon footprints. Absent a clear definition, responsibility for determining whose viewpoints on affordable energy services count has been squarely placed on the shoulders of national authorities. The outcomes of domestic debates between energy stakeholders situated quite differently in relation to political processes and power will consequently determine what, if any, affordability considerations matter in the drive for universal access. In other words, under this target, aspirations for access are universal, while considerations of affordability have been left up to national ambition or the lack thereof. The persistence of this discrepancy during the climate emergency could undercut progress on many of the equity-oriented SDGs.

Correspondingly, national authorities are left to determine the specific meaning of "reliable" access to energy services. Public and private utility firms that generate and distribute power certainly have their own ideas about acceptable levels of load shedding and the appropriate durations of targeted and rolling blackouts. So too do households that require reliable energy access to power up the computers necessary for their children's education. At present, the arbiters of reliable access in some contexts include national monopolies and privatized oligopolies whose interests diverge radically from those at the household level. While political debates over what is considered reliable will necessarily have unique dynamics in different country contexts, minimalist understandings of reliability have a clear global advantage. The first indicator on this target (7.1.1) entrenches an exceedingly low universal benchmark for energy access. It directs needed attention to the proportion of the population with access to electricity, but it defines access solely in relation to an electricity source that can provide very basic lighting, charge a phone, or power a radio for only four hours per day (Our World in Data team 2023). This remarkably low international standard facilitates the production of flattering statistics on energy access in countries where access remains unreliable. It also fuels a divergence between what the statistics will show regarding progress towards energy for all, and the reality of persistently deficient energy access in many remote, rural, and informal contexts. The fact that this target stuck with the existing ultra-low criterion for household energy access and did not introduce an ambitious new standard is troubling. It bolsters the interests of energy stakeholders at the national level who can reap benefits from bare-bones approaches to reliable service provision.

This target's failure to specify the meaning of "modern" energy services also has political consequences. Some energy sector stakeholders may believe that households enjoy access to modern energy if they are connected to a national, regional, or local electricity grid and have the capacity to gener-ate back-up power. Others consider modern energy to be primarily about off-grid solutions. Many environmentalists now link the idea of modern energy directly to the greater household use of renewables and the latest energy-efficient technologies, which reduce greenhouse gas emissions. The absence of a specific vision for modern energy under this target downloads responsibility for defining "modern" energy services to authorities at the national level. That said, a particular understanding of modern energy animates this target's second indicator (7.1.2). Aiming to ensure universal access to clean fuels and technologies for cooking by 2030, governments have committed to reporting on the proportion of the population with primary reliance on clean fuels and technology. Clean cookstoves powered by solar or electric power, or by wood pellets, can reduce pollution and prevent health problems that are caused by the indoor burning of wood, coal, and charcoal. This indicator clearly favours the use of some modern fuels and cooking technologies more than others. Its orientation is based on sound rationales and is clearly linked to other goals. Even so, the failure to provide any parameters for modern energy opens the door to abuse. Those with an interest in purveying dirtier fuels or technologies, such as so-called clean coal, can still claim that they are providing modern energy. In countries that produce oil and gas, some might similarly characterize their push to connect more households to gas pipelines as a modern improvement that aligns with this goal. Here again, the first target's deficient definitions enable political interpretations that could impede the realization of energy for all.

The second target (7.2) seeks to substantially increase the share of renewable energy in the global energy mix, and it too suffers from big political problems. This objective contends directly with the rise of organized transnational and domestic pressure groups that trumpet talking points from the fossil fuel industry. While commitment to the greater use of renewables in electricity, transportation, and cooking and heating may be universal under target 7.2, political contests over this priority have not disappeared. Fierce debates over the types of energy that can be accurately labelled as "renewable" remain unresolved. In this context, firms in the extractive industry have made many efforts to rebrand and position themselves in relation to renewables. The indicator (7.2.1) that underpins the renewable energy target unfortunately reflects the broader politics. It directs attention to the share of renewable energy in total final energy consumption. The latter stipulation is particularly consequential, as it excludes an effort under this target to monitor the consumption of renewables by the energy sector itself. Furthermore, the inclusion of hydropower in a list of renewable power sources under this target (alongside solar, wind, geothermal, bioenergy, and marine) is especially controversial. The World Commission on Dams concluded over twenty years ago that the benefits of hydropower have not outweighed the social and environmental costs of dam construction (Chen and Landry 2018). While developed countries have in some instances moved away from this technology, many developing countries have voiced increasing support for large hydropower investments. The exclusion of pertinent data and inclusion of a questionable "renewable" technology underserve the second target's ambitions. If these aims are to be taken seriously, new indicators related to the carbon intensity and broader environmental footprint of the production and trade of renewables will be essential.

Efforts to double the global rate of improvement in energy efficiency under the third target (7.3) are also not immune from politics. Focusing on primary energy supply, the indicator (7.3.1) for this target emphasizes the ratio between the quantity of kilowatt-hours produced and GDP. As many oil- and gas-producing nations currently have higher than average ratios, data collection under this target could be used to encourage their efforts to lower the amount of energy used to keep their economies going. Despite this potential, the lack of any further indicators related to trends in the global production and trade of energy-inefficient technologies is worrying. Energy-inefficient oil and gas producers are also global purveyors of energy-inefficient technologies. As the world draws down its reliance on fossil fuel technologies, governments will face domestic pressure from this sunset industry to build the global market for older energy production technology. Better knowledge on the direction of these trends is clearly needed if this third target is to be taken seriously. Many legacy enterprises that produce antiquated upstream, refining, and generation technology have a direct interest in securing new clients. This target's failure to capture the economic importance of outdated and SDG-noncompliant technology to energy-inefficient economies is highly discouraging. It belies the eager efforts many powerful stakeholders have made to characterize the Global Goals as a "data-driven" exercise.

The goal's first implementation target (7.a) could be portrayed as a corrective, but it too suffers from its own political deficiencies. This target aims to promote investments in clean energy and calls for stronger international cooperation to enhance global access to clean energy research and technology. Be that as it may, the target focuses not only on renewables and energy-efficient technologies but also on cleaner fossil fuel technologies. It offers no definition of what those technologies might be. In addition, the target simultaneously encourages the promotion of investment in energy infrastructure and "clean" energy technology. This problematic orientation opens the door for those with an interest in linking obsolete legacy technologies to the clean energy investment agenda. The indicator (7.a.1) associated with this target reflects these challenges directly. It focuses on international financial flows to developing countries in support of clean energy research and development and renewable energy production, including hybrid systems. This measure seems sound in relation to many renewable technologies. Financing for the development of solar technologies and the establishment of solar energy fields, for instance, can clearly advance the implementation target. But can the same be said for investments in hybrid technologies that enable the "cleaner" operation of coal-fired electricity generation and prolong their operation? Put another way, are investments in solar energy and investments in carbon capture and sequestration technologies truly equivalent in terms of their contributions to advancing this goal? Under this target, no mechanisms direct attention to trends in the composition of the clean energy investment push. The underlying assumption is that all types of "cleaner" investment can make a difference.

The presumption that investments in this area will produce universal benefits is especially problematic at a time when many governments seek greater energy access, particularly in African contexts. China, for example, is more likely to form investment partnerships with oil-producing countries than with non-oil-producing countries (Lee 2019). This comprehensive effort to achieve energy security and resource access subsumes all the investments that China might make to enable cleaner energy technology and build better energy infrastructure (Aggarwal 2022). Technology transfers and financing for at least seventeen Chinese-backed hydropower development projects across Africa, for instance, might technically count as a contribution to the cleaner energy technology and investment agenda (Chen and Landry 2018). But these controversial projects do not exist independently of China's continent-wide investment footprint in genuine renewables, hybrid "clean" coal systems, or straight-up oil and gas production technology and infrastructure. And China is certainly not the only powerful state with a diversified footprint in Africa's energy future (Taliotis et al. 2014). The United States also has its own comprehensive initiative, called Power Africa. Encouraging the scaling up of investments in cleaner technologies and infrastructure without drawing attention to the broader impact that states have on the maintenance and expansion of dirty energy production is a recipe for failure.

The final implementation target (7.b) is similarly deficient. At first glance, it sounds reasonable, calling to expand infrastructure and upgrade technology for the supply of modern and sustainable energy services for all in developing countries. The associated indicator (7.b.1) initially called for data on investments in energy efficiency as a proportion of GDP. Yet that is where clarity and good sense come to a grinding halt, as the original language included in the indicator is a telling example of unintelligible "UN-ese." As part of the drive to expand energy services for developing countries, the indicator called for efforts to track "the amount of foreign direct investment in financial transfer for infrastructure and technology to sustainable development services" (Our World in Data team 2023).

The insertion of this confusing bafflegab might be excusable on a topic of lesser importance. Year-on-year data related to trends in the foreign direct investment (FDI) component of the push for investment in cleaner energy technologies and infrastructure would be very useful. These statistics could speak to the performance of the overall investment push in relation to local capacity-building needs. Countries that benefit from technology transfers and rely less on FDI over time might be able to reap more from the overall investment push. Others that continue to depend on foreign firms to build technologies or to execute infrastructure development over the years might underperform. Regardless, numbers on this sensitive topic are not directly available at present. Instead, new language for this indicator was developed in 2021, and statistics on installed electricity generation capacity from renewables are being used as a proxy.

According to the UN secretary-general's midpoint assessment of this goal, the world has not moved fast enough to ensure universally reliable access to electricity or to eliminate the use of polluting cooking fuels by 2030 (UNSG 2023). Unfortunately, the secretary-general's report did not detail the root causes of the sluggish pace or spell out the ways that SDG 7's political orientation could have contributed to it. Simply put, this goal is overly reliant on major corporate actors in the energy sector and on private sector innovations. It encourages a massive financial and investment push to transition energy systems. Consequently, it seeks to entrench corporate interests in reforming the global energy sector and bolstering the liberal international economic order. This political position is now incredibly controversial. Right-wing populists decry all global ideas and agenda setting related to energy system reform. For their part, progressives and greens oppose this goal's light-touch, corporate-friendly reform agenda *and* push back against the rent seekers and cronies who seek to entrench fossil fuel dependence.

References

Aggarwal, P. 2022. *China's Energy Security: The Journey from Self-Sufficiency to Global Investor*. Singapore: Palgrave Macmillan.

Chen, Y., and D. Landry. 2018. "Capturing the Rains: Comparing Chinese and World Bank Hydropower Projects in Cameroon and Pathways for South-South and North-South Technology Transfer." *Energy Policy* 115.

Lee, C-y. 2019. "China's Energy Diplomacy: Does Chinese Foreign Policy Favour Oil-Producing Countries." *Foreign Policy Analysis*, 15, 4.

Our World in Data team. 2023. "Ensure Access to Affordable, Reliable, Sustainable and Modern Energy for All." ourworldindata.org/sdgs/affordable-clean-energy.

Taliotis, C., M. Bazilian, M. Welsch, et al. 2014. "Grand Inga to Power Africa: Hydropower Development Scenarios to 2035." *Energy Strategy Reviews* 4.

UN (United Nations). 2020. *Affordable and Clean Energy: Why It Matters*. un.org/sustainabledevelopment/wp-content/uploads/2016/08/7_Why-It-Matters-2020.pdf.

———. 2022. *The Sustainable Development Goals Report 2022*. New York: UN.

———. 2023. "Goal 7: Ensure Access to Affordable, Reliable, Sustainable and Modern Energy." un.org/sustainabledevelopment/energy.

UNSG (United Nations Secretary-General). 2023. *Progress towards the Sustainable Development Goals: Towards a Rescue Plan for People and Planet. Report of the Secretary-General (Special Edition)*. New York: United Nations General Assembly and Economic and Social Council.

Goal **8**
Decent Work and Economic Growth

What They Tell Us

> **Mission statement:** Promote sustained, inclusive, and sustainable economic growth, full and productive employment, and decent work for all.

The basic social contract that underpins democratic societies requires all people to share in the fruits of economic progress (UN 2020). To ensure the health of our societies and socioeconomic systems, we must promote inclusive and sustainable economic growth, employment, and decent work for all (UN 2023). Without more opportunities for dignified work and people-centred investments, social exclusion could destabilize even the most prosperous societies. The economic crises of the past few years have "reversed progress" on decent work for all (UN 2022, 42). Average employment growth since 2008 has declined significantly compared with the rates that were evident in the early 2000s, and over 60 per cent of all workers lack any kind of employment contract (ILO n.d.). The global unemployment rate continues to grow, permanent full-time work is in decline, and the least developed countries have not reached the 7 per cent growth rate target. Together we must work to correct the course.

Work and Growth Targets		Indicators	
8.1	Sustain per capita economic growth in accordance with national circumstances and, in particular, at least 7 per cent gross domestic product growth per annum in the least developed countries	8.1.1	Annual growth rate of real GDP per capita
8.2	Achieve higher levels of economic productivity through diversification, technological upgrading and innovation, including through a focus on high-value added and labour-intensive sectors	8.2.1	Annual growth rate of real GDP per employed person

Work and Growth Targets	Indicators
8.3 Promote development-oriented policies that support productive activities, decent job creation, entrepreneurship, creativity, and innovation, and encourage the formalization and growth of micro-, small-, and medium-sized enterprises, including through access to financial services	8.3.1 Proportion of informal employment in total employment, by sector and sex
8.4 Improve progressively, through 2030, global resource efficiency in consumption and production and endeavour to decouple economic growth from environmental degradation, in accordance with the 10-year framework of programmes on sustainable consumption and production, with developed countries taking the lead	8.4.1 Material footprint, material footprint per capita, and material footprint per GDP 8.4.2 Domestic material consumption, domestic material consumption per capita, and domestic material consumption per GDP
8.5 By 2030, achieve full and productive employment and decent work for all women and men, including for young people and persons with disabilities, and equal pay for work of equal value	8.5.1 Average hourly earnings of employees, by sex, age, occupation, and persons with disabilities 8.5.2 Unemployment rate, by sex, age, and persons with disabilities
8.6 By 2020, substantially reduce the proportion of youth not in employment, education, or training	8.6.1 Proportion of youth (aged 15–24 years) not in education, employment, or training
8.7 Take immediate and effective measures to eradicate forced labour, end modern slavery and human trafficking, and secure the prohibition and elimination of the worst forms of child labour, including recruitment and use of child soldiers, and by 2025 end child labour in all its forms	8.7.1 Proportion and number of children aged 5–17 years engaged in child labour, by sex and age
8.8 Protect labour rights and promote safe and secure working environments for all workers, including migrant workers, in particular women migrants, and those in precarious employment	8.8.1 Fatal and non-fatal occupational injuries per 100000 workers, by sex and migrant status 8.8.2 Level of national compliance with labour rights (freedom of association and collective bargaining) based on International Labour Organization (ILO) textual sources and national legislation, by sex and migrant status
8.9 By 2030, devise and implement policies to promote sustainable tourism that creates jobs and promotes local culture and products	8.9.1 Tourism direct GDP as a proportion of total GDP and in growth rate
8.10 Strengthen the capacity of domestic financial institutions to encourage and expand access to banking, insurance, and financial services for all	8.10.1 (a) Number of commercial bank branches per 100000 adults and (b) Number of automated teller machines (ATMs) per 100000 adults 8.10.2 Proportion of adults (15 years and older) with an account at a bank or other financial institution or with a mobile-money-service provider

Work and Growth Targets		Indicators
8.a	Increase Aid for Trade support for developing countries, in particular Least Developed Countries, including through the Enhanced Integrated Framework for Trade-Related Technical Assistance to Least Developed Countries	**8.a.1** Aid for Trade commitments and disbursements
8.b	By 2020, develop and operationalize a global strategy for youth employment and implement the Global Jobs Pact of the International Labour Organization	**8.b.1** Existence of a developed and operationalized national strategy for youth employment, as a distinct strategy or as part of a national employment strategy

The Hidden Politics

SDG 8 embeds efforts to realize the Global Goals with an ideological drive to achieve sustained economic growth. In so doing, it exudes and imposes a political perspective that could undercut the capacity of future generations to enjoy sustainable development (Birdthistle and Hales 2022). No attempt was made to integrate the goal's first three targets with sustainability considerations. Instead, these targets are baldly presented as necessary without any reference to their climate impacts, or to the challenges they pose for life on land or below water. The first target (8.1) and associated indicator (8.1.1) encourage governments to meet their commitments to grow, and to track the growth of real GDP per capita. This emphasis effectively disregards many ongoing scientific and policy debates over the necessity of limitless growth (Hickel and Kallis 2020). Similarly, the next target (8.2) endorses the historic efforts that developing countries have made to diversify their economies and upgrade towards higher value-added and labour-intensive sectors without any reference to the environment. While it could be argued that efforts to achieve the other SDGs could "green" approaches to economic diversification, this target does not directly endorse the development of greener economies. It simply encourages governments to focus on the growth of GDP per employed person (8.2.1), not on the sustainability impacts of the work that employed people do while on the job. Moreover, the target (8.3) on entrepreneurship, innovation, and the formalization of micro and small businesses lacks an indicator linked to the development of greener enterprises or economies. Governments are only directed to reduce the proportion of informal employment (8.3.1) in the hope of yielding greater social inclusion and better work conditions. By failing to link entrepreneurship, innovation, and enterprise directly to the overarching sustainability challenge, this target is set to underperform.

The political perspective that informed the first three targets of SDG 8, and that worked against the explicit inclusion of political considerations linked to the environment, has been termed green growth. This understanding assumes that efforts to achieve "greener" growth are ongoing, and that growth is becoming more environmentally friendly over time. This viewpoint animates the goal's fourth target (8.4) on the need to improve global resource efficiency in consumption and production, and to decouple economic growth from environmental degradation. The influence of this approach cannot be understated — in fact, SDG 12 is mainly focused on disconnecting growth from despoliation and achieving more efficiencies in production and consumption. True believers in green growth assert that environmental externalities can be reduced in ways that enhance well-being and allow for the continued growth of GDP (Bowen and Hepburn 2014). According to this viewpoint, if the correct prices and green technologies are in place, GDP can grow without similar levels of growth in the amount of material resources that economies consume (Hussain et al. 2022). In other words, economic expansion is compatible with the planet's ecology, and technological change and substitution can reduce humanity's material footprint (Hickel and Kallis 2020).

This political agenda rests on seriously shaky foundations. Questions have been raised regarding its congruence with the World Commission on Environment and Development's call for development that meets the needs of the present without compromising the ability of future generations to meet their own needs (Lorek and Spangenberg 2014). The idea that green growth is the best path to "greening" resource-intensive areas of consumption such as food, housing, and transportation disregards looming ecological catastrophes. It also downplays the roles that treaty-based, statutory, and regulatory measures could play in securing inclusive sustainable development for future generations. Moreover, as Hickel and Kallis (2020) have shown, no empirical evidence indicates that absolute reductions in the rate of resource use per unit of economic activity are possible at the global scale if economic growth as endorsed by SDG 8 persists. Governments will also face difficulties in tracking any efforts to lower the total global material footprint of the resources that national economies consume (8.4.1) and to reduce domestic material consumption (8.4.2). Data on both indicators remain in many cases outdated and unavailable (Our World in Data team 2023). According to Hickel and Kallis (2020), the available evidence suggests that many countries have reduced the growth of domestic material consumption relative to the growth of GDP. However, global material footprints of consumption have been rising at rates equal to or greater than GDP growth.

Beyond the data limitations on both indicators, the target itself is beholden to growthism. It does not include any quantitative objectives to reduce resource use per capita, and it fails to provide any guidance on what level of material footprint might be sustainable (Hickel 2019). Ultimately, this target bakes in the ideology that has driven environmental catastrophe, undermining the SDGs' orientation towards sustainable development (Hickel 2021).

The alarming politics that envelop SDG 8 are also evident in relation to the subsequent targets on full employment and decent work. Experts have expressed serious concerns over the 2030 Agenda's treatment of labour and have sought clarification about whether it enshrines decent work as a human right (Frey 2017). They have also decried how labour and employment rights have been tagged on to the growth agenda as seemingly derivative considerations. For instance, indicators for the fifth target (8.5) on full, productive, and decent work for all and equal pay for work of equal value focus solely on hourly earnings (8.5.1) and the unemployment rate by sex, age, and disability (8.5.2). The emphasis on wages and employment status falls short insofar as it obscures other aspects of compensation that are fundamental to the realization of decent work. Benefits associated with full-time employment, including health- and pension-related measures, tend to correlate with outcomes such as better job and life satisfaction. Furthermore, relying on the unemployment rate to provide insight on decent work is troubling at a time when a decreasing proportion of workers around the world enjoy full employment and its related benefits. As more and more workers cobble together short-term contracts or multiple part-time jobs, trends in the unemployment rate reveal less and less about progress towards decent work for all. Furthermore, the pursuit of economic growth remains only one of the possible means to achieve full employment (Frey 2017). This target's lack of indicators related to the range of government measures and guarantees that can expedite full employment is consequently political. Over the ninety years that have passed since the New Deal programs were first implemented in the United States, social policies have helped secure decent work in many global contexts. Targets under SDG 8 exclude government initiatives from the data while enshrining a drive for more economic growth.

Weak language and indicators also impair the other employment-related targets. The sixth target (8.6) calls for a substantial reduction in the proportion of youth not in employment, education, or training. At first glance, this emphasis might seem worthy and rather innocuous, but on second reading the limitations become obvious. The target and associated indicator (8.6.1) do not prioritize the education and training of young people (15–24 years) over their employment status. Further, no mention is made of moving young people out of low- and lower-skilled employment. The clear aim of this target is to simply formalize the status of more youth in relation to employment, education, or training. While this push could expedite the realization of decent work, it represents a missed opportunity to reinforce SDG 4's aspirations for education. A weak indicator (8.7.1) also compromises the subsequent target's (8.7) aim to eradicate forced labour, modern slavery, human trafficking, and all forms of child labour, as governments are asked to report progress in relation to ending child labour only (Our World in Data team 2023). The failure to develop and include indicators on forced labour, modern slavery, and human trafficking, or to mandate better data production on these challenges, shows a clear lack of ambition. Although many nongovernmental organizations and academics work diligently to produce quality data on these challenges, official assessments of performance are not required to include these numbers.

The absence of data on these global and highly consequential phenomena will also undercut the eighth target's (8.8) ambition to protect labour rights and promote safe working environments. The tens of millions of people around the world who are forced to work, or who are bought, sold, or trafficked, can suffer fatal and nonfatal injuries (8.8.1) and obviously do not enjoy freedom of association or collective bargaining rights (8.8.2). Yet their plight remains invisible when statistics do not capture occupational injuries beyond the formal economic sector. The persistence and growth of the informal sector and the rise of digital work also pose problems for the accurate assessment of national progress on the achievement of core labour rights. Data collection in support of this target will not track the intensification of corporate legal strategies and union-busting practices that are used to curtail the core rights of gig economy workers. Taken together, the employment targets are inattentive to dynamics of the contemporary global economy and its governance that have serious consequences for workers everywhere.

The ninth target (8.9) exemplifies SDG 8's overemphasis on growth. Promoting beneficial and sustainable tourism that generates jobs and supports local culture and products does sound the right note. However, the tourism sector is known for its poor records related to servile employment and a lack of enduring linkages with local food, furniture, and other supply industries. Even so, the indicator for this target (8.9.1) focuses exclusively on raising the proportionate share of tourism in total GDP and in GDP growth. The dubious idea that pursuit of this indicator can be compatible with many of the other Global Goals is a product of green growth ideology. The assumption is that all actors in the tourism industry will take the other SDGs seriously, and in so doing, enhance tourism's sustainability credentials and ensure the development of more beneficial and enduring connections with local economies. The notion that some might choose to double down on unsustainable high-volume and low-cost models seems to have been wished away. While evidence does suggest that tourism businesses are thinking more about sustainability, their approaches to this topic have largely been voluntary and had highly variable impacts (Panzer-Krause 2019). The target also does not acknowledge the evident governance and performance gaps, and does not problematize fallout from those gaps, such as the profusion of greenwash in tourism marketing and promotions. Global procurement systems that enable cheap, emissions-intensive, and homogeneous holidays have not been slated for elimination. No quantitative targets for local employment and sourcing have been established. Tourism is simply put forward as a priority for global growth in the hope that sustainability will be simultaneously achieved.

To serve SDG 8's aspirations for growth, the final outcome-oriented target (8.10) seeks to ensure access to banking, insurance, and financial services for all. It aims to strengthen the capacity of domestic financial services and promote better access to financial services. Here, too, the indicators are quite telling. The number of commercial bank branches and ATMs per 100,000 people (8.10.1) and the proportion of adults with an account at a bank, other financial institution, or mobile money service (8.10.2) are to be watched. This focus essentially mandates the expansion of finance to new frontiers, clearly advancing commercial and financial interests (Weber 2017). The underlying message is clear: the potential to maximize growth increases when more people can access formal financial services. Efforts to pull savings and lending out of informal and illicit economies and into the light can obviously liberate many people. But the drive to build capacity in and access to formal financial services can also be associated with the decline of savings and the rise of consumer indebtedness. In many cases, higher levels of personal debt can bolster economic growth in the near term (Valckx 2017). The target's silence on this challenge, and on the role of savings and debt over longer time horizons more generally, raises serious questions about its alignment with the 2030 Agenda. Is debt now about much more than personal choices or obligations? Does Agenda 2030 effectively enshrine the capacity to access debt as a human right in order to contribute to "greening" growth?

To implement SDG 8, the 2030 Agenda encourages two further political actions. First, it calls for governments to increase their support for Aid for

Trade (8.a), a program led by the World Trade Organization, in terms of commitments and disbursements to developing countries (8.a.1). This approach reflects the dated and highly contentious viewpoint that the growth of international trade accelerates overall growth rates. It fails to engage with the decades-old counterargument that economies tend to trade more as they grow (Rodrik 1997). Furthermore, the emphasis on increasing trade capacity and infrastructure could undermine ambitions to achieve more responsible production and consumption. The growth-first lens also contradicts and will ultimately circumscribe efforts to develop and operationalize an effective global strategy for youth employment and to implement the International Labour Organization's Global Jobs Pact, as outlined in the second implementation target (8.b).

In his midpoint assessment of the lack of progress made to date on SDG 8, the UN secretary-general blamed a confluence of escalating global crises (UNSG 2023). The secretary-general's report called for financial system reform but neglected to mention the many ways that this goal advances financial sector interests. The analysis presented above leaves no doubt that the goal's multifaceted growth agenda can be characterized as an effort to reform the liberal international economic order. This political orientation towards solidifying support for the global economy is anything but uncontroversial. Many nationalist and populist demagogues consider economic growth and employment to be fundamentally domestic concerns. Social progressives and greens challenge SDG 8's growth-oriented reformism *and* the nationalist and capitalist voices that seek autonomy from global agenda setting.

References

Birdthistle, N., and R. Hales. 2022. *Attaining the 2030 Sustainable Development Goal of Climate Action.* Bingley, UK: Emerald Publishing.

Bowen, A., and C. Hepburn. 2014. "Green Growth: An Assessment." *Oxford Review of Economic Policy* 30, 3.

Frey, D.F. 2017. "Economic Growth, Full Employment and Decent Work: The Means and Ends in SDG 8." *The International Journal of Human Rights* 21, 8.

Hickel, J. 2019. "The Contradiction of the Sustainable Development Goals: Growth Versus Ecology on a Finite Planet." *Sustainable Development* 27.

———. 2021. "What Does Degrowth Mean? A Few Points of Clarification." *Globalizations* 18, 7.

Hickel, J., and G. Kallis. 2020. "Is Green Growth Possible?" *New Political Economy* 25, 4.

Hussain, Z., B. Mehmood, M.K. Khan, and R.S.M. Tsimisaraka. 2022. "Green Growth, Green Technology, and Environmental Health: Evidence From High-GDP Countries." *Frontiers in Public Health* 9.

ILO (International Labour Organization). n.d. "Goal #8: Decent Work and Economic Growth." ilo.org/global/topics/sdg-2030/goal-8/lang--en/index.htm.

Lorek, S., and J.H. Spangenberg. 2014. "Sustainable Consumption within a Sustainable Economy — Beyond Green Growth and Green Economies." *Journal of Cleaner Production* 63.

Our World in Data team. 2023. "Promote Sustained, Inclusive and Sustainable Economic Growth, Full and Productive Employment and Decent Work for All." ourworldindata.org/sdgs/economic-growth.

Panzer-Krause, S. 2019. "Networking towards Sustainable Tourism: Innovations between Green Growth and Degrowth Strategies." *Regional Studies* 53, 7.

Rodrik, D. 1997. *Has Globalization Gone Too Far?* Washington, DC: Institute for International Economics.

UN (United Nations). 2020. *Decent Work and Economic Growth: Why It Matters.* un.org/sustainabledevelopment/wp-content/uploads/2018/09/Goal-8.pdf.

———. 2022. *The Sustainable Development Goals Report 2022.* New York: UN.

———. 2023. "Goal 8: Promote Inclusive and Sustainable Economic Growth, Employment and Decent Work for All." un.org/sustainabledevelopment/economic-growth. un.org/sustainabledevelopment/wp-content/uploads/2016/08/8_Why-It-Matters-2020.pdf.

UNSG (United Nations Secretary-General). 2023. *Progress towards the Sustainable Development Goals: Towards a Rescue Plan for People and Planet. Report of the Secretary-General (Special Edition).* New York: United Nations General Assembly and Economic and Social Council.

Valckx, N. 2017. "Rising Household Debt: What It Means for Growth and Stability." *IMF Blog*, October 3. imf.org/en/Blogs/Articles/2017/10/03/rising-household-debt-what-it-means-for-growth-and-stability.

Weber, H. 2017. "Politics of 'Leaving No One Behind': Contesting the 2030 Sustainable Development Goals Agenda." In *The Politics of Destination in the 2030 Sustainable Development Goals: Leaving No-One Behind?*, edited by C. Gabay and S. Ilcan. London: Routledge.

Goal ⑨
Industry, Innovation, and Infrastructure

What They Tell Us

Mission statement: Build resilient infrastructure, promote inclusive and sustainable industrialization, and foster innovation.

Industry is at the centre of the global agenda to advance sustainable development (UN 2020). Companies must collaborate with governments and nongovernmental organizations to ensure the sustainable management of their initiatives and to promote sustainable growth everywhere. In many developing countries, basic infrastructure remains woefully inadequate. Where and when industry is inclusive, sustainable, and innovative, resilient infrastructure can be built (UN 2023). In turn, improved infrastructure can foster cleaner development, technological innovation, and economic dynamism. The pandemic underscored the importance of industrialization, technological innovation, and resilient infrastructure (UN 2022, 44). Countries with diversified industrial sectors and robust infrastructure experienced faster recoveries (UN 2023). Similarly, higher-technology industries performed better through the shock and recovered faster. Absolutely no doubt remains that knowledge-driven economies are more resilient and inclusive. This goal encourages businesses and governments to show leadership and unite behind the idea of extending the benefits from industry, innovation, and infrastructure to all (UN 2020).

Industry and Infrastructure Targets		Indicators	
9.1	Develop quality, reliable, sustainable, and resilient infrastructure, including regional and transborder infrastructure, to support economic development and human well-being, with a focus on affordable and equitable access for all	9.1.1	Proportion of the rural population who live within 2 km of an all-season road
		9.1.2	Passenger and freight volumes, by mode of transport

Industry and Infrastructure Targets	Indicators
9.2 Promote inclusive and sustainable industrialization and, by 2030, significantly raise industry's share of employment and gross domestic product, in line with national circumstances, and double its share in least developed countries	9.2.1 Manufacturing value added as a proportion of GDP and per capita 9.2.2 Manufacturing employment as a proportion of total employment
9.3 Increase the access of small-scale industrial and other enterprises, in particular in developing countries, to financial services, including affordable credit, and their integration into value chains and markets	9.3.1 Proportion of small-scale industries in total industry value added 9.3.2 Proportion of small-scale industries with a loan or line of credit
9.4 By 2030, upgrade infrastructure and retrofit industries to make them sustainable, with increased resource-use efficiency and greater adoption of clean and environmentally sound technologies and industrial processes, with all countries taking action in accordance with their respective capabilities	9.4.1 CO_2 emission per unit of value added
9.5 Enhance scientific research, upgrade the technological capabilities of industrial sectors in all countries, in particular developing countries, including, by 2030, encouraging innovation and substantially increasing the number of research and development workers per 1 million people and public and private research and development spending	9.5.1 Research and development expenditure as a proportion of GDP 9.5.2 Researchers (in full-time equivalent) per million inhabitants
9.a Facilitate sustainable and resilient infrastructure development in developing countries through enhanced financial, technological, and technical support to African countries, least developed countries, landlocked developing countries and small island developing States	9.a.1 Total official international support (official development assistance plus other official flows) to infrastructure
9.b Support domestic technology development, research, and innovation in developing countries, including by ensuring a conducive policy environment for, inter alia, industrial diversification and value addition to commodities	9.b.1 Proportion of medium and high-tech industry value added in total value added
9.c Significantly increase access to information and communications technology and strive to provide universal and affordable access to the Internet in least developed countries by 2020	9.c.1 Proportion of population covered by a mobile network, by technology

The Hidden Politics

Efforts to develop quality, reliable, sustainable, and resilient infrastructure that people can access affordably and equitably are inherently political. For starters, loading six controversial terms into SDG 9's first target (9.1) without providing any definitions seems more of an invitation to politics than a call to action. For instance, who or what gets to define the specifics of "quality" infrastructure? Governments sign infrastructure development contracts with foreign and domestic firms that tend to include clear language on quality specifications and standards. But governments seeking debt-based agreements to fund infrastructure projects are not generally in a strong position to dictate contractual terms. If a government wishes to introduce considerations related to the quality of materials, and the financial backer or development firm is unwilling or unable to accommodate such considerations, the infrastructure project will underperform in relation to the SDGs. Put another way, to secure willing investors, governments that favour the use of certified responsibly sourced concrete might have to settle for lower-grade concretes that do not include "green" or less carbon-intensive cement.

The failure to define the other terms that appear in the first target is also consequential. Expectations related to "reliable" infrastructure may vary between smaller one-off national transportation projects and massive transboundary projects that bundle numerous projects to create infrastructure corridors. The latter type can include the simultaneous development of highways, railways, and pipelines. In resource-constrained contexts, reliability considerations for infrastructure dedicated to the movement of resources, goods, and people may not be given equal weight. Furthermore, is infrastructure development truly "sustainable" or "resilient" if it advances business as usual in the industries that are most responsible for the climate emergency, such as oil and gas extraction? And what of "affordable" and "equitable" access to infrastructure? The lack of detailed criteria related to these two terms opens the door to political controversy. Stakeholders in infrastructure development do not generally engage in political processes on equal terms. Specific ideas about equity and affordability that governments take seriously do not exist in a political vacuum. Powerful voices shape the access considerations that are ultimately deemed to matter.

Two indicators accompany this target, and both are a rather uncomfortable fit with ambitions for more inclusive and sustainable development. The first (9.1.1) focuses on the proportion of rural populations that live within two kilometres of an all-season road. The second (9.1.2) endorses efforts to increase passenger and freight volumes by mode of transport. Both measures fly in the face of concerns that rural land users have expressed in many contexts over how infrastructure development stands to alter their access to and control over land (Enns 2019; Thomas 2018). Roads are not universal liberators of human potential when they come packaged with land-intensive infrastructure that serves distant others, or when their locations reflect the needs of more powerful interest groups. According to research conducted by Dr. Charis Enns in Kenya, power dynamics associated with the mobilization of expert knowledge have shaped land deals, in some cases favouring conservationists over other rural land users. How exactly this target's focus on building roads and moving more people, goods, and raw materials can be taken to indicate progress towards sustainable development remains unclear. People in rural areas that are subjected to large-scale projects and the drive for more infrastructure might find that these ambitions undercut their capacity to benefit from other dimensions of the 2030 Agenda.

The subsequent target (9.2) seeks to advance inclusive and sustainable industrialization. Here, too, the selective, weak, and political use of language will shape and constrain efforts to achieve the desired ends. This target aims to significantly raise industry's share of employment and GDP in line with national circumstances, and to double its share in the least developed countries. However, the associated indicators define inclusive industrialization in exceedingly narrow terms, as inclusion matters only in two senses. First, manufacturing value added as a proportion of GDP and per capita (9.2.1): if the net output of industry constitutes a growing share of GDP and outpaces population growth, industrialization is held to be more inclusive. Second, manufacturing employment as a proportion of total employment (9.2.2): if the proportion increases, industry is deemed to be more inclusive, full stop. Thus, this target dispenses with all other challenges related to inclusion in the manufacturing industry, under the assumption that efforts to achieve the other goals, including SDG 8 on growth and decent work, will advance other aspects of inclusion. The target also presumes that the manufacturing industry will become more sustainable as it employs more people and grows in economic importance. This dubious premise is evident in the failure of the indicators to include any sustainability criteria whatsoever. Consequently, under this target, governments that prioritize industrialization might be able to claim success regardless of the quality of employment or industry that their efforts generate. Politically expedient approaches to increasing the importance of industry for employment and the overall national economy will not be universally congruent with the Global Goals. Strategies for industrialization that double down on sweatshops and polluting industries obviously do not align with other SDGs. On these matters, the silence of the target on inclusive and sustainable industrialization is deafening.

The third target (9.3) and its associated indicators also overemphasize aggregate growth and downplay the composition of industry. On the surface, this target's focus on advancing the position of small-scale industrial and other enterprises in developing countries by improving their access to value chains and markets seems rather innocuous. It reflects a soft liberal agenda related to global integration and financial capacity building. The two associated indicators also appear inoffensive. These seek to increase the proportion of small-scale industries in total industry value added (9.3.1), and to improve the proportion of these industries with a loan or credit line (9.3.2). Yet there is a massive problem here. This target and its indicators do not include any language related to priority areas within the industrial sector, or to sources of finance, standards, or to any other criteria of business quality. Thus, a surge of new small businesses that depend on outsourcing arrangements and contingent workers could feasibly advance this target on their own terms. Similarly, when more and more small-scale industrial firms become reliant on expensive and contingent loans disbursed by formal lenders or buyers in other countries, this trend could be interpreted as advancing "progress." Simply put, this target has a quality problem. It is inattentive to the quality of value-added businesses and to the quality of their financial connections and reliance. This deficiency could undercut progress on many of the other SDGs that intersect with small-scale industrial activities.

SDG 9's fourth target (9.4) prioritizes upgrades and retrofits that aim to ensure the sustainability of infrastructure and industries. By advocating the adoption of new technologies and processes alongside greater resource-use efficiency, this target does insert green objectives into the drive to build infrastructure and intensify industry. Yet only one indicator has been associated with this target's green agenda, and it focuses attention solely on carbon emissions per unit of value added (9.4.1). While this emphasis could encourage efficiencies and the uptake of greener approaches to construction and industrial production, data on the carbon emission intensity of economies are currently incomplete. At present, the data do not include emissions that result from land-use changes, such as the development of resource corridors and other land-intensive infrastructure projects (Our World in Data team 2023). This inadequacy is politically disconcerting. Infrastructure development has been shown to drive carbon emissions and forest loss while threatening the rights of communities in forested areas (Bebbington et al. 2018). Leading researchers have found that the construction of roads, railways, port facilities, and waterways make significant contributions to emissions by facilitating in-migration, settlement, and subsequent land-use changes. The indicator for this target remains insensitive to the ways that the development of infrastructure continues to fuel the extraction of resources. Even if all firms in the industrial and construction sectors were to adopt greener practices, the true carbon intensity of economies increases when new infrastructure corridors enable extraction and intensify and change land use.

The failure to include any additional indicators or quantitative objectives also speaks to the limitations of the fourth target. Statistics on the uptake of technologies that enable greener industrial process and production methods are not being collected. Similarly, there is no indicator to measure the efforts that infrastructure development firms are making to adopt greener sourcing. Nor is there an indicator to track the carbon and broader sustainability impacts of government procurement contracts on industry and infrastructure. Beyond these concerning oversights, the expansion of infrastructure undoubtedly contributes to accelerating biodiversity loss and ecosystem decline (Enns and Sneyd 2021). This target is resoundingly silent on the fact that infrastructure projects often do violence to nonhuman species. In the ostensibly "greener" development of the Chad-Cameroon Petroleum Development and Pipeline Project, for instance, many fish species disappeared after a reef was blasted and replaced with an artificial underwater structure. While SDGs 14 and 15 explicitly emphasize biodiversity, life under water, and life on land, data collection on infrastructure excludes the violent impacts that new corridors can have on the environment and the nonhuman world. The absence of any explicit or implicit language on this known challenge is damning, reflecting the goal's ideological overemphasis on the growth of industry and infrastructure in toto.

The next target's (9.5) emphasis on enhancing scientific research, upgrading technological capabilities, and increasing spending on research and development in all countries seems aligned with genuine aspirations for a fairer and more inclusive world. Both indicators under this target will provide useful snapshots of highly consequential trends. Statistics on research and development spending as a proportion of GDP (9.5.1) and on the number of full-time researchers per million inhabitants (9.5.2) direct attention to two essentials for the creation and application of knowledge. Still, intentions to grow domestic research spending and the number of researchers can come up against a serious political impediment. If these efforts are successful, they will increase the global pool of available research talent and put downward pressure on research worker wages and compensation. The target also does not acknowledge the possibility that the push for investment in research and development could amplify the so-called brain drain of talent from developing countries. Absolute growth of the brain drain phenomenon could undercut the drive to establish relatively higher numbers of researchers domestically and generate persistent inefficiencies in research spending. Data on overseas research work and the migration of researchers are consequently missing in action. Moreover, while many ongoing multistakeholder development initiatives aim to correct this phenomenon, trends in their financing or successes are not being tracked.

This target faces numerous additional stumbling blocks. The faltering post-COVID trajectory of a transnational effort to build centres of scientific and research excellence and bolster research communities in the African context is telling. Mercantilist and nationalistic thinking undermined several linked initiatives that had idealistically aimed to create transborder scientific communities to advance African research excellence (T. Zomahoun, personal communication, September 15, 2023). Similarly troubling is the prospect that a big push for enhanced research capacities will privilege Western-based approaches to science over other forms of knowledge creation. Furthermore, the digital business models that drive the virtual economy rely heavily on innovations that are protected by monopolistic intellectual property rights such as copyright (Denoncourt 2020). This target fails to address the consequences that monopoly power can have for scientific research in developing countries. Its indicators also gloss over the development challenges that are associated with patent-protected innovations. As a whole, these obstacles highlight the limitations of a push to build research capacity that focuses solely on expenditures and numbers of people. On their own, these ends will not deliver on the promise of research and science for all.

The goal's first implementation target (9.a) seeks to enhance official financial, technological, and technical support for infrastructure development in developing countries. Increases of total official development assistance and other official flows (9.a.1) can contribute to improving the sustainability and resilience of infrastructure projects. This can be possible when donors encourage their development partners to use more stringent criteria and requirements related to consultation, oversight, reporting, and sourcing. The fact nonetheless remains that official flows are a very small component of overall infrastructure investment. For example, the financing that China's state-backed banks provided during Africa's recent infrastructure boom dwarfed the disbursements made by official bilateral lenders (*The Economist* 2022). Relying on official sources to scale up sustainability and resilience, as this target seems to do, is also politically naive. Private sector–led infrastructure development partnerships, and even host governments, can and do shun the participation of donors that might seek to impose exacting quality standards. And official donors themselves can be wary of the political risks associated with participation in megaprojects.

The subsequent implementation target (9.b) also exhibits a veneer of respectability that fades in the light of political reality. This target supports domestic technology and industrial diversification and has an indicator

(9.b.1) that will yield insights. Its focus on the proportion of medium and high-tech industry in total value added can speak to progress on industrial diversification and efforts to add more value to commodities. That said, the latter two policy aspirations have underperformed for decades. As the introduction to this book recounts, international initiatives led by developing countries on these topics have faced considerable political resistance, and many continue to depend on exports of low value-added commodities. As it stands, under this target, the investments made by commodity trading firms and their global buyers to diversify and add more value in developing countries are not being counted. Likewise, the ways that these firms and their operations impede developing country efforts to increase the proportion of medium and high-tech industry in their total value added also remain cloaked in darkness. More broadly, this target is also woefully inattentive to the increasing reliance of least developed, landlocked, and small island developing states on imports of manufactured goods (Gutmann and Adesina 2022). This dependence stunts the development of medium and high-tech industries and does nothing to enhance sustainability and resilience. The final implementation target's emphasis on information and communication technology (9.c) and the coverage of mobile networks (9.c.1) mirrors many of these consequential shortcomings.

The UN secretary-general's SDG midpoint review trumpeted some regional successes related to manufacturing value added per capita and called for efforts to promote innovation and the transfer of technology (UNSG 2023). The report was not candid about the ways that SDG 9 bolsters the liberal international economic order and global capitalism. As reviewed above, this goal is permeated with liberal understandings of the potential for infrastructure, innovation, and industry to advance the human condition and contribute to maintaining and sustaining life on Earth. From this perspective, more infrastructure projects and more industrial development, coupled with the application of technological innovations, are compatible with greater social inclusion and better environmental practices. To say the least, this orientation optimistically overlooks the opportunity for nationalists to exploit SDG 9's agenda. Progressives and greens challenge this goal's excessive liberalism *and* fight the efforts states make to advance national power and interests at the expense of local populations and environments. They also promote the regulatory and legal frameworks necessary to better align business activities in these areas with human needs and planetary boundaries (Stockholm Resilience Centre 2023).

References

Bebbington, A.J., D.H. Bebbington, L.A. Sauls, et al. 2018. "Resource Extraction and Infrastructure Threaten Forest Cover and Community Rights." *PNAS* 115, 52.

Denoncourt, J. 2020. "Companies and UN 2030 Sustainable Development Goal 9 Industry, Innovation and Infrastructure." *Journal of Corporate Law Studies* 20, 1.

The Economist. 2022. "Chinese Loans and Investment in Infrastructure Have Been Huge." *The Economist*, May 20.

Enns, C. 2019. "Infrastructure Projects and Rural Politics in Northern Kenya: The Use of Divergent Expertise to Negotiate the Terms of Lease Deals for Transport Infrastructure." *The Journal of Peasant Studies* 46, 2.

Enns, C., and A. Sneyd. 2021. "More-Than-Human Infrastructural Violence and Infrastructural Justice: A Case Study of the Chad-Cameroon Pipeline Project." *Annals of the American Association of Geographers* 111, 2.

Gutmann, M., and O. Adesina. 2022. "SDG 9 — Historicizing Production, Innovation, and Infrastructure, from the Industrial Revolution to Contemporary African Strategies of Industrialization." In *Before the UN Sustainable Development Goals*, edited by M. Gutmann and D. Gorman. Oxford: Oxford University Press.

Our World in Data team. 2023. "Build Resilient Infrastructure, Promote Inclusive and Sustainable Industrialization and Foster Innovation." sdg-tracker.org/infrastructure-industrialization.

Stockholm Resilience Centre. 2023. "Planetary Boundaries." stockholmresilience.org/research/planetary-boundaries.html.

Thomas, D.P. 2018. *Bombardier Abroad: Patterns of Dispossession*. Black Point, NS: Fernwood Publishing.

UN (United Nations). 2020. *Industry, Innovation and Infrastructure: Why it Matters*. un.org/sustainabledevelopment/wp-content/uploads/2018/09/Goal-9.pdf.

———. 2022. *The Sustainable Development Goals Report 2022*. New York: UN.

———. 2023. "Goal 9: Build Resilient Infrastructure, Promote Sustainable Industrialization and Foster Innovation." un.org/sustainabledevelopment/infrastructure-industrialization.

UNSG (United Nations Secretary-General). 2023. *Progress towards the Sustainable Development Goals: Towards a Rescue Plan for People and Planet. Report of the Secretary-General (Special Edition)*. New York: United Nations General Assembly and Economic and Social Council.

Goal ⑩
Reduced Inequalities

What They Tell Us

Mission statement: Reduce inequality within and among countries.

To achieve the Global Goals, we must ensure that no one is left behind as we strive to reduce inequalities (UN 2023). Income equality within and between countries has persisted and fostered concerning levels of social exclusion. That said, income is not the only source of inequality that should preoccupy policy- and decision-makers. Inequalities based on sex, age, disability, sexual orientation, race, class, ethnicity, religion, and opportunity have also been stubbornly incessant (UN 2020). Transformative change will be required to reduce inequality of all types. Governments must pursue inclusive social and economic growth, and decision-making on global issues must become more genuinely cooperative and representative. Prior to the pandemic, "encouraging signs across a number of indicators" suggested a narrowing of income inequality (UN 2022, 46). Positive trends seem now to have gone into reverse, and structural and systemic discrimination have intensified (UN 2023). Inequality within emerging and developing countries is rising, and income inequality between countries has also increased. The path to improving the situation of labour and displaced people and to realizing a fairer, more inclusive world has become more difficult.

Inequality Targets	Indicators
10.1 By 2030, progressively achieve and sustain income growth of the bottom 40 per cent of the population at a rate higher than the national average	10.1.1 Growth rates of household expenditure or income per capita among the bottom 40 per cent of the population and the total population
10.2 By 2030, empower and promote the social, economic, and political inclusion of all, irrespective of age, sex, disability, race, ethnicity, origin, religion, or economic or other status	10.2.1 Proportion of people living below 50 per cent of median income, by sex, age and persons with disabilities

Inequality Targets	Indicators
10.3 Ensure equal opportunity and reduce inequalities of outcome, including by eliminating discriminatory laws, policies, and practices and promoting appropriate legislation, policies, and action in this regard	10.3.1 Proportion of population reporting having personally felt discriminated against or harassed in the previous 12 months on the basis of a ground of discrimination prohibited under international human rights law
10.4 Adopt policies, especially fiscal, wage, and social protection policies, and progressively achieve greater equality	10.4.1 Labour share of GDP 10.4.2 Redistributive impact of fiscal policy
10.5 Improve the regulation and monitoring of global financial markets and institutions and strengthen the implementation of such regulations	10.5.1 Financial Soundness Indicators
10.6 Ensure enhanced representation and voice for developing countries in decision-making in global international economic and financial institutions in order to deliver more effective, credible, accountable, and legitimate institutions	10.6.1 Proportion of members and voting rights of developing countries in international organizations
10.7 Facilitate orderly, safe, regular, and responsible migration and mobility of people, including through the implementation of planned and well-managed migration policies	10.7.1 Recruitment cost borne by employee as a proportion of monthly income earned in country of destination 10.7.2 Proportion of countries with migration policies that facilitate orderly, safe, regular, and responsible migration and mobility of people 10.7.3 Number of people who died or disappeared in the process of migration towards an international destination 10.7.4 Proportion of the population who are refugees, by country of origin
10.a Implement the principle of special and differential treatment for developing countries, in particular least developed countries, in accordance with World Trade Organization agreements	10.a.1 Proportion of tariff lines applied to imports from least developed countries and developing countries with zero-tariff
10.b Encourage official development assistance and financial flows, including foreign direct investment, to States where the need is greatest, in particular least developed countries, African countries, small island developing States and landlocked developing countries, in accordance with their national plans and programmes	10.b.1 Total resource flows for development, by recipient and donor countries and type of flow (e.g. official development assistance, foreign direct investment, and other flows)
10.c By 2030, reduce to less than 3 percent the transaction costs of migrant remittances and eliminate remittance corridors with costs higher than 5 per cent	10.c.1 Remittance costs as a proportion of the amount remitted

The Hidden Politics

SDG 10 was developed partly in response to a global political backlash against rising inequalities related to income and wealth around the world (Oestreich 2018). Even so, it encourages the pursuit of a broad range of legal, social, and economic reforms to reduce many different sources of inequality beyond income. This expansive approach to reducing inequalities includes targets that can be linked to the advancement of civil and political rights, as well as economic, social, and cultural rights. At first glance, the goal's framing appears to be comprehensive and unifying. However, a deep dive into the associated indicators contradicts this impression and reveals the goal's minimalist political intentions.

The first target's (10.1) call for governments to prioritize the growth of incomes and household expenditures for the bottom 40 per cent of the population is clearly redistributionist. This focus is a necessary first step on the path towards reducing the social ills associated with persistently high economic inequality. Yet this emphasis on flows remains exceedingly basic, and on its own is a woefully insufficient means to pursue equality (Piketty 2019). Reflecting the World Bank's preferred framing, this target fails to spotlight or problematize trends at the top of the distribution, and entirely omits consideration of inequalities related to the stock of accumulated wealth (Dalby et al. 2019). Thus, imploring governments to pursue reforms that grow the per capita incomes or household expenditures of the bottom two quintiles could yield superficial appeasement (10.1.1). This push could readily degenerate into a drive to raise the purchasing power that poorer people command in the consumer economy. After all, lower- income people tend to spend unexpectedly higher incomes on consumable and durable goods. Increased sales volumes at the lower end of those markets are often linked to fatter corporate profits and heftier executive compensation. Policies that put more money into the hands of poorer people can reduce inequality in the short term. But they can also induce inflationary price setting and profiteering. These and other challenges associated with income redistribution and the ways that globally mobile executives tend to respond to it are well known. Without simultaneous consideration of high-income earners, and to the strategies they can apply to mitigate the potential impact of redistributionist policies, this target is not fit for purpose. Its failure to spur governments to participate in international taxation initiatives, or to embrace fiscal and policy measures that could curb wealth inequality, is telling. At worst, this orientation is conducive to the interest that so-called ultra-high-net-worth individuals can have in framing economic inequality as a consumption challenge facing the poor. It neglects the ways that wealth inequality contributes to intergenerational inequities or class building. And it is also calamitously silent on wealth-maintenance practices, including capital flight, investment strike, dual citizenship, trust structures, and offshore tax havens.

The subsequent target (10.2) injects lofty ambitions on other dimensions of inequality into the goal, but these are similarly constrained by a weak indicator. The second target's bold call to empower and promote the social, economic, and political inclusion of all draws attention to inequalities associated with age, sex, disability, race, ethnicity, origin, religion, and economic or other status. However, the transformative potential of this language is vastly curtailed by the associated indicator's (10.2.1) emphasis only on the proportion of people living below 50 per cent of median income by sex, age, and persons with disabilities. World-level data on this highly restricted indicator remain unavailable (Our World in Data team 2023). Beyond this challenge, the indicator fails to include any language whatsoever on Indigenous and racialized peoples, religious minorities, ethnic groups, or status related to caste. Authorities at the national level remain free to turn their attention to the income-related challenges faced by members of those groups, but they have not been advised to do so. The emphasis on median income also restricts the scope for action under this target. In societies where income inequality is persistently high, the median income tends to be much lower than the average or mean income. Improving the lot of the poorest and most marginalized groups is an obviously sound priority. That said, this approach could preclude consideration of the plight of equity-seeking groups whose incomes might hover just above the 50 per cent cap.

The goal's third target (10.3) moves beyond the economic dimension of inclusion and engages directly with social and political inequalities. Its aspirations are nevertheless subdued. Under this target, governments are advised to *ensure* equal opportunities but to only *reduce* inequalities of outcome. They are directed to *eliminate* discriminatory laws, policies, and practices but to only *promote* the legislation, policies, and action that they deem appropriate. Exceedingly restricted language also infuses the associated indicator (10.3.1), narrowing its scope to the elimination of discriminatory practices prohibited under international human rights law. This framing highlights the proportion of people who report having personally felt discriminated against or harassed in the past year. Though data on this topic can surely catalyze needed actions, the failure of this target to include any indicators related to the structural and systemic barriers that equity-seeking groups continue to face beyond direct instances of discrimination is worrying. It excludes much of the work that these groups continue to do to advance social, economic, and political equality. Less ambitiously, indicators under this target could have encouraged governments to be attentive to the share of political and economic leadership positions held by members of equity-seeking groups.

The fourth target (10.4) on government policies and greater equality is also loaded with ambiguous language. Governments are advised to adopt fiscal, wage, and social protection policies, and to pursue the progressive achievement of greater equality. This admonition is presented without any stipulations whatsoever related to the target level or type of equality that they should aim for. The time horizon associated with the "progressive" achievement of greater equality is similarly undefined. This maximalist language is consequently open to abuse. Cost-cutting governments that retrench universal social protection policies and introduce highly restricted means-tested social assistance systems, for example, could associate their efforts with this target. If cutbacks and welfare reforms coincide with a surge of employment-generating growth, austere policy agendas could be congruent with increasing the labour share of GDP, as specified in the first associated indicator (10.4.1). The only other associated indicator (10.4.2) encourages a focus on the redistributive impact of fiscal policy. However, in any context where the total compensation of employees as a percentage of GDP continues to inch upwards, governments can rightly or disingenuously construe their fiscal policies to be progressive. The possible limitations of these indicators are especially worrying in contexts where informal employment dominates. Policies that aim to make street vendor employees or informal home workers more legible to authorities for the purposes of taxation clearly do not have the same potential to generate equality as policies that introduce a universal child benefit. Both policies could nonetheless contribute to increasing the labour share of GDP or be framed as "redistributionist."

The subsequent target (10.5) also features a notable imbalance between idealistic language and inadequate measures. Its pertinent call for stronger regulation and monitoring of global financial markets is outweighed by its inattention to the persistence of practices that have swollen the size and importance of financial sectors relative to overall economic activity. This target leaves the consequences of such financialization untouched, and simply urges governments to ensure heightened performance in relation to the International Monetary Fund's so-called Financial Soundness Indicators (10.5.1). Thus, it accentuates a need for financial stability, and underscores trends in short-term liabilities, nonperforming loans, and return on assets in this sector. Placing exclusive stress on the need to better monitor the status quo is hugely constraining. It ensures that efforts under this target are unconcerned with the continuation of unsound financial practices beyond those that are directly related to short-term solvency and financial performance. Consequently, this target does not aim to address financial sector bloat, nor does it seek to rein in the dangerous potential for financial alchemists to develop "innovative" products that pose long-term threats to the system. It is also unconcerned with the ways that banks and financial services firms contribute to inflating the value of asset markets, such as real estate. Players in the financial sector have direct interests in profiting as much as possible from the massive ongoing intergenerational transfer of wealth from baby boomers to their children and in averting regulatory attention from this new money-making frontier. The target remains silent on this matter and on the broader reality that interests in the financial sector can align against SDG 10 and many other goals

The sixth target (10.6) reiterates a long-standing appeal to enhance the representation and voice of developing countries in global economic and financial decision-making. At first glance, the weight that the associated indicator (10.6.1) places on the membership and voting rights of developing countries in international organizations seems well placed. Efforts in this area have been ongoing for decades and could yield more inclusive and legitimate decision-making practices. Still, the emphasis on ensuring that more developing countries can contribute to financial and economic governance within public international organizations is insufficient. It simply takes as given the current lack of UN oversight over the powers and scope of the principal multilateral financial institutions. The Bretton Woods Institutions are technically considered specialized agencies of the UN system. As such, they should be answerable to the vast majority that developing countries command in the UN, and their leaders should also welcome governance innovations that enable greater UN oversight over their operations. This target does not strive to create new mechanisms that would permit the UN majority to hold decisions taken by specialized agencies such as the World Bank or the International Monetary Fund to better account. Rather, it takes the existing distribution of responsibilities as given, and fails to create structures that could check or balance the outsized power of international financial and economic institutions. Moreover, the exclusive stress that this target places on voting shares and membership in existing public institutions fails to address other factors that continue to exclude developing countries from decision-making. It does not call for the G7, the BRICS group, or other influential intergovernmental and bilateral agenda-setting processes to recognize or respect the perspectives of developing or least developed countries. Furthermore, it leaves untouched the global power imbalances that constrain the capacity of developing countries to make truly independent economic and financial decisions.

The next target's (10.7) plea for all countries to facilitate the orderly, safe, regular, and responsible migration and mobility of people also fails to directly address some of the leading political and economic drivers of unequal outcomes. The indicators draw needed attention to persistent challenges including the high recruitment costs that many migrants face (10.7.1) and disappearances and deaths in the process of migration (10.7.3). They also encourage the production of data that will allow citizens and civil society groups to hold governments to better account. Statistics on the implementation of well-managed migration policies (10.7.2) and on the proportion of the population who are refugees, by country of origin (10.7.4), can be readily used to fight for migrant rights. The ease with which these indicators can be used politically is atypical. That said, efforts under this target do not seek to tackle the political challenge head-on. Governments have not been encouraged to collect data on trends in anti-immigrant sentiment or crimes against migrants and refugees. They have also not been advised to report on their efforts to regulate transnational networks that "assist" fee-paying migrants, or to shut down illicit immigrant smugglers. Data under this target also fail to capture the many ways that skilled migration can generate unequal outcomes. The threats that individual migrants face in pursuing their own interests have clearly been prioritized over the structural development challenges and inequalities that migration can generate in countries of origin.

Unfortunately, the three implementation targets under SDG 10 have at best a very limited potential to directly reduce inequalities. The call for special and differential treatment for developing countries in the world trading system (10.a) renews a decades-old imperative that continues to face numerous stumbling blocks. Many initiatives to improve the fairness of world trade have engendered considerable political pushback and underperformed. The only indicator (10.a.1) associated with this target focuses exclusively on tariff reduction, and that restriction is highly political. Reducing the proportion of tariff lines that are applied to imports from the least developed countries and developing countries to zero could be impactful. But this emphasis neglects the reality that tariffs are not the only consequential barrier to trade. Nontariff barriers, including quotas, licensing, and sanitary regulations, are persistently used to exclude imports from developing countries. Over twenty years into the push for zero tariffs, nontariff measures remain a principal source of asymmetrical outcomes in the trading system. The weight placed on tariffs also obscures other trade-related issues that continue to fuel inequalities, such as intrafirm trade, transfer pricing strategies, and the origin of what is being traded (Basnett et al., 2019).

The second implementation target (10.b) optimistically assumes that more flows of development assistance, portfolio investment, and foreign direct investment to poorer countries will reduce inequalities. Aiming to grow the resources available for development and to better align their use with national plans could make progress on inequality possible. Knowing more about whether this agenda is doing so in particular places would nonetheless require in-depth case study research in all countries. As it stands, this target's assertion that bigger pies and better management are an inequality silver bullet is highly political. Growth is the overarching priority, and the target is entirely inattentive to the reality that in some cases, lower volumes of any one of these flows might yield inclusive results. This faith-based stance radiates a strong system maintenance bias, ignoring entirely the ways that aid, financial flows, and direct investments continue to generate inequalities for all. The final implementation target's narrow appeal to lower the transaction costs that migrants face when they send remittances home is, at the very least, more aligned with efforts to reduce inequality (10.c). But it too leaves untouched many other types of transaction costs related to finance and logistics that can create unequal outcomes.

The UN secretary-general's SDG midpoint analysis argued that factors such as the pandemic and uneven recoveries in different regions of the world threatened to further reverse progress on global inequality (UNSG 2023). While the report included some language on the need to address the sources of wage disparities and unequal resource access, it remained silent on the politically controversial positions embedded in SDG 10. This goal advances an agenda that if implemented would buttress the liberal international economic order over the short to medium terms. It proposes measures that would only mitigate inequality and does not address sources of inequality that could generate instability over longer time horizons, such as wealth inequality, financialization, nontariff barriers to trade, and skilled migration. Moreover, SDG 10 overemphasizes measures that aim to put more money into the pockets of less fortunate people and underplays the need for policy action at the very top of global income and wealth distributions. The goal's drive to achieve inclusive growth through redistribution could also promote corporate interests across a range of consumer-facing sectors. Even so, right-wing populists tend to flatly reject liberal redistributionism. They mercilessly and deceptively portray any measures to raise government revenues as being against "the people" and misleadingly suggest that government redistribution schemes create inequality. Progressives and greens stand opposed to SDG 10's lack of courage regarding wealth inequality *and* to the posturing of populist and nationalist opportunists who seek to make political capital by fighting social inclusion and redistribution. For them, SDG 10 is simply not a source of system transformation. Rather, this goal has a deep system maintenance bias (Telleria and Garcia-Arias 2021).

References

Basnett, B.S., R. Myers, and M. Elias. 2019. "SDG 10: Reduced Inequalities — An Environmental Justice Perspective On Implications for Forests and People." In *Sustainable Development Goals: Their Impacts on Forests and People*, edited by P. Katila, C.J.P. Colfer, W. de Jong, et al. Cambridge: Cambridge University Press.

Dalby, S., S. Horton, and R. Mahon. 2019. "Global Governance Challenges in Achieving the Sustainable Development Goals." In *Achieving the Sustainable Development Goals: Global Governance Challenges*, edited by S. Dalby, S. Horton, R. Mahon, and D. Thomaz. London: Routledge.

Oestreich, J.E. 2018. "SDG 10: Reduce Inequality in and Among Countries." *Social Alternatives* 37, 1.

Our World in Data team. 2023. "Reduce Inequality within and among Countries." ourworldindata.org/sdgs/reduced-inequalities.

Piketty, T. 2019. *Capital and Ideology*. Cambridge, MA: Harvard University Press.

Telleria, J., and J. Garcia-Arias. 2021. "The Fantasmatic Narrative of 'Sustainable Development': A Political Analysis of the 2030 Global Development Agenda," *Environment and Planning C: Politics and Space* 40, 1.

UN (United Nations). 2020. *Reduced Inequalities: Why It Matters*. un.org/sustainabledevelopment/wp-content/uploads/2018/01/10_Why-It-Matters-2020.pdf.

———. 2022. *The Sustainable Development Goals Report 2022*. New York: UN.

———. 2023. "Goal 10: Reduce Inequality Within and Among Countries." un.org/sustainabledevelopment/inequalities.

UNSG (United Nations Secretary-General). 2023. *Progress towards the Sustainable Development Goals: Towards a Rescue Plan for People and Planet. Report of the Secretary-General (Special Edition)*. New York: United Nations General Assembly and Economic and Social Council.

Goal ⑪
Sustainable Cities and Communities

What They Tell Us

Mission statement: Make cities and human settlements inclusive, safe, resilient, and sustainable.

Cities currently generate inequality and consume vast quantities of energy (UN 2023). The costs of the status quo take the form of slums and informal settlements, traffic inefficiencies, carbon emissions, air pollution, and sprawling suburbs (UN 2020). Urban development must be well planned and sustainable to generate inclusive growth. Investments in public transport, solid waste management, air quality, and disaster risk management are urgently needed. As cities expand, we can and must pursue better sustainability planning and execution. The preparedness and resilience of cities must be strengthened (UN 2022, 48). High-quality infrastructure and universal access to basic services facilitate quicker recoveries and improve the capacity of human settlements to respond to future crises. We must all take an active interest in the governance and management of cities. If we each develop a vision for our streets and neighbourhoods, and act on that vision, we can have a big impact on our communities and on our quality of life (UN 2020).

Sustainable City Targets	Indicators
11.1 By 2030, ensure access for all to adequate, safe, and affordable housing and basic services and upgrade slums	11.1.1 Proportion of urban population living in slums, informal settlements, or inadequate housing
11.2 By 2030, provide access to safe, affordable, accessible, and sustainable transport systems for all, improving road safety, notably by expanding public transport, with special attention to the needs of those in vulnerable situations, women, children, persons with disabilities, and older persons	11.2.1 Proportion of population that has convenient access to public transport, by sex, age, and persons with disabilities

Sustainable City Targets	Indicators
11.3 By 2030, enhance inclusive and sustainable urbanization and capacity for participatory, integrated, and sustainable human settlement planning and management in all countries	11.3.1 Ratio of land consumption rate to population growth rate 11.3.2 Proportion of cities with a direct participation structure of civil society in urban planning and management that operate regularly and democratically
11.4 Strengthen efforts to protect and safeguard the world's cultural and natural heritage	11.4.1 Total per capita expenditure on the preservation, protection, and conservation of all cultural and natural heritage, by source of funding (public, private), type of heritage (cultural, natural), and level of government (national, regional, and local/municipal)
11.5 By 2030, significantly reduce the number of deaths and the number of people affected and substantially decrease the direct economic losses relative to global gross domestic product caused by disasters, including water-related disasters, with a focus on protecting the poor and people in vulnerable situations	11.5.1 Number of deaths, missing persons, and directly affected persons attributed to disasters per 100,000 population 11.5.2 Direct economic loss attributed to disasters in relation to global gross domestic product (GDP) 11.5.3 (a) Damage to critical infrastructure and (b) number of disruptions to basic services, attributed to disasters
11.6 By 2030, reduce the adverse per capita environmental impact of cities, including by paying special attention to air quality and municipal and other waste management	11.6.1 Proportion of municipal solid waste collected and managed in controlled facilities out of total municipal waste generated, by cities 11.6.2 Annual mean levels of fine particulate matter (e.g. PM2.5 and PM10) in cities (population weighted)
11.7 By 2030, provide universal access to safe, inclusive, and accessible green and public spaces, in particular for women and children, older persons, and persons with disabilities	11.7.1 Average share of the built-up area of cities that is open space for public use for all, by sex, age, and persons with disabilities 11.7.2 Proportion of persons victim of physical or sexual harassment, by sex, age, disability status, and place of occurrence, in the previous 12 months
11.a Support positive economic, social, and environmental links between urban, peri-urban, and rural areas by strengthening national and regional development planning	11.a.1 Number of countries that have national urban policies or regional development plans that (a) respond to population dynamics; (b) ensure balanced territorial development; and (c) increase local fiscal space
11.b By 2020, substantially increase the number of cities and human settlements adopting and implementing integrated policies and plans towards inclusion, resource efficiency, mitigation and adaptation to climate change, resilience to disasters, and develop and implement, in line with the Sendai Framework for Disaster Risk Reduction 2015–2030, holistic disaster risk management at all levels	11.b.1 Number of countries that adopt and implement national disaster risk reduction strategies in line with the Sendai Framework for Disaster Risk Reduction 2015–2030 11.b.2 Proportion of local governments that adopt and implement local disaster risk reduction strategies in line with national disaster risk reduction strategies
11.c Support least developed countries, including through financial and technical assistance, in building sustainable and resilient buildings utilizing local materials	11.c.1 [The indicator is currently under development]

The Hidden Politics

On first reading, the language of SDG 11's first target (11.1) seems politically innocuous. The call to ensure adequate, safe, and affordable housing and basic services and to upgrade slums evokes images of social improvement and inclusion. Still, the use of terms that are highly contested in debates on urban housing, living, and land-use upgrades is worrying. This target offers no guidance whatsoever related to the adequacy of dwellings. It sets no objectives related to square or cubic living space requirements per person, or to the adequacy of building materials. The insertion of considerations related to safe housing also open the door to wide-ranging interpretations, which could include a need for effective building inspection services or a much more problematic push for concerted efforts to better police the poor. Similarly, while the emphasis on affordable housing is seductive, it too is actively contested. Landlords, developers, tenants, city officials, authorities, organized criminals, bankers, and other stakeholders never share the same perspective on housing costs. Efforts to redevelop tenements and to elimi-nate extortionary housing and "protection" rents might cut out profiteers and enhance affordability for some people. But these campaigns can also further enrich established builders, mortgage lenders, and service providers and impose punishing long-term liabilities on marginalized populations. This target's sole indicator (11.1.1) directs attention only to the proportion of the urban population that lives in slums, informal settlements, or inadequate housing. Governments have not been advised to monitor the proportion of slums that have been cleared and redeveloped through participatory processes, nor have they been directly asked to put an end to nonconsulta-tive or top-down slum clearance decision-making practices. Consequently, to bolster "progress" on this target, some governments could continue to employ the unethical strategy of bulldozing slums and informal settlements without warning under the cover of darkness. In sum, the implicit message of this target is that the urban poor are a potential source of destabilization and that housing improvements and the associated rise of indebtedness can help better manage this risk (Soederberg 2017).

The subsequent target's (11.2) emphasis on improving urban movement is also unavoidably political. The push for safe, affordable, accessible, and sustainable transport systems for all explicitly prioritizes the expansion of public transport and the needs of vulnerable people. Yet these abstract aims are open to considerable interpretation. Those with a commercial interest in moving their goods more quickly through cities, for example, might consider the development of new toll roads to be fully aligned with this target. They could highlight the ways that exclusionary tollways improve road safety, reduce drive time and transportation costs, and make roads more accessible for business. Others whose communities are bisected or cut off by these roads, or who are unable to afford the price to use them, could have different interpretations. Efforts to address persistent gridlock on arterial roads in ways that favour business interests are nonetheless congruent with this target's solitary indicator (11.2.1). It encourages governments only to monitor the proportion of the population that has convenient access to public transport. This metric excludes considerations related to safety, affordability, and sustainability, and does not define what distance is truly convenient for elders or persons with disabilities. It also offers no guidance regarding the types of vehicle or models of service delivery. These omissions matter. For instance, independent motorcycle taxis remain an accessible, affordable, and lower-emission public transport option in many cities. Local governments that nonetheless move to eliminate this cheap and often informal transit alternative could argue that their preference is aligned with the indicator. Even if they were to prioritize an unreliable private bus network run by politically connected cronies, they could portray any expansion in formal bus stops or routes as enhancing accessibility. Data related to this indicator are currently unavailable, but statistical trends might obscure more than they reveal about the scale and scope of the challenges facing inclusive urban transportation.

The third target (11.3) seeks to reduce hierarchical and opaque urban decision-making processes. Where these practices persist, they tend to inflame the range of political challenges identified above. The target directly encourages governments to develop urban planning and management processes that are participatory, inclusive, and sustainable. Here, too, however, the indicators tell a different tale. The first (11.3.1) focuses attention only on the rate of sustainable urbanization defined as the ratio of land consumed to the population growth rate. In other words, it reemphasizes efforts to intensify urban land use. The other indicator (11.3.2) encourages national governments to track the proportion of cities with urban planning and management systems that have structures to enable civil society participation. At its most inoffensive, participation in urban development can take the form of formal and equitable public consultation related to the relaxation of rules that govern backyard apartments or cottages. But in many global contexts, business interests tend to dominate debates about land-use intensification (Soederberg 2017). In practice, formal structures of participation can be made inoperative or effectively sidelined where local officials have an interest in doing so. Taken together, both indicators express ideals that remain subject to active political interpretation and to interest-based political manipulation. There is no necessary connection between the simultaneous realization of intensified land use and the uptake of participatory decision-making, on the one hand, and the achievement of inclusive or sustainable outcomes, on the other.

The fourth target (11.4) on strengthening efforts to protect and safeguard the world's cultural and natural heritage has similar shortcomings. To advance this broadly shared ideal, the target's sole indicator (11.4.1) prompts governments to track public and private expenditures per capita on the preservation, protection, and conservation of all cultural and natural heritage. This orientation overemphasizes the aggregate availability of financial resources and trivializes the challenges that the urban development agenda can pose for specific heritage sites and practices. What exactly gets preserved, protected, or conserved in urban settings is never apolitical. For instance, the necessity of preserving culturally significant marketplaces remains a matter of perspective. Drives to intensify and formalize land use can readily disappear long-standing fish markets or the spaces where artisanal handicraft traders operate. Sites that Indigenous Peoples or minority ethnic groups consider sacred are also not immune from these pressures. The indicator is so weak that governments can portray any actions that they take on heritage in a positive light. If public and private heritage expenditures per capita were to grow, and the additional resources were solely allocated to efforts to preserve symbols of imperial and colonial heritage, the data would still indicate technical progress. They would also do so if increased disbursements for heritage expedited gentrification and amplified inequalities. The divide between ambition and political reality on this target remains vast.

On the face of it, the subsequent target's (11.5) call to mitigate the impact of disasters on urban populations and economies is straightforward and sensible. That said, while the associated indicators directly link to this objective, they focus solely on the domestic level of analysis. This constraint opens the door to the politicization of data, and seemingly downloads responsibility for progress onto national and local authorities. Specifically, the first indicator (11.5.1) looks to reduce the number of deaths, missing persons, and directly affected persons attributed to disasters. It does not aim to measure any determinantal impacts associated with the mobilization of global disaster response interventions. Since challenges in this area were comprehensively articulated by the Tsunami Evaluation Coalition (Telford and Cosgrave 2006), some international and nongovernmental organizations have developed systems to ensure that their disaster responses better align with local priorities and capacity. Still, it cannot simply be assumed that global disaster response interventions and resources necessarily contribute to reducing the numbers of affected people. The diversity of global responders must also be considered, as the effectiveness of disparate organizations such as World Central Kitchen and the World Food Programme can vary widely on the ground. The failure to include measures to assess the relative capabilities of global disaster responders or their alignment or harmonization with local authority structures shrinks this target's ambition. So too does the second associated indicator's (11.5.2) exclusive focus on direct economic losses attributed to disasters in relation to GDP. Data on this topic can certainly raise awareness of the vulnerable disaster-prone states that experience disproportional losses over time. It can also serve as a catalyst for future global interventions. But it ultimately detracts attention from the realities of disaster capitalism (Klein 2007). When parasitic profiteers and the global media converge on disaster sites, their activities tend to stimulate economic growth. They can exert strong influence over subsequent government decisions and redirect policy in ways that undermine disaster preparedness. Thus, the emphasis on aggregate disaster losses should have been coupled with additional measures to assess the distribution of gains.

Weak indicators and a neglect of day-to-day political realities also undermine the sixth target's (11.6) objective to reduce the adverse per capita environmental impact of cities. Efforts to improve waste management systems and air quality within cities can obviously advance this target and enhance public health outcomes (Rebecchi 2021). Even so, the associated indicators obscure key aspects of the metabolism of cities. They focus only on the proportion of urban solid waste that is regularly collected and adequately discharged (11.6.1), and on annual mean levels of fine particulate matter (11.6.2). The first measure fails to account for the fact that many cities continue to export their solid waste to other national and international destinations. It is also indifferent to the known deficiencies of the world's recycling system and to the operations of precarious waste pickers and recycling cooperatives (Gutberlet 2021; Hook and Reed 2018). Improved waste collection may beautify cities but will not necessarily reduce their per capita environmental impact. Likewise, cities might improve local air quality even as they host industries that produce machines known to reduce air quality when operated. Campaigns for cleaner air in cities might also push polluting industries out and inadvertently facilitate the export of dirty industries to other cities that are all too willing to host them. This target remains insensitive to these phenomena even though it is possible to measure related trends, such as the percentage of cities that welcome inward investments from dirty industries. In sum, the ecological footprint of many industries that are based in cities and metropolitan areas is much broader than solid waste generation or air pollution. This target's political insistence on prioritizing improvements to the lived experience of individual city dwellers is telling. It shows that SDG 11 is not serious about the ways that human settlements amplify planetary challenges.

This lack of sincerity also contaminates the seventh target (11.7) on safe, inclusive, and accessible urban public and green space. Here, the emphasis does not fall on the ways that urban green spaces can increase biodiversity, improve urban microclimates, and decrease pollution and noise (Riechers et al. 2018). Rather, concerns simply centre around ensuring that these spaces are available and open to public use for all. In other words, these spaces matter to the extent that they serve as sources of social stability. The first indicator (11.7.1) deemphasizes green space and draws attention only to the share of the built-up area of cities that is open space for public use. In this light, public spaces are social goods to the extent that they enable people to pursue recreational activities inclusively. The second indicator's (11.7.2) stress on physical safety doubles down on this orientation. It highlights only the need for urban public space to be free from criminal activity and does not address the underlying socioeconomic factors that can perpetuate crime. Conceptualizing these spaces as needed release valves that must be policed is a far cry from endorsing their use to support the achievement of other SDGs. This target is acutely indifferent to the ways that urban public and green spaces can be used to enhance the sustainability of urban food systems, for example. Yet, on a more positive note, its call for more public space can enable opportunities for political mobilization to advance the Global Goals or other civic agendas. The target's political myopia is in this case a two-way street: green urban spaces can be used to challenge status quo inequalities.

The implementation targets under SDG 11 include a smattering of policies that could improve the sustainability of cities. The first (11.a) seeks to expand the uptake of urban and regional development planning, while the second (11.b) calls for the development and implementation of disaster risk reduction strategies at all levels. If realized, both objectives could build the capacity of cities to address future challenges. That said, these ambitions are inattentive to the many political factors that can undermine urban planning, and do not problematize the political and economic interests that benefit from the disaster recovery status quo. Moving beyond planning and strategy, the third implementation target (11.c) adds a political priority related to improving the sustainability and resilience of buildings in the least developed countries. Increased financial support in this area could yield more resource-efficient buildings that have been constructed or retrofitted with local materials. The key terms associated with this objective nonetheless remain undefined, and an indicator for this target is still being debated and developed. It consequently remains open to politicized use and abuse.

In the SDGs midpoint report, the UN secretary-general lamented that factors such as the pandemic, climate change, and conflicts have disproportionately and negatively impacted cities, and that slum populations have continued to grow (UNSG 2023). The report drew no attention whatsoever to the politics of SDG 11's aim to bolster the ways that cities can function as engines of global economic growth (Colenbrander 2016). The view that kinder and cleaner cities can contribute to the legitimacy of the liberal international economic order and global capitalism is not broadly shared. Right-wing populists equate this goal's approach with a shadowy global agenda to introduce greater oversight of cities and to transform their social and economic life. For their part, social progressives and greens condemn this goal's blatant pro-growth orientation *and* resist the right-wing forces that agitate to atomize and individualize the life of cities.

References

Colenbrander, S. 2016. *Cities as Engines of Economic Growth: The Case for Providing Basic Infrastructure and Services in Urban Areas.* London: IIED.

Gutberlet, J. 2021. "Grassroots Waste Picker Organizations Addressing the UN Sustainable Development Goals." *World Development* 138.

Hook, L., and J. Reed. 2018. "Why the World's Recycling System Stopped Working," *Financial Times,* October 25.

Klein, N. 2007. *The Shock Doctrine: The Rise of Disaster Capitalism.* Toronto: Knopf Canada.

Rebecchi, A., and S. Capolongo. 2021. "Healthy Design and Urban Planning Strategies Framing the SDG 11 Sustainable Cities and Communities." *European Journal of Public Health*, 33, 3.

Riechers, M., J. Barkmann, and T. Tscharntke. 2018. "Diverging Perceptions by Social Groups on Cultural Ecosystem Services Provided by Urban Green." *Landscape and Urban Planning* 175.

Soederberg, S. 2017. "Universal Access to Affordable Housing? Interrogating an Elusive Development Goal." In *The Politics of Destination in the 2030 Sustainable Development Goals: Leaving No-One Behind?*, edited by C. Gabay and S. Ilcan. London: Routledge.

Telford, J., and J. Cosgrave. 2006. *Joint Evaluation of the International Response to the Indian Ocean Tsunami: Synthesis Report.* Tsunami Evaluation Coalition.

UN (United Nations). 2020. *Sustainable Cities and Communities: Why It Matters.* un.org/sustainabledevelopment/wp-content/uploads/2019/07/11_Why-It-Matters-2020.pdf.

———. 2022. *The Sustainable Development Goals Report 2022*. New York: UN.

———. 2023. "Goal 11: Make Cities Inclusive, Safe, Resilient and Sustainable." un.org/sustainabledevelopment/cities.

UNSG (United Nations Secretary-General). 2023. *Progress towards the Sustainable Development Goals: Towards a Rescue Plan for People and Planet. Report of the Secretary-General (Special Edition)*. New York: United Nations General Assembly and Economic and Social Council.

Goal 12
Responsible Consumption and Production

What They Tell Us

Mission statement: Ensure sustainable consumption and production patterns.

Strong businesses have an interest in ending unsustainable patterns of consumption and production (UN 2023). Poor business practices are root causes of the triple planetary crisis of climate change, biodiversity loss, and pollution. We need to better understand the environmental and social impact of products and services. Working collaboratively to improve resource efficiency and shape a new circular economy will help us achieve sustainable consumption and production patterns. Economic activities in the circular economy will need to become much more socially and environmentally responsible. The triple planetary crisis threatens human well-being and the achievement of the Global Goals (UN 2022, 50). Total domestic material consumption rose rapidly in the twenty years before the pandemic, and the global material footprint also grew considerably (UN 2023). Governments and citizens should seize the opportunity to work together to shape the new circular economy. We should reduce the waste we produce and be more thoughtful about what we buy and choose sustainable options whenever possible. If we buy from sustainable and local sources and exercise pressure on businesses to adopt sustainable practices, we can make a difference (UN 2020).

Consumption and Production Targets	Indicators
12.1 Implement the 10-Year Framework of Programmes on Sustainable Consumption and Production Patterns, all countries taking action, with developed countries taking the lead, taking into account the development and capabilities of developing countries	12.1.1 Number of countries developing, adopting, or implementing policy instruments aimed at supporting the shift to sustainable consumption and production
12.2 By 2030, achieve the sustainable management and efficient use of natural resources	12.2.1 Material footprint, material footprint per capita, and material footprint per GDP

Consumption and Production Targets	Indicators
12.2 (Continued)	12.2.2 Domestic material consumption, domestic material consumption per capita, and domestic material consumption per GDP
12.3 By 2030, halve per capita global food waste at the retail and consumer levels and reduce food losses along production and supply chains, including post-harvest losses	12.3.1 (a) Food loss index and (b) food waste index
12.4 By 2020, achieve the environmentally sound management of chemicals and all wastes throughout their life cycle, in accordance with agreed international frameworks, and significantly reduce their release to air, water, and soil in order to minimize their adverse impacts on human health and the environment	12.4.1 Number of parties to international multilateral environmental agreements on hazardous waste, and other chemicals that meet their commitments and obligations in transmitting information as required by each relevant agreement 12.4.2 (a) Hazardous waste generated per capita; and (b) proportion of hazardous waste treated, by type of treatment
12.5 By 2030, substantially reduce waste generation through prevention, reduction, recycling, and reuse	12.5.1 National recycling rate, tons of material recycled
12.6 Encourage companies, especially large and transnational companies, to adopt sustainable practices and to integrate sustainability information into their reporting cycle	12.6.1 Number of companies publishing sustainability reports
12.7 Promote public procurement practices that are sustainable, in accordance with national policies and priorities	12.7.1 Number of countries implementing sustainable public procurement policies and action plans
12.8 By 2030, ensure that people everywhere have the relevant information and awareness for sustainable development and lifestyles in harmony with nature	12.8.1 Extent to which (i) global citizenship education and (ii) education for sustainable development are mainstreamed in (a) national education policies; (b) curricula; (c) teacher education; and (d) student assessment
12.a Support developing countries to strengthen their scientific and technological capacity to move towards more sustainable patterns of consumption and production	12.a.1 Installed renewable energy-generating capacity in developing countries (in watts per capita)
12.b Develop and implement tools to monitor sustainable development impacts for sustainable tourism that creates jobs and promotes local culture and products	12.b.1 Implementation of standard accounting tools to monitor the economic and environmental aspects of tourism sustainability
12.c Rationalize inefficient fossil-fuel subsidies that encourage wasteful consumption by removing market distortions, in accordance with national circumstances, including by restructuring taxation and phasing out those harmful subsidies, where they exist, to reflect their environmental impacts, taking fully into account the specific needs and conditions of developing countries and minimizing the possible adverse impacts on their development in a manner that protects the poor and the affected communities	12.c.1 Amount of fossil-fuel subsidies (production and consumption) per unit of GDP

The Hidden Politics

SDG 12's emphasis on the need for more responsible and sustainable consumption and production derives entirely from a separate and highly controversial international process. After the 2002 World Summit on Sustainable Development held in Johannesburg, countries worked to develop the 10-Year Framework of Programmes on Sustainable Consumption and Production Patterns (Gasper et al. 2019). Under the guidance of the UN Environment Programme, six programmes were ultimately agreed on: (i) sustainable public procurement; (ii) consumer information; (iii) sustainable tourism; (iv) sustainable lifestyles and education; (v) sustainable buildings and construction; and (vi) sustainable food systems. Countries then endorsed these programmes at the 2012 UN Conference on Sustainable Development held in Rio de Janeiro. From that point, serious political conflict emerged over whether to include these programmes in the Global Goals. During the dying days of Prime Minister Stephen Harper's regime in 2015, the Canadian government emerged as a leading voice opposed to their inclusion, according to a detailed political analysis conducted by Gasper et al. (2019). Despite this regressive counterattack, the sustainable consumption and production agenda was finally included as a standalone goal under the SDGs. The targets openly mirror the aims of the 10-Year Framework except for one notable change: the date for concrete action was delayed to 2030.

The political limitations of the programmes included in SDG 12 are now well known. Gasper et al. (2019) have shown that the understanding of sustainable consumption and production that animates this goal is not compatible with the Brundtland Commission's strong perspective on sustainable development. It does not aim to align consumption and production with ecological boundaries, nor does it seek to arrest unsustainable consumption patterns. Rather, in a business-friendly manner, it simply encourages a different kind of consumption. This viewpoint now infuses all efforts under SDG 12 and has pushed transformative ideas related to the elimination of certain types of unsuitable consumption to the margins. Worryingly, it exudes faith that technology and technical innovations could permit consumption and production to grow indefinitely (Gasper et al. 2019).

The first target's (12.1) appeal for all countries to take action on implementing the 10-Year Framework imposes additional constraints. The language explicitly recognizes the varied capabilities and levels of development that countries have to pursue meaningful implementation. Developed countries are encouraged to take the lead but are not directly instructed to address capacity gaps in developing countries. The message here is obvious.

Developing countries that fail to pursue or achieve meaningful change for any reasons whatsoever have an out. They can just claim that they lacked capacity and did not receive sufficient support. The indicator (12.1.1) under this target also gives governments inordinate latitude. Its focus on the number of countries with national action plans, or that are adopting or implementing policy instruments in this area, is troubling. This metric excludes any considerations related to the ambition, quality, content, or effectiveness of national plans or policy instruments (Our World in Data team 2023). Thus, the mere existence of plans or policies is enough to meet the standard.

The second target (12.2) has been treated with slightly more political importance. Its call to achieve the sustainable management and efficient use of natural resources was also included under SDG 8. As with the fourth target of the growth-related goal, the two indicators here are material footprint (12.2.1) and domestic material consumption (12.2.2). The politics of these indicators were discussed at length under SDG 8. To say the least, what level of material footprint is "sustainable" remains subject to serious political contestation (Gasper et al. 2019). Beyond the evident data challenges, sharply divided discourses on responsibility related to the sustainable management and use of natural resources continue to constrain progress (Sneyd et al. 2022). Stakeholders who are situated differently in relation to natural resource production and consumption hold vastly divergent ideas about who or what is responsible for the achievement of sustainability. On the production side, many corporations that extract raw materials from soils or forests argue that their operations are responsible and enhance sustainability. For their part, researchers and advocates in civil society often challenge these views on resource sustainability and produce research that showcases the persistence of irresponsible practices. Governments can also have direct interests in maintaining resource operations that lack a strong approach or commitment to sustainable management. On the consumption side, downstream buyers and retail consumers tend to hold disparate ideas about sustainable production and corporate responsibility claims. These divided realities matter. Natural resource products that increase material footprints or domestic material consumption might nonetheless be framed by some as sustainable or responsible (Sneyd et al. 2022). An entire industry now seeks to profit from the development of public relations and compliance strategies that enable clients to make such claims. The second target utterly fails to address these issues or to even recognize the extent of the underlying political challenge. While this inattentiveness does not openly invite politicization, it certainly leaves the door wide open to it.

The subsequent target's (12.3) emphasis on very narrow aspects of the global food waste problem reflects the 10-Year Programme's political commitment to changing consumption, not challenging it. This target does not seek to end the unsustainable consumption of waste-generating retail fast foods that have been grown using unsustainable practices and then transported over vast distances. Rather, it takes global food production and supply chains as given and leaves the broader sustainability challenges unaddressed. Its aim to halve per capita food waste at the retail and consumer levels might contribute to reducing the extensive growth of farmland and enhance food security. Nevertheless, the sole focus on reducing waste volumes remains problematic. The ecological footprint of the foods that drive waste production or overall consumption is overlooked. The ways that local and sustainable food production can contribute to reducing the ecological burden of farming have been similarly omitted. As it stands, the target's food waste loss indicator (12.3.1) showcases the scale of the household food loss problem, but only in relation to the volumes of food that are lost. This information could readily serve as a basis for calls to improve technologies to prevent postharvest losses; develop more effective cold chains, refrigeration, and storage and stocking systems; and increase access to refrigerators and freezers. If efforts under this target degenerate into a resource-intensive drive to produce more food and cold storage options, sustainability will clearly suffer. Moreover, the prominence of household losses in the data could be amenable to political attempts to demonize "wasteful" consumers. More policing of the individual behaviour of poorer people will certainly not deliver more sustainable production or consumption systems.

The next two targets on chemical and hazardous waste management (12.4) and on waste reduction (12.5) are also not unaffected by political limitations and data challenges. Indicators associated with the fourth target have the potential to enhance sustainable production and consumption. These focus on the number of parties to multilateral environmental agreements that meet their reporting commitments and obligations (12.4.1) and on the generation and treatment of hazardous waste (12.4.2). The first measure nonetheless offers an incomplete picture of compliance. It overlooks the ways that unsustainable practices have lingered in the face of numerous agreements. For instance, efforts under the Stockholm Convention related to the release of persistent organic pollutants from the spraying of herbicides and pesticides and the incineration of waste have consistently underperformed (Koloutsou-Vakakis and Chinta 2011). The failure to include any further measures related to curtailing these and other consequential and hazardous pollutants, such as so-called forever chemicals, is telling. Indicators under the fourth target remain wedded to legacy ambitions that were first articulated over twenty years ago. They overemphasize interstate initiatives and are animated by dated views on hazards and waste. The fifth target on waste reduction also reflects this challenge. Its indicator (12.5.1) draws attention only to recycling rates and to the amount of material recycled. Thus, the waste-related target does not prompt governments to monitor trends in the overall production of waste, its content, or safe disposal. Indicators related to waste exports, or to tracking the number of countries that adopt legal or policy measures to eliminate plastic bags, are similarly absent. These gaps show that relying on the 10-Year Programme's targets to stimulate action in the present is a political problem. Data that are effectively relics will not drive progress in this area. They will merely bring light to past challenges and fail to speak to contemporary waste-related hazards.

The sixth target's (12.6) call for companies to adopt sustainable practices and integrate sustainability information into their reporting could easily provoke political problems. It includes no measures to curb the persistence of unsustainable practices, or to define what constitutes sustainable practices. Instead, the indicator under this target (12.6.1) is solely attentive to the number of companies that publish sustainability reports. This appeal to scale up the production of glossy corporate public relations materials could encourage some companies to pursue better behaviours and become more accountable. That said, the focus on increasing the flow of corporate sustainability information is open to serious political abuse. No attention has to be paid to the actual content of what is reported. As such, firms have effectively been given the green light to frame their sustainability reporting as they see fit. If unscrupulous companies produce propaganda that distorts their sustainability accomplishments, the volume of sustainability reporting will still go up. There are no mechanisms under this target to prevent the use of public relations strategies that illegitimately bolster corporate images, such as greenwashing, social washing, and fair washing. Corporations that avoid these practices can nevertheless employ their reports politically. They can positively frame their participation in corporate-driven governance initiatives that ostensibly aim to improve sustainability-related outcomes, even if those voluntary processes consistently underperform (McKeon 2017).

The call for more sustainability reporting could encourage consumers to demand greener products and push companies to better deliver (Bernstein and Vos 2021). But this exceptionally weak objective represents the failure of the UN to promote the development of strong laws and enforcement tools that oblige corporations to pursue sustainability. The 10-Year Framework also does not seek to harmonize corporate sustainability reporting or align such reporting with veritable sustainability practices. Its antiquated ambitions are unsuitable for a world where sustainability metrics can bolster the market value of listed companies (Zhou et al. 2022). Corporations in sensitive or dirty industries are now all too wise to the ways that their reporting strategies on environmental, social, and governance performance can advance their interests (Garcia et al. 2017). The availability of more information could ultimately spur changes to production and consumption, but the assumption that it will necessarily accelerate the pace or extent of change in a world where multiple, overlapping, and conflicting approaches to sustainability proliferate is at best politically naive (Sneyd et al. 2022).

The subsequent two targets underscore a need for governments to pursue sustainability-oriented reforms to procurement policies (12.7) and increase education on sustainable lifestyles (12.8). This focus notably departs from the language of the previous target. Under the 10-Year Framework, government measures related to sustainable purchasing and education take priority over any government actions to ensure stronger corporate sustainability practices. Given the economic size and importance of government contracts, efforts to enhance the sustainability of public procurement systems could be impactful. Yet even in this area, new policies and action plans (12.7.1) will be shaped and constrained by the global glut of divergent approaches to measuring and achieving sustainability. Contracts to supply coffee that has been certified by independent and accredited third parties to meet organic and fair-trade standards, for instance, would advance sustainability. And they would do so in ways that deviate widely from coffee supply contracts that rely only on other certifications, "in-house" codes of conduct, or "trust us" approaches to sustainability (Fridell et al. 2021). The current parameters for sustainable procurement policy and planning simply do not capture these and many other possible discrepancies in sustainability practice. They overemphasize surface-level increases in the share of products and services that governments purchase "sustainably" and underplay the potential for underperformance.

Turning to the eighth target (12.8) regarding government education on sustainable lifestyles, the associated indicator (12.8.1) repeats the first indicator of the seventh target (4.7.1) under SDG 4. The political limitations of these ambitions for global education were discussed at length in the chapter on SDG 4, but their inattentiveness to the development of critical thinking skills is worth reiterating. If more people around the world can develop the capacity to think critically about the limits and possibilities of SDG 12, consumption and production might become much more sustainable.

However, enhancing student capacities to ask questions, acknowledge and challenge assumptions, and reflect on and justify positions related to the 2030 Agenda is certainly not a priority under this target.

The three implementation-related targets on sustainable consumption and production disregard the need for regulatory change to enforce and strengthen sustainability practices (Gasper et al. 2019). They do not direct attention to the regulation of corporate behaviours that unnecessarily bolster repeated and wasteful consumption and they fail to problematize any aspects of consumption whatsoever. Moreover, they scrupulously avoid any call to halt unsustainable production or resource extraction. The first target (12.a) seeks only to strengthen the scientific and technological capacity of developing countries in this area. Its indicator (12.a.1) can be interpreted as a simple plea to enable developing countries to scale up their use of environmentally sound technologies. The second target (12.b) on the global tourism industry narrowly aims to increase the number of implemented sustainability strategies, policies, and action plans that are subject to monitoring and evaluation systems (12.b.1). As such, it is concerned primarily with ensuring that the industry grows while efforts to mitigate its environmental impacts through offsets, conservation, and procurement are ongoing. The idea that international travel itself might in some cases be considered unsustainable consumption, or that travel-related overconsumption is a problem, is nowhere in evidence. The final implementation target's stress on rationalizing inefficient fossil fuel subsidies is similarly deficient (12.c). It glosses over the wide-ranging irrationalities associated with entrenched dependence on fossil fuels. Overall, the limitations of the implementation targets compound the political problems detailed above and show that commitments under SDG 12 are far behind the times.

The UN secretary-general's SDG midpoint analysis expressed support for a global shift towards more sustainable practices and the decoupling of economic growth from the use of natural resources (UNSG 2023). Nevertheless, the secretary-general's nice-sounding language did not draw attention to the associated politics and contrasted sharply with the actual content of SDG 12. This goal has a clear political perspective. It woefully downplays or disregards the state-based actions necessary to enforce corporate compliance with its purpose. And its overreliance on corporate sustainability narratives and initiatives bolsters business as usual in a world where major corporations now have serious interests in portraying themselves as sustainability leaders. Many right-wing nationalists forcefully oppose agendas that encourage businesses to prioritize sustainability. Social progressives and greens oppose this goal's pro-corporate, anti-regulatory orientation *and* forcefully challenge the right-wing assault on efforts to mainstream sustainability. Progressives and greens stress the failure of the UN system and its member states to promote the regulatory and legal frameworks needed to rein in corporate practices and consumer behaviours that despoil the planet.

References

Bernstein, J.M., and R.O. Vos. 2021. SDG 12 — *Sustainable Consumption and Production: A Revolutionary Challenge for the 21st Century.* Bingley, UK: Emerald Publishing.

Fridell, G., Z. Gross, and S. McHugh. 2021. *The Fair Trade Handbook: Building a Better World, Together.* Black Point, NS: Fernwood Publishing.

Garcia, A.S., W. Mendes-Da-Silva, and R.J. Orsato. 2017. "Sensitive Industries Produce Better ESG Performance: Evidence from Emerging Markets." *Journal of Cleaner Production* 150.

Gasper, D., A. Shah, and S. Tankha. 2019. "The Framing of Sustainable Consumption and Production in SDG 12." *Global Policy Volume* 10, 1.

Koloutsou-Vakakis, S., and I. Chinta. 2011. "Multilateral Environmental Agreements for Wastes and Chemicals: 40 Years of Global Negotiations." *Environmental Science and Technology* 45, 1.

McKeon, N. 2017. "Are Equity and Sustainability a Likely Outcome When Foxes and Chickens Share the Same Coop? Critiquing the Concept of Multistakeholder Governance of Food Security." In *The Politics of Destination in the 2030 Sustainable Development Goals: Leaving No-One Behind?*, edited by C. Gabay and S. Ilcan. London: Routledge.

Our World in Data team. 2023. "Ensure Sustainable Consumption and Production Patterns." ourworldindata.org/sdgs/responsible-consumption-production.

Saito, K. 2024. *Slow Down: The Degrowth Manifesto.* New York: Astra House.

Sneyd, A., S. Hamann, C. Enns, and L.Q. Sneyd. 2022. *Commodity Politics: Contesting Responsibility in Cameroon.* Montreal and Kingston: McGill-Queen's University Press.

UN (United Nations). 2020. *Responsible Consumption and Production: Why It Matters.* un.org/sustainabledevelopment/wp-content/uploads/2019/07/12_Why-It-Matters-2020.pdf.

———. 2022. *The Sustainable Development Goals Report 2022.* New York: UN.

———. 2023. "Goal 12: Ensure Sustainable Consumption and Production Patterns." un.org/sustainabledevelopment/sustainable-consumption-production.

UNSG (United Nations Secretary-General). 2023. *Progress towards the Sustainable Development Goals: Towards a Rescue Plan for People and Planet. Report of the Secretary-General (Special Edition).* New York: United Nations General Assembly and Economic and Social Council.

Zhou, G., L. Liu, and S. Luo. 2022. "Sustainable Development, ESG Performance and Company Market Value: Mediating Effect of Financial Performance." *Business Strategy and the Environment* 31, 7.

Goal ⑬
Climate Action

What They Tell Us

> **Mission statement:** Take urgent action to combat climate change and its impacts.

To achieve a low-carbon, climate-resilient transition to a carbon-neutral world, annual investments must be scaled up rapidly and substantially (UN 2020). If we fail in our efforts to keep the temperature around 1° above preindustrial levels, the impacts will be truly devastating for people and the planet. We are doomed to face glacier loss, rising sea levels, flooding, droughts, human displacement, poverty, hunger, health, and inequality unless we act now (UN 2023). The "world is on the brink of a climate catastrophe, and the window to avert it is closing rapidly" (UN 2022b, 52). Global greenhouse gas emissions need to peak before 2025 and must decline 43 per cent by 2030. Net zero is still within our grasp if we unite behind this goal (UN 2020).

Climate Action Targets	Indicators
13.1 Strengthen resilience and adaptive capacity to climate-related hazards and natural disasters in all countries	13.1.1 Number of deaths, missing persons, and directly affected persons attributed to disasters per 100,000 population 13.1.2 Number of countries that adopt and implement national disaster risk reduction strategies in line with the Sendai Framework for Disaster Risk Reduction 2015–2030 13.1.3 Proportion of local governments that adopt and implement local disaster risk reduction strategies in line with national disaster risk reduction strategies
13.2 Integrate climate change measures into national policies, strategies, and planning	13.2.1 Number of countries with nationally determined contributions, long-term strategies, national adaptation plans, and adaptation communications, as reported to the secretariat of the United Nations Framework Convention on Climate Change 13.2.2 Total greenhouse gas emissions per year

Climate Action Targets	Indicators
13.3 Improve education, awareness-raising and human and institutional capacity on climate change mitigation, adaptation, impact reduction and early warning	13.3.1 Extent to which (i) global citizenship education and (ii) education for sustainable development are mainstreamed in (a) national education policies; (b) curricula; (c) teacher education; and (d) student assessment
13.a Implement the commitment undertaken by developed-country parties to the United Nations Framework Convention on Climate Change to a goal of mobilizing jointly $100 billion annually by 2020 from all sources to address the needs of developing countries in the context of meaningful mitigation actions and transparency on implementation and fully operationalize the Green Climate Fund through its capitalization as soon as possible	13.a.1 Amounts provided and mobilized in United States dollars per year in relation to the continued existing collective mobilization goal of the $100 billion commitment through to 2025
13.b Promote mechanisms for raising capacity for effective climate change-related planning and management in least developed countries and small island developing States, including focusing on women, youth, and local and marginalized communities	13.b.1 Number of least developed countries and small island developing States with nationally determined contributions, long-term strategies, national adaptation plans, and adaptation communications, as reported to the secretariat of the United Nations Framework Convention on Climate Change

* Acknowledging that the United Nations Framework Convention on Climate Change is the primary international, intergovernmental forum for negotiating the global response to climate change.

The Hidden Politics

The language of the SDG 13 tacitly acknowledges the scale of the political challenge facing efforts to move its aspirations forward. This is the only Global Goal that initially included with its list of targets an asterisked proviso that was related to broader contextual factors or political limitations (UN 2022a). The previous goal on sustainable production and consumption, for example, does not include a similar statement that acknowledges it has been copied and pasted from other international processes. In a departure from the rest of the 2030 Agenda, a note attached to SDG 13 concedes that responsibility for global climate action falls primarily under the UN Framework Convention on Climate Change (UNFCCC). This clause can be interpreted as a limiting condition. By asserting that authority for progress in this area falls elsewhere in the UN system, it can be read as an attempt to place responsibility for potential shortcomings at the feet of participants in a separate international undertaking.

Consequently, the political perspectives and conflicts that animate the UNFCCC negotiations contribute to setting the limits of the possible for climate action. Analyses of the narrative positions of a diverse range of climate negotiators suggest that their priorities have not remained static (Blaxekjær and Nielsen 2015). Rather, as perspectives on negotiating imperatives have shifted, new alliances, forums, dialogues, and working groups have been formed by like-minded states. The proliferation of coalitions aiming to influence the direction of the UNFCCC has made it much more difficult to analyze the politics that can undermine progress. While powerful states might still work to persuade others to follow their lead, these interest-based efforts butt up against the multiplication of new political formations. Thus, it cannot be said with any degree of certainty that the political power, economic might, or strategies employed by any developed or emerging state are at the root of any setbacks or failings, or of overall stagnation. Divides on common and shared responsibilities for climate action are not fixed along North-South lines, and areas of agreement have become more fluid over time (Blaxekjær and Nielsen 2015). The sheer complexity of the shifting narrative positions and political configurations is now itself an impediment to progress. Political forces can temporarily align and overcome obstructions, as the 2015 Paris Agreement demonstrates. But these moments of relative alignment have continued to be fleeting, and their infrequency imposes a painfully substantial political constraint on ambitions under SDG 13. As seen at the 2023 UN Climate Change Conference in Dubai, divides over the adequacy of climate finance and the relative importance of funding adaptation agreements or mitigation strategies continue to animate stark political conflict (Carlin 2023).

Beyond the politics of SDG 13's asterisked proviso are the deeper politics of what was left out. No footnote acknowledged the ways that humans have radically changed the Earth's ecosystem since the early 1950s (Reid et al. 2017). Space was not allocated to recognize that SDG 13 and the 2030 Agenda more broadly are rooted in the present Anthropocene epoch. Although the Anthropocene remains an unofficial unit of geologic time, the term was widely used and hotly debated during the development of the SDGs. Whether the drafters deemed this contemporary turn of phrase to be too controversial is irrelevant. Their evident neglect of ecosystem health reflects a massive failing of political will. They did not take care to prioritize or expedite goals that seek to achieve healthier ecosystems, such as SDG 13, 14, and 15. Instead, governments worked together to create universal goals, and endeavoured to portray these goals as equally consequential. Thus, the limits of what was politically possible in 2015 now detract from efforts to address the ongoing climate emergency and redesign our societies and economies to promote healthy ecosystems.

Turning to the first target (13.1) under SDG 13, its narrow concentration on measures to strengthen resilience and adaptive capacity in relation to climate-related hazards and natural disasters is a political problem. This target simply rephrases the fifth target of SDG 11, on sustainable cities and communities. For that reason, some of the political limitations of its language and indicators were previously discussed in the chapter on SDG 11. The stress that the associated indicators place on reducing disaster-related deaths and displacements (13.1.1) and on broadening the uptake of disaster risk reduction strategies, including through the Sendai Framework for Disaster Risk Reduction (13.1.2 and 13.1.3), undeniably constitutes a call for concerted climate action. But the exclusive focus on crisis-related dimensions of resilience and adaptation is troubling and worthy of further elaboration. Resilience is about much more than the physical capacity to withstand immediate climate-related dangers. This concept has mental, emotional, and social dimensions that the target disregards. The recurrence of disasters can undermine the morale of individuals and entire populations, and eventually threaten their capacity to spring back. It is telling that this target includes no ambitions whatsoever related to mitigating the emotional, mental, and social toll that disasters can exact. It should go without saying that many other goals include targets that seek to enhance quality of life over longer time horizons.

Excessive short-termism is also evident in the way that this target has framed adaptation. Here, it is primarily defined in relation to preparedness for extreme weather-related events, and not to the longer-term impacts of human practices on the climate. Topsoil degradation, for instance, is exacerbated by the conventional agricultural practices that also disproportionately contribute to intensifying the climate emergency. Adaptations that aim to ward off the looming disaster of soil exhaustion, such as regenerative agriculture, can enhance soil health and draw down legacy carbon from the atmosphere. However, the Sendai Framework on Disaster Risk Reduction conspicuously fails to mention soil health or the adaptive strategies necessary to thwart this impending catastrophe. Adequate responses to the climate emergency will require a much broader lens on the need to move people out of harm's way and to adapt their behaviours and systems. The first target of the climate action goal frankly fails to provide needed leadership on this protracted challenge.

The political limitations of the subsequent target (13.2) relate less to definitions and more to the realities of domestic authority and political power. The idea that the enhanced integration of climate change measures into national policies, strategies, and planning might expedite domestic adaptation efforts, improve resilience, and lower emissions is obviously not wrongheaded. The emphasis on national-level innovations is quite sensible and applicable to at least 166 of the UN's 193 member states. In that group of unitary states, supreme authority is constituted at the national level and exercised by central governments. Thus, national policies, strategies, and plans in those contexts set the limits of the possible for climate action. But what is relevant for unitary states can pose serious political challenges in federated states. Perhaps unsurprisingly, countries with federal systems of government are disproportionately prominent in the list of the world's leading oil producers. The United States, Russia, Canada, Iraq, the United Arab Emirates, Brazil, Mexico, Nigeria, Venezuela, India, Argentina, Malaysia, and Australia all feature federal systems of government. Authority in each of these oil producers is consequently devolved to federated units including states, regions, provinces, emirates, governorates, oblasts, and islands. In federal states, national policies, strategies, and plans are invariably subject to constitutional limits. Constitutions explicitly establish the range of exclusive powers that national-level and devolved authorities wield, and supreme courts render final decisions pertaining to the compliance of legislation with constitutional distributions of power.

Efforts to operationalize national climate change adaptation strategies unavoidably face constitutional limits and possible legal challenges in federal states. Canada is a textbook case. Its national adaptation strategy does not endorse any measures that could be interpreted as intruding upon the authority of its provinces to govern natural resources. As such, this strategy recommends adaptation innovations but does not set hard targets or issue the kinds of strong directives that are possible in unitary states. Without a national-level energy policy or wealth fund linked to resource extraction, Canada's adaptation approach is simply not comparable to those produced by strong central governments. The first associated indicator (13.2.1) is nevertheless insensitive to the potential for widely divergent performance on adaptation. It aims only to count the numbers of countries with policies, strategies, or plans in place at the national level. This restriction stands in stark contrast to the previous target's intent to scale up subnational planning related to disasters. Given the inordinate reliance of many federated states on oil production, this oversight is much more than a simple curiosity. Powerful oil-producing regions absolutely constrain the scale and effectiveness of national climate actions related to adaptation and undermine national efforts to reduce greenhouse gas emissions, which is the focus of the second indicator (13.2.2), but data under the second target remain insensitive to this political reality.

The subsequent target's (13.3) appeal for efforts to improve education, awareness raising, and human and institutional capacity to address all dimensions of climate change faces similar stumbling blocks. Its indicator (13.3.1) shrinks these aims considerably. No data are collected on the number of countries with effective public information campaigns or capacity-building programs. Furthermore, the indicator does not zero in on the number of countries that have integrated education related to mitigation, adaptation, impact reduction, and early warning into primary, secondary, and tertiary curricula. It also notably excludes any mention of a need to incorporate these topics into teacher training or student assessments. Instead, the indicator just repeats the language of the SDG 4 and 12 indicators (4.7.1 and 12.8.1) related to education for sustainable development, lifestyles, and global citizenship. These topics simply cannot be considered equivalent to climate change education, and any attempt to do so would unhelpfully amplify the political challenges facing sustainable development, lifestyle, and global citizenship education. Additionally, where subnational authorities exercise full responsibility over education and national-level education ministries do not exist, the efficacy of any climate change–related materials that are integrated into student learning could vary widely. As it stands, data on progress related to this target remain unavailable. All in all, this goal's intentions related to climate change education are at best unserious.

The two implementation targets for climate action intend to mobilize finance (13.a) and capacity-building support (13.b) for adaptation, mitigation, planning, and management in developing and vulnerable countries. The indicator associated with the first target (13.a.1) seeks to track the funds that developed country parties to the UNFCCC mobilize annually for the Green Climate Fund. In so doing, data under this target can be used to name and shame individual donors that shirk their pledges to the collective effort to disburse US$100 billion per year to the fund. This indicator stands out for its aim to prevent political backsliding on commitments to the Paris Agreement. Vigilance regarding climate-related disbursements has been framed as empowering action (Campbell et al. 2018), but this orientation is far from comprehensive. It is openly unconcerned with any considerations related to outcomes, leaving others to determine whether the mobilization of funds expedites needed transformative actions. The assumption that more money will automatically yield more effective action is increasingly problematic as the "dark side" of the energy transition becomes ever more apparent (Kramarz 2021 et al.). For instance, climate change and sustainability considerations are likely to drive the next global mining and metals boom, as demand for the metals (lithium, copper, cobalt, nickel, platinum) and rare earth elements that underpin battery technologies surges (Hodgkinson and Smith 2021). The transition is also empowering new stakeholders that may have political interests in minimizing effective climate actions or detracting from demonstrated successes (Louman et al. 2019). Likewise, certain stakeholders who stand to benefit from climate finance are shaping the limits of the possible for climate action. A focus on international commitments diverts attention from the rise and diversification of corporate interests linked to the energy transition.

The capacity-building implementation target (13.b) calls for enhanced and specialized support for climate change–related planning and management in least developed countries and small island developing states. This agenda, if implemented effectively, could help address a big political challenge facing climate action in vulnerable contexts. Many least developed and small island countries face complicated synergies and potential trade-offs between their SDG 13 climate commitments and their broader efforts to realize the 2030 Agenda (Thapa et al. 2023). Efforts to improve the capacity of vulnerable countries to assess these dilemmas could be highly impactful. Even so, the indicator (13.b.1) merely stresses the number of countries that are receiving this type of support, and the amount of support. As a result, the target remains indifferent to the forces and factors that can easily intervene and undercut climate change–related planning and management. When lucrative resource investment deals are on the line, for instance, political interpretations of the "national interest" can be weaponized to sideline effective plans and well-trained managers. Capacity building in this area remains subject to political will and sovereign authority.

The UN secretary-general's review at the SDG midpoint called for urgent and transformative action to avert climate catastrophe and meet commitments under the Paris Agreement (UNSG 2023). This framing of the political challenge dodged the multilevel politics that hold SDG 13 and broader climate initiatives back. The goal simply restates or endorses the intentions of other interstate, intergovernmental processes that have repeatedly failed to produce adequate responses to the climate emergency. Many right-wing populists can score political points with voters by dubiously portraying climate action as a nefarious foreign agenda to raise taxes, kill jobs, and hurt so-called good people. These ill-conceived takes on climate action pander to inefficient fossil fuel producers and downstream industry players who want to keep black gold flowing for as long as possible, regardless of the consequences. Social progressives and greens challenge the limits of the UN's agenda for climate action *and* confront mendacious right-wing critiques of climate initiatives.

References

Blaxekjær, L.Ø., and T.D. Nielsen. 2015. "Mapping the Narrative Positions of New Political Groups Under the UNFCCC." *Climate Policy* 15, 6.

Campbell, B., J. Hansen, J. Rioux, et al. 2018. "Urgent Action to Combat Climate Change and its Impacts (SDG 13): Transforming Agriculture and Food Systems." *Current Opinion in Environmental Sustainability* 34.

Carlin, D. 2023. "Your Quick Guide to the Outcomes of COP28," *Forbes*, December 13. forbes.com/sites/davidcarlin/2023/12/13/your-quick-guide-to-the-outcomes-of-cop-28.

Hodgkinson, J.H., and M.H. Smith. 2021. "Climate Change and Sustainability as Drivers for the Next Mining and Metals Boom: The Need for Climate-Smart Mining and Recycling." *Resources Policy* 74.

Kramarz, T., S. Park, and C. Johnson. 2021. "Governing the Dark Side of Renewable Energy: A Typology of Global Displacements." *Energy Research and Social Science* 74.

Louman, B., R.J. Keenan, D. Kleinschmit, et al. 2019. "SDG 13: Climate Action — Impacts on Forests and People." In *Sustainable Development Goals: Their Impacts on Forests and People*, edited by P. Katila, C.J.P. Colfer, W. de Jong, et al. Cambridge: Cambridge University Press.

Reid, A.J., J.L. Brooks, L. Dolgova, et al. 2017. "Post-2015 Sustainable Development Goals Still Neglecting Their Environmental Roots in the Anthropocene." *Environmental Science and Policy* 77.

Thapa, P., B. Mainali, and S. Dhakal. 2023. "Focus on Climate Action: What Level of Synergy and Trade-Off Is There Between SDG 13; Climate Action and Other SDGs in Nepal?" *Energies* 16, 1.

UN (United Nations). 2020. *Climate Action: Why It Matters*. un.org/sustainabledevelopment/wp-content/uploads/2019/07/13_Why-It-Matters-2020.pdf.

_____. 2022a. "Climate Change." New York: Sustainable Development Goals Knowledge Platform. sustainabledevelopment.un.org/topics/climatechange.

———. 2022b. *The Sustainable Development Goals Report 2022*. New York: UN.

———. 2023. "Goal 13: Take Urgent Action to Combat Climate Change and Its Impacts." un.org/sustainabledevelopment/climate-change.

UNSG (United Nations Secretary-General). 2023. *Progress towards the Sustainable Development Goals: Towards a Rescue Plan for People and Planet. Report of the Secretary-General (Special Edition)*. New York: United Nations General Assembly and Economic and Social Council.

Goal ⑭
Life below Water

What They Tell Us

> **Mission statement:** Conserve and sustainably use the oceans, seas, and marine resources for sustainable development.

Overfishing, ocean plastic, acidification, and rising temperatures are threatening marine species and negatively impacting marine ecosystem services (UN 2023). Life below water is at risk, but we have the tools to correct course if we act now. With greater cooperation and focused effort, we can clean the waters and realize the promise of sustainable development (UN 2020). There is no doubt that "human activity is endangering the planet's largest ecosystem" and affecting the livelihoods of billions of people (UN 2022, 54). Sustainability and the protection of vulnerable habitats requires increased international cooperation to protect open ocean and deep-sea areas. Government-protected areas can also conserve biodiversity and ensure a sustainable future for the fishing industry. Individuals should select certified products and work to eliminate plastic usage and organize beach clean-ups (UN 2020). During the pandemic, ocean plastic and overfishing continued to rise at alarming rates. To realize this goal, we must do better.

Life Below Water Targets	Indicators
14.1 By 2025, prevent and significantly reduce marine pollution of all kinds, in particular from land-based activities, including marine debris and nutrient pollution	14.1.1 (*a*) Index of coastal eutrophication; and (*b*) plastic debris density
14.2 By 2020, sustainably manage and protect marine and coastal ecosystems to avoid significant adverse impacts, including by strengthening their resilience, and take action for their restoration in order to achieve healthy and productive oceans	14.2.1 Number of countries using ecosystem-based approaches to managing marine areas
14.3 Minimize and address the impacts of ocean acidification, including through enhanced scientific cooperation at all levels	14.3.1 Average marine acidity (pH) measured at agreed suite of representative sampling stations

Life Below Water Targets	Indicators
14.4 By 2020, effectively regulate harvesting and end overfishing, illegal, unreported, and unregulated fishing, and destructive fishing practices, and implement science-based management plans, in order to restore fish stocks in the shortest time feasible, at least to levels that can produce maximum sustainable yield as determined by their biological characteristics	**14.4.1** Proportion of fish stocks within biologically sustainable levels
14.5 By 2020, conserve at least 10 per cent of coastal and marine areas, consistent with national and international law and based on the best available scientific information	**14.5.1** Coverage of protected areas in relation to marine areas
14.6 By 2020, prohibit certain forms of fisheries subsidies which contribute to overcapacity and overfishing, eliminate subsidies that contribute to illegal, unreported, and unregulated fishing, and refrain from introducing new such subsidies, recognizing that appropriate and effective special and differential treatment for developing and least developed countries should be an integral part of the World Trade Organization fisheries subsidies negotiation	**14.6.1** Degree of implementation of international instruments aiming to combat illegal, unreported, and unregulated fishing
14.7 By 2030, increase the economic benefits to small island developing States and least developed countries from the sustainable use of marine resources, including through sustainable management of fisheries, aquaculture, and tourism	**14.7.1** Sustainable fisheries as a proportion of GDP in small island developing States, least developed countries, and all countries
14.a Increase scientific knowledge, develop research capacity, and transfer marine technology, taking into account the Intergovernmental Oceanographic Commission Criteria and Guidelines on the Transfer of Marine Technology, in order to improve ocean health and to enhance the contribution of marine biodiversity to the development of developing countries, in particular small island developing States and least developed countries	**14.a.1** Proportion of total research budget allocated to research in the field of marine technology
14.b Provide access for small-scale artisanal fishers to marine resources and markets	**14.b.1** Degree of application of a legal/regulatory/policy/institutional framework which recognizes and protects access rights for small-scale fisheries
14.c Enhance the conservation and sustainable use of oceans and their resources by implementing international law as reflected in the United Nations Convention on the Law of the Sea, which provides the legal framework for the conservation and sustainable use of oceans and their resources, as recalled in paragraph 158 of "The future we want"	**14.c.1** Number of countries making progress in ratifying, accepting, and implementing through legal, policy, and institutional frameworks, ocean-related instruments that implement international law, as reflected in the United Nations Convention on the Law of the Sea, for the conservation and sustainable use of the oceans and their resources

The Hidden Politics

This goal's first target (14.1) is a tall political order. It ostensibly aims to prevent and significantly reduce marine pollution of all kinds. Yet it singularly stresses the need for governments to prioritize efforts to reduce pollution from land-based activities. This stipulation narrows the scope for actions considerably, as seen in the associated indicator on coastal eutrophication and plastic debris (14.1.1). Tough measures to abate the unnecessary and indiscriminate overuse of inorganic fertilizers and tilling in agriculture could curtail erosion and limit runoff that disrupts aquatic life. Prohibitions on single-use plastics and strategies to scale up sewage and wastewater treatment could be similarly impactful. Stricter rules for industrial effluent, the introduction of more rigorous enforcement mechanisms, and campaigns that raise public awareness and encourage accountability could also be effectual. However, while these and other measures to mitigate land-based impacts related to coastal eutrophication and plastic debris are clearly necessary, they will by no means be sufficient.

International commerce also drives fertilizer runoff, plastic pollution, and ocean contamination more broadly. The growth of transboundary trade in industrial and consumer products and wastes that are potential pollutants can drive the persistence of damaging land-based practices. Specifically, trade opportunities can give companies and countries incentives to maintain the production and export of known pollutants. If dirty industries can reap consistent profits from selling their products to overseas buyers, they have political and economic interests in upholding the status quo. So too do maritime shipping and logistics firms. The failure to include any indicators that could be used to fight the political interests aligned against robust changes to land-based activities is troubling. And it is not the target's only political oversight. Ocean-based extractive activities, including deep sea mining and offshore drilling, have the potential to spur contamination at sea and on land. Products derived from metals or fossil fuels that are extracted from ocean floors can directly exacerbate marine pollution. The exclusion of language of any kind related to deep sea extractives or maritime shipping showcases this target's worrying political limitations.

The subsequent target (14.2) also skirts the politics of national and private sector interests in the maintenance and expansion of polluting ocean-based activities. Still, its emphasis on the sustainable management and protection of marine and coastal ecosystems could be an entry point for change. Its appeal for management systems that can ward off significant adverse impacts and its call for restorative actions set the right tone on ocean defence. That said, ambiguities in the target's language could readily undermine these intentions. It offers no guidance on just how adverse the impacts on marine life or ecosystem health would have to be to be considered "significant." The target's insistence on restoration is also constrained by language that seems to direct such action only towards ocean productivity. It should go without saying that efforts to restore the ocean's productive capacity for humans do not necessarily align with the imperative of transforming human practices to maximize ecosystem health. The nebulous jargon of "productive oceans" takes as given the imperative of maintaining current ocean-based economic activities. It cedes the ground entirely to the political interests that governments and firms can have in maintaining business as usual at sea. The target's sole indicator (14.2.1) seeks only to increase the proportion of national exclusive economic zones that are managed using ecosystem-based approaches. These governance approaches can improve ecosystem health, but they are not a panacea. Most often, they are applied to mitigate human impacts, not with an eye towards curtailing dated economic practices that amplify the climate emergency.

While the third target (14.3) does underscore an urgent climate action imperative, its aspirations are also woefully inattentive to the associated politics. Getting states to agree on the crucial need to minimize and address the impacts of ocean acidification, and to further their scientific cooperation in this area, is one thing. Ensuring that countries follow through on this commitment is quite another. Reducing average marine acidity (14.3.1) will require not only a massive reduction in carbon emissions but also substantial retrofits and innovations in waste disposal, land management, and industrial systems. This target is an exemplar of the ways that the 2030 Agenda's idealist intentions can collide with entrenched interests. States agree to cooperate scientifically, not to collaborate in any way to expedite best practices. No indicators related to international initiatives or domestic laws, policies, regulations, or strategies to reduce ocean acidification have been included. Governments have simply paid lip service to the idea that ocean acidification is a serious threat to marine food chains and reefs.

SDG 14's fourth target (14.4) can now be considered an early artefact of political failure under the Global Goals. Despite its pledge to end overfishing by 2020, the practice remains rampant. According to the Our World in Data team (2023), based on the Food and Agriculture Organization's analysis, more than one-third of global fisheries are overexploited. Illegal, unreported, and unregulated fishing and destructive fishing practices have also not ceased. In hindsight, this target overplayed measures related to sustainable management plans and glossed over the stark political economy challenges.

Its only indicator (14.4.1) magnified the importance of industry-friendly nar-ratives on the restoration of fish stocks to levels that can produce maximum sustainable yields. This approach assumed that belief in the "need" to ensure perpetual exploitation was nearly universal, and that effective regulation and enforcement could discipline free riders and end overconsumption. It did not anticipate that the depth of commitments to this very narrow understanding of sustainability would fall far short of global expectations. No indicators were developed to facilitate assessments of state or industry-based efforts to curb unsustainable practices. Faith in the universality of aspirations for sustainable yet unrelenting exploitation also unduly obscured the range of perspectives that vied to inform sustainable fisheries policy and regulation. The target excluded the views of ocean conservationists and advocates who sought to better align consumption and production patterns with deeper visions of sustainability than just the durability of the fishing industry. Many with stakes in managing and profiting from the global fishing industry failed to heed even minimalist business-oriented standpoints on sustainability. Despite notable sustainable successes in this space, the target was not achieved and the overarching tragedy of the commons persists.

The subsequent target (14.5) on coastal and marine conservation has an indicator (14.5.1) that includes the most expansive globally accepted definition of "protected" areas possible. Conserving at least 10 per cent of coastal and marine areas will undeniably require greater scrutiny of the coverage of protected areas in relation to marine areas. The International Union for Conservation of Nature (IUCN) considers protected areas to be "clearly defined geographical spaces, recognized, dedicated, and managed through legal or other effective means, to achieve the long-term conserva-tion of nature" (Our World in Data team 2023). Thus, what counts as a marine protected area is open to considerable political interpretation and action. Governments apply divergent language, legal mechanisms, and criteria in relation to protected areas (Owens 2023). The IUCN definition includes seven categories of protected areas, each of which permit different levels of human activity. For example, marine conservation areas that are managed as strict nature reserves have a vastly higher potential to ensure biodiversity than those managed by "other effective means." The former approach prohibits all commercial fishing and industrial activities, whereas the latter type can include military areas and renewable energy sites with so-called de facto conservation benefits (Diz et al. 2018). If governments rely disproportionately on areas subject only to private, local, community, or other nonstatutory informal management to bolster marine protection, any progress they do make towards this target could be more apparent than real. On that front, efforts to expand coastal and marine protection of any type have underperformed globally. This target's emphasis on marine conservation was not an original call to action, but a simple recognition of the failure of many states to perform on previous commitments. It overtly repeated language from the Convention on Biological Diversity's Aichi Target 11 from 2011 and articulated no further ambitions.

Turning to the sixth target (14.6) on illegal, unreported, and unregulated fishing and overfishing, its language has been open to political interpretation and abuse. Some have claimed the target focuses solely on the reduction or prohibition of fishery subsidies, which remain wide-ranging and can include government payouts that enhance capacity and fuel overcapacity (Schuhbauer 2020). Subsidies for boat construction or modernization, and market and storage infrastructure, along with various tax exemptions, are still used to maintain, grow, and expand fisheries. As such, these benefits and bounties can amplify problems. Where heavily subsidized fleets from one country intrude on the exclusive economic zones of other states, illegal, unreported, and unregulated fishing can be exacerbated. Given these realities, the World Trade Organization understandably claimed a significant victory when its Agreement on Fisheries Subsidies was finally adopted in June 2022 (WTO 2022). At that time, the World Trade Organization Secretariat also dubiously asserted that this achievement had been accomplished through multilateral agreement and ensured that the sixth target of SDG 14 had been fully met. The inaccuracy of these claims is beyond doubt and reflects simple unawareness or willing ignorance of how progress on this target is monitored. The associated indicator (14.6.1) is concerned with the degree of implementation of *all* international instruments that aim to combat illegal, unreported, and unregulated fishing. In this case, the indicator does not shrink the scope of an SDG target but expands it by an order of magnitude. The target's language on subsidies might have been convenient for World Trade Organization officials, but the indicator is clear on the matter. The Food and Agriculture Organization maintains a comprehensive list of the relevant international measures, which include the UN Fish Stocks Agreement, the Code of Conduct for Responsible Fisheries, the International Plan of Action, and a range of other voluntary and regional measures. (FAO n.d.). Data on the implementation of these measures is at best patchy. To say the least, officials from the Food and Agriculture Organization are not trumpeting progress in this area as an SDG success story (Our World in Data team 2023).

Unlike the previous target, the seventh target (14.7) of SDG 14 is not an outlier, and its political ambitions clearly shrink from the broad language of the target to its narrow indicator. Here, the intention is to increase the economic benefits that flow to small island developing states and least developed countries from the sustainable use of marine resources. The target highlights several ways to achieve this result, including through the growth of sustainable fisheries, aquaculture, and tourism. However, the indicator (14.7.1) focuses solely on sustainable fisheries as a proportion of GDP. If data on this topic become fully available, they could showcase developments in the relative economic importance of sustainable fishing over time. But these statistics would not speak to the overall economic benefits to be had from the uptake of more sustainable approaches to the use of other marine resources. This gap is another example of the ways that SDG indicators can fail to adequately measure relevant sustainability innovations or social impacts. Specifically, this indicator relies on a "blue economy" orientation that numerous social scientists have critiqued for being relatively inattentive to social justice considerations (Germond-Duret et al. 2023).

As it stands, progress on the seventh target is not being judged through a range of relevant indicators. No effort is being made to count the number of countries that adopt sustainable management plans to ensure that the health of coral reefs remains stable under increased tourism (Hafezi et al. 2020). Data showcasing how the pursuit of sustainability in this area is helping small island developing states and least developed countries to break out of economic enclaves are similarly missing in action (Wilkinson et al. 2021). How this push could relate to the maintenance of traditional knowledge also remains unknown (Moncada et al. 2021). Moreover, indicators linked to the implementation of commitments made under relevant multilateral agreements, including the Small Island Developing States Accelerated Modalities of Action Pathway, are nowhere to be found (Dubrie et al. 2019). Last but certainly not least, statistics that respect and capture the dynamism and diversity of ecosystems and cultures in many small island developing states and least developed countries are unavailable (Kelman 2018). These gaps confirm that indicators and targets under SDG 14 are relatively slipshod. They are often politically inadequate, and they open the door to massive politicization.

The goal's three implementation targets do not correct this course. The first (14.a) calls for more scientific knowledge, research capacity, and transfer of marine technologies to small island developing states and least developed countries. Yet its indicator (14.a.1) focuses only on the proportion of research budgets allocated to the field of marine technology. As such, it simply assumes that higher research budgets will eventually contribute to improving the global distribution of marine technologies. This premise carelessly overlooks the range of barriers that continue to impede technology transfers, including patents, licences, costs, capacity, and a lack of political will. The second implementation target (14.b) prioritizes small-scale fishers and their access to marine resources and markets. On this target, governments have agreed to an indicator (14.b.1) that puts the spotlight directly on their legal, regulatory, policy, and institutional frameworks. If they had endorsed a similar level of oversight for all targets under SDG 14, this chapter might have told a very different political story. The indicator (14.c.1) associated with the final implementation target (14.c) is potentially of greater consequence. Data related to the progress that countries make on ratifying, accepting, and implementing ocean-related international law can be used to hold governments to better account. Still, the gulf between implementation and the effective enforcement of international instruments can remain vast in many contexts. Where laws, policies, and frameworks look good on paper, practices can still persistently undermine life under water.

The UN secretary-general's review at the SDG midpoint reiterated that acidification, eutrophication, the depletion of fish stocks, and the scourge of plastic pollution necessitate urgent action to support life under water (UNSG 2023). Though the secretary-general downplayed the seeming "success" story on overfishing, his report was less clear about the political assumptions that animate SDG 14. This goal includes targets and indicators that exude the growth orientation of the 2030 Agenda and do not challenge the ways that corporations continue to use oceans, seas, and marine resources to advance their own interests at the expense of ecosystem health. National governments continue to face domestic political pressure to maximize the benefits that can be reaped from ocean-based activities. Social progressives and greens take issue with this goal's liberal limitations *and* combat those that seek to advance extractive practices and national interests. Progressives and ecologists are committed to reducing the ecological and social footprint of the rich on oceans and ocean-dependent people.

References

Diz, D., D. Johnson, M. Riddell, et al. 2018. "Mainstreaming Marine Biodiversity into the SDGs: The Role of Other Effective Area-Based Conservation Measures (SDG 14.5)." *Marine Policy* 93.

Dubrie, A., E. Thorne, L.F. de Meira, et al. 2019. *Synthesis of the Caribbean Subregion Midterm Review Report of Small Island Developing States (SIDS) Accelerated Modalities of Action (SAMOA) Pathway*. Santiago: ECLAC.

Food and Agriculture Organization (FAO). n.d. "Other Related Agreements." fao.org/fishery/en/166350/en.

Germond-Duret, C., C. P. Heidkamp, and J. Morrissey. 2023. "(In)justice and the Blue Economy." *The Geographical Journal* 189, 2.

Hafezi, M., O. Sahin, R.A. Steward, et al. 2020. "Adaptation Strategies for Coral Reef Ecosystems in Small Island Developing States: Integrated Modellng of Local Pressures and Long-Term Climate Changes." *Journal of Cleaner Production*, 253.

Kelman, I. 2018. "Islandness within Climate Change Narratives of Small Island Developing States." *Island Studies Journal* 13, 1.

Moncada, S., L. Briguglio, H. Bambrick, et al. (eds). 2021. *Small Island Developing States: Vulnerability and Resilience Under Climate Change*. Cham, Switzerland: Springer Nature.

Our World in Data team. 2023. "Conserve and Sustainably Use the Oceans, Seas and Marine Resources." ourworldindata.org/sdgs/life-below-water.

Owens, B. 2023. "Marine Protected Areas, Explained." *Hakai Magazine*, June 8. hakaimagazine.com/features/marine-protected-areas-explained.

Schuhbauer, A., D.J. Skerritt, N. Ebrahim, et al. 2020. "The Global Fisheries Subsidies Divide between Small- and Large-Scale Fisheries." *Frontiers of Marine Science* 7.

UN (United Nations). 2020. *Life below Water: Why It Matters*. un.org/sustainabledevelopment/wp-content/uploads/2019/07/14_Why-It-Matters-2020.pdf.

———. 2022. *The Sustainable Development Goals Report 2022*. New York: UN.

———. 2023. "Goal 14: Conserve and Sustainably Use the Oceans, Seas and Marine Resources." un.org/sustainabledevelopment/oceans.

UNSG (United Nations Secretary-General). 2023. *Progress towards the Sustainable Development Goals: Towards a Rescue Plan for People and Planet. Report of the Secretary-General (Special Edition)*. New York: United Nations General Assembly and Economic and Social Council.

Wilkinson, E., M. Scobie, C. Lindsay, et al. 2021. *Sustaining Developing in Small Island Developing States*. London: ODI.

WTO (World Trade Organization). 2022. *Agreement on Fisheries Subsidies*. wto.org/english/tratop_e/rulesneg_e/fish_e/fish_e.htm.

Goal ⑮
Life on Land

What They Tell Us

> **Mission statement:** Protect, restore, and promote sustainable use of terrestrial ecosystems, sustainably manage forests, combat desertification, and halt and reverse land degradation and halt biodiversity loss.

This goal is about conserving life on land and protecting and restoring terrestrial ecosystems (UN 2023). Ensuring the health of our ecosystems and the maintenance of biological diversity is essential for life on land (UN 2020). Together, we can secure the ecosystem services that support life on Earth for generations to come. Unfortunately, "biodiversity has been largely neglected" in postpandemic recovery spending, and the world's forested area continues to decline (UN 2022, 56). While more countries are incorporating ecosystem and biodiversity values into their accounting and reporting systems, agricultural expansion and logging are encroaching on habitats (UN 2023). More than half of key biodiversity areas remain unprotected. Nonetheless, individuals can do some things to help. We can recycle, eat a locally based and sustainably sourced diet, and consume only what we need (UN 2020). We must redouble our efforts to protect species at risk and prioritize the achievement of land degradation neutrality.

Life on Land Targets	Indicators
15.1 By 2020, ensure the conservation, restoration, and sustainable use of terrestrial and inland freshwater ecosystems and their services, in particular forests, wetlands, mountains, and drylands, in line with obligations under international agreements	15.1.1 Forest area as a proportion of total land area 15.1.2 Proportion of important sites for terrestrial and freshwater biodiversity that are covered by protected areas, by ecosystem type
15.2 By 2020, promote the implementation of sustainable management of all types of forests, halt deforestation, restore degraded forests, and substantially increase afforestation and reforestation globally	15.2.1 Progress towards sustainable forest management

Life on Land Targets	Indicators
15.3 By 2030, combat desertification, restore degraded land and soil, including land affected by desertification, drought, and floods, and strive to achieve a land degradation-neutral world	**15.3.1** Proportion of land that is degraded over total land area
15.4 By 2030, ensure the conservation of mountain ecosystems, including their biodiversity, in order to enhance their capacity to provide benefits that are essential for sustainable development	**15.4.1** Coverage by protected areas of important sites for mountain biodiversity **15.4.2** (*a*) Mountain Green Cover Index and (*b*) proportion of degraded mountain land
15.5 Take urgent and significant action to reduce the degradation of natural habitats, halt the loss of biodiversity, and, by 2020, protect and prevent the extinction of threatened species	**15.5.1** Red List Index
15.6 Promote fair and equitable sharing of the benefits arising from the utilization of genetic resources and promote appropriate access to such resources, as internationally agreed	**15.6.1** Number of countries that have adopted legislative, administrative, and policy frameworks to ensure fair and equitable sharing of benefits
15.7 Take urgent action to end poaching and trafficking of protected species of flora and fauna and address both demand and supply of illegal wildlife products	**15.7.1** Proportion of traded wildlife that was poached or illicitly trafficked
15.8 By 2020, introduce measures to prevent the introduction and significantly reduce the impact of invasive alien species on land and water ecosystems and control or eradicate the priority species	**15.8.1** Proportion of countries adopting relevant national legislation and adequately resourcing the prevention or control of invasive alien species
15.9 By 2020, integrate ecosystem and biodiversity values into national and local planning, development processes, poverty reduction strategies, and accounts	**15.9.1** (*a*) Number of countries that have established national targets in accordance with or similar to Aichi Biodiversity Target 2 of the Strategic Plan for Biodiversity 2011–2020 in their national biodiversity strategy and action plans and the progress reported towards these targets; and (*b*) integration of biodiversity into national accounting and reporting systems, defined as implementation of the System of Environmental-Economic Accounting
15.a Mobilize and significantly increase financial resources from all sources to conserve and sustainably use biodiversity and ecosystems	**15.a.1** (*a*) Official development assistance on conservation and sustainable use of biodiversity; and (*b*) revenue generated and finance mobilized from biodiversity-relevant economic instruments
15.b Mobilize significant resources from all sources and at all levels to finance sustainable forest management and provide adequate incentives to developing countries to advance such management, including for conservation and reforestation	**15.b.1** (*a*) Official development assistance on conservation and sustainable use of biodiversity; and (*b*) revenue generated and finance mobilized from biodiversity-relevant economic instruments
15.c Enhance global support for efforts to combat poaching and trafficking of protected species, including by increasing the capacity of local communities to pursue sustainable livelihood opportunities	**15.c.1** Proportion of traded wildlife that was poached or illicitly trafficked

The Hidden Politics

This goal's first target (15.1) on conservation, restoration, and sustainable use of terrestrial and inland freshwater ecosystems and their services simply erases the associated politics. It is woefully inattentive to the ways that power dynamics and hierarchies influence conservation efforts. Specifically, it does not promote the rights of residents to participate in decision-making related to conservation, and it fails to enshrine a commitment to respect Indigenous perspectives and act on their priorities (Krauss 2021). By omitting the human context within which conservation objectives are contested, this target opens the door to the persistence of colonial practices that often perpetuate socioecological injustices. Many conservationists now reject the dated and racist notion that pristine nature exists and can be treated independently of local lives and livelihoods. They seek to decolonize the field and put land and water users at the centre of conversations about interdependencies and alternatives. According to Judith E. Krauss (2021), the failure of this target and of SDG 15 more generally to recognize the human dimensions of conservation openly invites governments to replicate the problematic dynamics of exclusion and restriction.

Beyond this vast political problem, the target's two indicators also shrink its ambitions. The first indicator (15.1.1) condenses the target's encompassing language on conservation, restoration, and sustainable use of forests, wetlands, mountains, and drylands down to an exacting focus on forest area as a proportion of total land. Efforts to monitor trends in virgin forests and tree plantations can provide some insight on these objectives, but reliance on this narrow indicator will tell only a small part of the conservation story. Similarly, the second indicator (15.1.2) draws attention only to the proportion of terrestrial and freshwater biodiversity sites that are covered by protected areas. This stress on the expansion of protected areas will produce needed data on conservation trends by type of ecosystem. But it also neglects the politics of protected area designations detailed above under SDG 14. Technical progress or the lack thereof in relation to the growth or coverage of protected areas is one thing. Whether areas that are subject to different types of protection are indeed effective for conservation and for communities is quite another. If the growth of more effective types of protected area stalls, or relatively more ineffective types proliferate, those eventualities could have serious ramifications for progress under this target.

The next target (15.2) on the promotion and implementation of sustainable forest management obscures the politics that can amplify deforestation and impede forest restoration, afforestation, and reforestation. The indicator

(15.2.1), which measures progress towards sustainable forest management through five subindicators, is just not robust. Constructively, its focus on the expansion of forested areas (15.2.1.1) and on above-ground forest biomass (15.2.1.2) can speak to the progress of reforestation and efforts to curtail forest degradation. These subindicators nonetheless gloss over the inequitable human practices and political conflict that can accompany campaigns to expand forests and forest biomass. Similarly, the third subindicator's (15.2.1.3) emphasis on the protection of forest biodiversity draws needed attention to trends in protected areas and in the abundance of selected species and numbers of threatened or endangered species. But it is also not vigilant about the relative effectiveness of protection or the politics that can lead biodiversity protection efforts to look better on paper than they do on the ground. For instance, in many biodiversity hotspots, forest-dependent people can rely on the collection of forest products for their livelihoods (L.Q. Sneyd 2013). While wild food gatherers can make durable contributions to biodiversity conservation, their practices can also undermine progress. In some contexts, authorities do not have the enforcement capabilities or political incentives necessary to accurately document biodiversity losses. Consequently, the third subindicator could offer a far rosier view on biodiversity trends than is warranted.

The fourth subindicator (15.2.1.4) of sustainable forest management is similarly problematic. It spotlights only the availability of long-term management plans. Many national and subnational forest laws have included language on the former focus for decades, and forest planning has certainly proliferated (Chia et al. 2019). Even so, the existence of laws that mandate forest management planning has not been a cure-all (A. Sneyd 2011). Illegal logging practices have persisted in numerous countries that have strong forest laws. Forested areas that are remote or near borders or conflict zones continue to be susceptible to practices including bribery, permit forging, and the illegal felling, mixing, and relabelling of logs. This subindicator also downplays the financial and other incentives that legal operators in better governed contexts can have to disregard forest plan stipulations. It consequently exaggerates the importance of plan availability and needlessly fails to consider the adequacy of forest plans or the levels of adherence to them.

A similar story can be told about the final subindicator (15.2.1.5). It is attentive only to the proportion of forested areas where compliance with a set of national or international standards is independently verified. This focus overstates the importance of trends in forested areas while dismissing the relevant political challenges. The scope, potential impact, and effectiveness of forest management standards, codes, and systems that are overseen by accredited third parties vary widely. Some systems fuel the growth of forested areas that are subjected to audits and verification but persistently underperform. If governments rely on those systems, and not on other more rigorous certifications that have the demonstrated potential to improve practice, headline trends in sustainably managed and verified areas will not tell the full story. They could be used to obscure the growth of weaker governance approaches. For example, the European Union's Forest Law Enforcement, Governance and Trade (FLEGT) initiative can improve governance and harvesting practices and ensure the legality of timber (Neupane et al. 2019). Its monitoring, reporting, and verification systems can also shake up nontransparent practices (Tegegne et al. 2018). Yet other evidence suggests that local elites can and do capture the benefits that flow from this system, and that enforcement and community engagement problems persist (Appau and Derkyi 2022). FLEGT has also reinforced hierarchies in downstream industries and generated an illicit trade in licences (Maryudi and Myers 2018). In countries with poor enforcement of forest legislation, this verification system has also fuelled other kinds of rent-seeking behaviour (Andong and Ongolo 2020). Taken together, these difficulties suggest that FLEGT might underachieve relative to other systems that independently verify sustainable forest management practices. The Forest Stewardship Council's long-standing certification system has not been a silver bullet, but its standards and control systems are relatively more comprehensive in relation to sustainability (A. Sneyd 2011). Thus, the oversight provided by FLEGT and the Forest Stewardship Council cannot be taken as equivalent.

The subsequent targets also face significant political challenges stemming from indicators that redact the human dimensions of conservation. These targets are among the most complex in the 2030 Agenda. They nonetheless fail to engage substantively with relevant governance gaps, asymmetrical partnerships, and subnational authorities (Sayer et al. 2019). Evidence now suggests that the intricacies of these objectives and their seeming disconnect from people might deter government action. Governments are certainly free to act upon their own sovereign priorities, but the abstract and fragmented presentation of the targets may disincentivize engagement. According to Sayer et al. (2019), the national SDG implementation team in at least one incredibly biodiverse country has produced a strategy that treats these targets as optional. The national secretariat and SDG working groups in Indonesia created an action plan that cherry-picks only three targets from this goal, dispensing with at least five targets.

The third target's objectives to combat desertification, restore degraded land and soil, and achieve a land degradation-neutral world are undeniably necessary (15.3). Still, these ambitions have only been associated with subindicators on land cover (15.3.1.1), land productivity (15.3.1.2), and carbon stocks (15.3.1.3). They could have been more fruitfully connected to other indicators that intersect more directly with human practices. For instance, an indicator related to land under large-scale conventional agriculture could have linked this target more fully to a principal source of the looming soil exhaustion disaster. The intersections of this target with SDG 2 and SDG 13 could have also been made more readily apparent to nonexperts and decision-makers. Similarly, the indicators associated with the target (15.4) on mountain ecosystem conservation for sustainable development draw attention only to the coverage of protected areas (15.4.1) and to mountain green cover and degraded mountain land (15.4.2). Here again, indicators under SDG 15 neglect the importance of the type of protected areas that predominate. Moreover, they obscure important connections with human activities that other goals seek to expand, such as sustainable tourism under SDG 8. The lack of an indicator on this intersection point is distressing, as the growth of mountain-based eco-hotels and so-called low-impact ski resorts may not be compatible with ecosystem conservation.

The next target's (15.5) aim to stop the degradation of natural habitats, halt biodiversity loss, and protect threatened species has wide-ranging contradictions with several other goals. These ends are incompatible with energy development aspirations under SDG 7 and the push for new infrastructure under SDG 9. Infrastructure projects for renewable energy can and do create entry points for practices that degrade natural habitats and fuel biodiversity and species loss. Encouraging governments to be cognizant of extinction risk trends in the Red List Index (15.5.1) while also urging them to develop infrastructure that will drive resource extraction is antithetical. The target features no indicators that could help governments unpack this vast contradiction or the profit-oriented practices that drive planetary devastation and extinctions.

To a certain degree, the next four targets stand apart from the previous targets. They each feature indicators that can highlight trends in relevant government actions. Even so, their attentiveness to the uptake of legal and policy measures at the national level is by no means sufficient. They overlook power dynamics and potential governance gaps at the international and subnational levels of analysis. The sixth target (15.6) on the fair and equitable sharing of benefits from the use of genetic resources, for example, includes an indicator (15.6.1) that considers only the number of countries with relevant legislation or policy. Data that underscore the national uptake of relevant international protocols and treaties are good. But this is not the only metric relevant to the many Indigenous Peoples and forest-dependent people whose territories and practices are often the source for valuable genetic resources. In contexts where the rule of law underperforms and courts are politically compromised, other measures for assessing the fair and equitable sharing of benefits are clearly required. Subnational factors also work against the seventh target's urgent call to end poaching, the trafficking of protected species, and the illegal wildlife product trade (15.7). Its indicator (15.7.1) is attentive only to the proportion of traded wildlife that was poached or illicitly trafficked. This indicator assumes national capacity on poaching, trafficking, and the illegal trade that simply does not exist in many contexts. Internationally comparable data on this indicator remain unavailable (Our World in Data team 2023).

Likewise, the eighth (15.8) target's call to prevent and reduce the impacts of invasive alien species includes an indicator (15.8.1) that focuses only on national legislation and the resourcing of control efforts. No data are collected on the participation of countries in any nascent international or multistakeholder processes related to controlling the global spread of invasive species. By contrast, the ninth target's (15.9) appeal for countries to integrate ecosystem and biodiversity values into their national planning does include language on subnational processes. Yet here, too, the underlying indicator (15.9.1) exclusively emphasizes the introduction of national targets and national accounting and reporting systems. It thus excludes the reality that stakeholders can and do work against the integration of ecosystem and biodiversity values into local planning or development processes.

SDG 15's three implementation targets also have indicators that overemphasize national-level capacity and initiative. The first's broad call to mobilize financial resources from all sources to conserve and sustainably use biodiversity and ecosystems is representative (15.a). Its indicator (15.a.1.b) shrinks these ambitions down to a primary focus on total official development assistance flows for biodiversity conservation. This shrinkage detracts attention from other possible sources of finance (15.b.1.b), including charitable donations, fundraising for ecosystem services, and biodiversity taxes on portfolio and direct investments. For years, many governments have overemphasized the former, and failed to collect relevant data on the latter. The second implementation target's push to mobilize financial resources for sustainable forest management (15.b) is undermined by an indicator (15.b.1.a) that overemphasizes trends in official flows. For its part, the final implementation target aims to combat poaching and the trafficking of protected species (15.c) but its indicator on the illegal wildlife trade calls for internationally comparable data that remain unavailable.

Overall, the implementation targets and indicators obscure the politics that hold back biodiversity measures, forest management, and action on illegal practices at the national level and beyond. They also neglect the reality that work to improve life on land in many contexts is decentralized and driven by local communities (Sayer et al. 2019). And they say nothing about the serious trade-offs between SDG 15 and other goals that could impact resource mobilization and use. This goal's aspirations have not been cohesively integrated into the 2030 Agenda.

According to the UN secretary-general's SDG midpoint assessment, the triple planetary crisis of biodiversity loss, pollution, and climate change had intensified, and human-environment relations needed to shift dramatically to achieve this goal (UNSG 2023). The secretary-general's call for a conspicuous break with the existing state of life on land stands in stark contrast with the political content of SDG 15. This goal is infused with an overly optimistic liberal take on the policies necessary to halt land degradation and preserve life on land. Its targets are not all attentive to the relevant politics. Beyond the troubling political oversights detailed above, some right-wing nationalists with stakes in a range of extractive and industrial land uses have characterized the many environmental ideals associated with this goal as inappropriate. Social progressives and greens work to address the limitations of SDG 15 *and* mobilize against nationalist dogma that escalates planetary crises. Faced with misleading liberal platitudes and nationalist political posturing, greens and progressives continue to fight for a deeper transformation of human-environment relations.

References

Andong, S., and S. Ongolo. 2020. "From Global Forest Governance to Domestic Politics: The European Forest Reforms in Cameroon." *Forest Policy and Economics* 111.

Appau, Y., and M.A.A. Derkyi. 2022. "Local Communities' Knowledge and Perception of FLEGT-VPA —Insights from Ghana." *Forest Policy and Economics* 144.

Chia, E.L., D. Hubert, S. Carudenuto, and O. Sene. 2019. "Evolution in the Enabling Factors for Transformational Change in Forestry and Land Use Policy Processes: The Case of REDD+ in Cameroon." *International Forestry Review* 21, 1.

Krauss, J.E. 2021. "Decolonizing, Conviviality, and Convivial Conservation: Towards a Convivial SDG 15, Life on Land?" *Journal of Political Ecology* 28, 1.

Maryudi, A., and R. Myers. 2018. "Renting Legality: How FLEGT is Reinforcing Power Relations in Indonesian Furniture Production Networks." *Geoforum* 97.

Neupane, P.R., C.B. Wiati, E.M. Angi, et al. 2019. "How REDD+ and FLEGT-VPA Processes are Contributing Towards SFM in Indonesia — the Specialist's Viewpoint." *International Forestry Review* 21, 4.

Our World in Data team. 2023. "Sustainably Manage Forests, Combat Desertification, Halt and Reverse Land Degradation, Halt Biodiversity Loss." ourworldindata. org/sdgs/life-on-land.

Sayer, J., D. Sheil, G. Galloway, et al. 2019. "SDG 15: Life on Land — the Central Role of Forests in Sustainable Development." In *Sustainable Development Goals: Their Impacts on Forests and People*, edited by P. Katila, C.J.P. Colfer, W. de Jong, et al. Cambridge: Cambridge University Press.

Sneyd, A. 2011. "Governing African Cotton and Timber Through CSR: Competition, Legitimacy, and Power." *Canadian Journal of Development Studies* 33, 2.

Sneyd, L.Q. 2013. "Wild Food, Prices, Diets, and Development: Sustainability and Food Security in Urban Cameroon." *Sustainability* 5, 11.

Tegegne, Y.T., M. Cramm, and J. Van Brusselen. 2018. "Sustainable Forest Management, FLEGT, And REDD+: Exploring Interlinkages to Strengthen Forest Policy Coherence." *Sustainability* 10, 12.

UN (United Nations). 2020. *Life on Land: Why It Matters.* un.org/ sustainabledevelopment/wp-content/uploads/2019/07/15_Why-It-Matters-2020.pdf.

———. 2022. *The Sustainable Development Goals Report 2022.* New York: UN.

———. 2023. "Goal 15: Sustainably Manage Forests, Combat Desertification, Halt and Reverse Land Degradation, Halt Biodiversity Loss." un.org/ sustainabledevelopment/biodiversity.

UNSG (United Nations Secretary-General). 2023. *Progress towards the Sustainable Development Goals: Towards a Rescue Plan for People and Planet. Report of the Secretary-General (Special Edition).* New York: United Nations General Assembly and Economic and Social Council.

Goal 16
Peace, Justice, and Strong Institutions

What They Tell Us

Mission statement: Promote peaceful and inclusive societies for sustainable development, provide access to justice for all, and build effective, accountable, and inclusive institutions at all levels.

Governments, civil society, and communities should collaborate and implement solutions that reduce violence, deliver justice, fight corruption, and ensure inclusive participation (UN 2020). We must build a world where people everywhere are free of fear from all forms of violence (UN 2023). Armed violence and insecurity are destructive long after conflicts cease. We can and must work together and do more to enable people to feel safe and included as they go about their lives. As of May 2022, the number of people forced to flee conflict, violence, human rights violations, and persecution had surpassed 100 million (UN 2022, 58). The previous year, fatal attacks on human rights defenders, journalists, and trade unionists occurred at least 320 times (UN 2023). As governments aim to achieve more peaceful and inclusive societies, justice for all, and more inclusive institutions at all levels, individuals can also take related actions. We can exercise our right to hold our elected officials to account. We can also exercise our right to freedom of information and share our opinion with our elected representatives. We can and must achieve this goal together (UN 2020).

Peace, Justice, and Institutions Targets	Indicators
16.1 Significantly reduce all forms of violence and related death rates everywhere	16.1.1 Number of victims of intentional homicide per 100,000 population, by sex and age
	16.1.2 Conflict-related deaths per 100,000 population, by sex, age, and cause
	16.1.3 Proportion of population subjected to (a) physical violence, (b) psychological violence, and (c) sexual violence in the previous 12 months

Peace, Justice, and Institutions Targets	Indicators
16.1 (continued)	16.1.4 Proportion of population that feel safe walking alone around the area they live after dark
16.2 End abuse, exploitation, trafficking, and all forms of violence against and torture of children	16.2.1 Proportion of children aged 1–17 years who experienced any physical punishment and/or psychological aggression by caregivers in the past month 16.2.2 Number of victims of human trafficking per 100,000 population, by sex, age, and form of exploitation 16.2.3 Proportion of young women and men aged 18–29 years who experienced sexual violence by age 18
16.3 Promote the rule of law at the national and international levels and ensure equal access to justice for all	16.3.1 Proportion of victims of violence in the previous 12 months who reported their victimization to competent authorities or other officially recognized conflict resolution mechanisms 16.3.2 Unsentenced detainees as a proportion of overall prison population 16.3.3 Proportion of the population who have experienced a dispute in the past two years and who accessed a formal or informal dispute resolution mechanism, by type of mechanism
16.4 By 2030, significantly reduce illicit financial and arms flows, strengthen the recovery and return of stolen assets, and combat all forms of organized crime	16.4.1 Total value of inward and outward illicit financial flows (in current United States dollars) 16.4.2 Proportion of seized, found, or surrendered arms whose illicit origin or context has been traced or established by a competent authority in line with international instruments
16.5 Substantially reduce corruption and bribery in all their forms	16.5.1 Proportion of persons who had at least one contact with a public official and who paid a bribe to a public official, or were asked for a bribe by those public officials, during the previous 12 months 16.5.2 Proportion of businesses that had at least one contact with a public official and that paid a bribe to a public official, or were asked for a bribe by those public officials during the previous 12 months
16.6 Develop effective, accountable, and transparent institutions at all levels	16.6.1 Primary government expenditures as a proportion of original approved budget, by sector (or by budget codes or similar) 16.6.2 Proportion of population satisfied with their last experience of public services
16.7 Ensure responsive, inclusive, participatory, and representative decision-making at all levels	16.7.1 Proportions of positions in national and local institutions, including (a) the legislatures; (b) the public service; and (c) the judiciary, compared to national distributions, by sex, age, persons with disabilities, and population groups 16.7.2 Proportion of population who believe decision-making is inclusive and responsive, by sex, age, disability, and population group

Peace, Justice, and Institutions Targets	Indicators
16.8 Broaden and strengthen the participation of developing countries in the institutions of global governance	16.8.1 Proportion of members and voting rights of developing countries in international organizations
16.9 By 2030, provide legal identity for all, including birth registration	16.9.1 Proportion of children under 5 years of age whose births have been registered with a civil authority, by age
16.10 Ensure public access to information and protect fundamental freedoms, in accordance with national legislation and international agreements	16.10.1 Number of verified cases of killing, kidnapping, enforced disappearance, arbitrary detention, and torture of journalists, associated media personnel, trade unionists, and human rights advocates in the previous 12 months 16.10.2 Number of countries that adopt and implement constitutional, statutory, and/or policy guarantees for public access to information
16.a Strengthen relevant national institutions, including through international cooperation, for building capacity at all levels, in particular in developing countries, to prevent violence and combat terrorism and crime	16.a.1 Existence of independent national human rights institutions in compliance with the Paris Principles
16.b Promote and enforce non-discriminatory laws and policies for sustainable development	16.b.1 Proportion of population reporting having personally felt discriminated against or harassed in the previous 12 months on the basis of a ground of discrimination prohibited under international human rights law

The Hidden Politics

This controversial goal includes a wide range of targets that unite the UN's peace and security agenda with UN efforts to promote governance innovations that advance more inclusive and just societies (McDermott et al. 2019). Its sweeping aims to improve practices and outcomes that are subject to national control challenges decision-makers to take concrete actions and embrace reforms. As such, this push to harmonize and align national interests with UN ideals faces numerous political stumbling blocks. Governments in many countries may not have the capacity to adequately act on its assorted targets. Some may also have direct stakes in being highly selective about which targets to prioritize. It is also by no means clear that government actions or inaction are the sole sources of many of the problems this goal seeks to address. Consequently, this goal may raise false hopes and lead to broken dreams. Its targets and indicators direct attention to the need to curtail certain problems and achieve better results, but this drive for peace and good governance remains inattentive to the ways that bad practices and outcomes can empower certain stakeholders and disempower others. The goal has simply not been informed by an adequate analysis of the power relations that shape and constrain its aspirations.

The first target's (16.1) objective to reduce all forms of violence and related death rates everywhere is case in point. Many governments may have an interest in interpreting data related to the associated indicators differently than their citizens do. Trends in the number of victims of intentional homicide, for instance, are necessarily subject to political interpretation (16.1.1). Upward movement in the homicide rate can readily be construed by some as a rationale to empower and weaponize police forces. Others might view this trend as a symptom of social or economic injustice. Notably, an additional indicator on deaths resulting from police violence was not included with this target. Data that detail the proportion of populations that are subject to violence (16.1.3) and that highlight perceptions of public safety (16.1.4) can also be used to bolster calls for higher police budgets. Statistics on violence committed by authorities or their surrogates, and on the contributions that public order forces make to perceptions of safety, are not collected. Furthermore, the call to reduce conflict-related deaths (16.1.2) might draw attention to a vital aspect of the peace agenda, but it remains deficient without an examination of military expenditures or deployments. Warring parties commonly believe that their efforts to procure more arms or hire "independent" military contractors will ultimately reduce conflict-related deaths. The data exclude the interests of those that have a monopoly on violence and are authorized to legally use force. Overall, this target's selective indicators disproportionately empower states and are woefully inattentive to the violence they can perpetrate.

The second target's (16.2) noble intention to end all forms of violence against children is also diminished by weak indicators and an inattentiveness to power dynamics. The indicators included with this target also clearly shrink its broad ambitions to end abuse, exploitation, trafficking, and all forms of violence. The first (16.2.1) focuses only on the proportion of children who have experienced violent or aggressive care at home over the past month. This measure faces serious limitations related to the accuracy and coverage of reporting and excludes all forms of violence that children might have experienced outside of the home. An indicator on the coverage of programs that can empower children to report abuse was not included with this target. Similarly, determining the number of victims of human trafficking by sex, age, and form of exploitation (16.2.2) is incredibly difficult. The data rely on instances where victims have been detected, and enforcement can lag far behind the development of new forms of trafficking. This target lacks indicators related to the investigative and enforcement capacity of antitrafficking agents, or to the number of countries that adopt policies to empower reporting. Moreover, the final indicator (16.2.3) cannot be taken as a unidirectional sign of child and youth empowerment. It focuses only on the proportion of young women and men (ages eighteen to twenty-nine) who experienced sexual violence by the age of eighteen. An array of identity, social, and economic factors can disempower young adults and dissuade them from reporting instances of sexual violence they experienced as children. The exclusion of reports of child sexual violence made by adult and elder victims from the data is a worrying oversight. Concerns related to the persistence and impact of intergenerational trauma stemming from child sexual abuse have simply been omitted from the statistics.

Indicators associated with the third target's aim to promote the rule of law and ensure equal justice for all (16.3) also obscure relevant power dynamics. Each indicator overemphasizes individual interactions with law enforcement and justice systems. At best, they offer a highly indirect guide to knowing about the status of the rule of law, which might not be applicable in some contexts. In countries where governments and other institutions respect the rule of law, sound knowledge about trends in the proportion of victims who file reports of their victimization with competent authorities can be valuable (16.3.1). It can be used to identify persistently unreported crimes and to pursue reforms and programs that encourage greater reporting. However, in many authoritarian countries and in contexts where dubious policing persists, the true extent of unreported crime tends to remain unknown. Victims of organized political, business, or crime networks, or of legal authorities themselves, are not generally forthcoming. As such, this indicator does not capture the true extent of policing problems. In many countries where those challenges are entrenched, data on this topic remain unavailable, and many powerful people have interests in keeping it that way. Indicators related to the existence or effectiveness of independent or third-party police oversight systems could have helped correct this gap. Similarly, the third target's second indicator (16.3.2) is far from adequate. Trends in the proportion of unsentenced detainees in the overall prison population can be used to develop arguments about the effectiveness of criminal justice systems. In countries where courts exist independently of political power, this information can be used to draw attention to the need for legal aid programs, increased resourcing, or the reform of excessively punitive laws. On the other hand, governments at the authoritarian end of the spectrum tend to treat information on unsentenced detainees with the utmost political sensitivity. Secret prisons and the systematic undercounting of unsentenced political detainees persist. It is consequently troubling that this target includes no further indicators related to the oversight of prisons or courts, or to the politicization of justice systems.

Weak indicators also inhibit the fourth target's (16.4) drive to rein in flows of illicit finance and arms, strengthen the recovery of stolen assets, and combat all forms of organized crime. Better data on the total value of inward and outward illicit financial flows (16.4.1) are clearly needed (Cobham and Jansky 2020). The difficulties of tracing and identifying dirty money in the global economy have now been recounted in numerous bestselling books and Hollywood films (Burgis 2020). As data on the true value of illicit flows remain problematic and subject to highly contested methodologies, this target's failure to include other relevant indicators is disturbing. For instance, it is possible to count government efforts to tackle the extractive practices and elaborate corporate structures that enable illicit funds to be siphoned out of some countries and squirreled away elsewhere. Government participation in related international initiatives and attempts to introduce and enforce laws that address known and new criminal practices can be readily tracked. Country-level data on the numbers of prosecutions pursued by type of financial crime could also bolster this target's ambition. As it stands, the only additional indicator included under this target pertains to the proportion of seized, found, or surrendered illicit arms whose origin has been traced or established (16.4.2). While this measure injects a needed focus on conflict-related financing, it too is limiting. For instance, no data are collected on the value of private military companies, or on the ways that their activities can intersect with financial crime or the illicit arms trade (Transparency International UK 2022). Operatives linked with these groups are now involved in numerous countries where the rule of law is in abeyance or coups d'état have recently occurred (Engels 2022). The governance of illicit financial flows requires much more vigilance than a superficial effort to monitor their value.

The subsequent target's (16.5) call for substantial reductions in all forms of corruption and bribery is similarly diminished by poor metrics. Its indicators are attentive only to the proportion of persons (16.5.1) or businesses (16.5.2) that have paid or been asked for a bribe by public officials over the past year. This priority needlessly overemphasizes one side of corrupt transactions. It unjustly erases the contributions that private individuals and corporations make to the persistence of bribery and corruption. Those that willingly pay bribes to advance their interests and corrupt the decisions made by public authorities are never the first in line to report their side of the bargain. Given that data on this topic are systematically underreported, a range of more robust indicators could have been added.

For example, data on the existence of independent anticorruption czars and on the implementation of laws or policy necessary to empower their actions would be informative. So too would statistics on the successful prosecution of bribery and corruption by sector. Knowing if anticorruption agencies or nongovernmental organizations are free to pursue their work, and if robust mechanisms for their participation are in place, could also clarify the picture. The failure to include these and other similar measures of progress under this target empowers individuals with an interest in maintaining corrupt practices. If they keep their lips sealed, the data might show improvements where none in fact exist. The insensitivity of these indicators to power relations is unsettling.

The subsequent target (16.6) on the development of effective, accountable, and transparent institutions exhibits similar failings. Its indicators do not align with its intentions. These indicators consider only government expenditures as a proportion of approved budgets (16.6.1) and the proportion of the population satisfied with their last experience of public services (16.6.2). Both benchmarks now seem remarkably out of place and inappropriate in the aftermath of the COVID-19 pandemic. Effective governments allocated considerable extrabudgetary funds to public health and health care systems during the crisis (Hsu et al. 2022). Simultaneously, the surge of demand for health services and the rapid uptake of virtual public service delivery had an impact on popular perceptions of public services. As such, these indicators are not at all calibrated to account for crisis responses. Out of necessity, effective and transparent governments that face existential external threats often make extrabudgetary allocations and reallocate public service personnel. These actions cannot accurately be characterized as irresponsible. Indicators that are more directly related to transparent and accountable decision-making, such as the existence of independent ombuds that have investigative powers, would have been far more appropriate.

Likewise, the seventh target's (16.7) call for responsive, inclusive, participatory, and representative decision-making is compromised by a failure to acknowledge political reality. This push for better decision-making practices is associated with indicators that overaccentuate social inequities and understate political and economic factors. The proportion of public positions that are held by sex, age, disability status, and population groups in relation to national distributions clearly matters for inclusion (16.7.1). So too does public opinion data on the perceptions of marginalized groups on the status of inclusive decision-making (16.7.2). However, the exclusion of considerations such as party membership or membership in politically aligned fraternal organizations or industry associations is a considerable weakness. Where party and fraternal organization membership are directly or implicitly required to participate in decision-making processes, it makes little sense to focus solely on identity-based perceptions of inclusion or participation. In other words, treating political or economic memberships as considerations that are independent of inclusive and representative decision-making is simply wrongheaded.

The subsequent three targets do not deviate from this trend. The eighth (16.8) merely reiterates ambitions articulated under the sixth target of SDG 10 (10.6) to improve the participation of developing countries in global governance institutions. The political limitations of this push, including its overarching failure to address many global power imbalances, were detailed above under SDG 10. For its part, the ninth target's (16.9) expansive call to provide legal identity for all is more apparent than real. Its only indicator (16.9.1) seeks to motivate birth registration efforts. This orientation to the problem entirely neglects the political barriers and powerful gatekeepers that adults can face when they attempt to acquire valid legal identity documents. On the other hand, the goal's tenth target (16.10) does include indicators that can enable the exercise of unchecked power to be showcased and called out. Aiming to improve public access to information and better protect fundamental freedoms, the first indicator (16.10.1) spotlights verified cases of the extrajudicial killing, kidnapping, enforced disappearance, arbitrary detention, and torture of politically active people. This well-intended measure nonetheless fails to account for the ways that data on this topic remain subject to political manipulation and contestation. Additional indicators that could compensate for this reality are missing. For example, it is possible to evaluate the strength of government commitments to implement the recommendations of the relevant UN special rapporteurs or procedures of the Human Rights Council. The target's only other indicator (16.10.2), on public access to information, compounds its disregard of relevant power relations. The data conflate constitutional guarantees in this area with statutory and policy language that "guarantees" public access to information. This approach creates unnecessary confusion by promoting the perception that nice-sounding policy language can advance this target as readily as hard constitutional rights.

The goal's two implementation targets are also inadequate to the task of reining in unchecked power. At best, they only scratch the surface of the power relations that hold back progress on peace, justice, and strong institutions. The first (16.a) seeks to strengthen the capacity of relevant national institutions. However, its indicator (16.a.1) is attentive only to the operationalization of independent national human rights institutions. This minimalist approach fails to cover the gamut of independent entities that are needed to advance each of the above targets. It also does not speak to the effectiveness of investigative and enforcement efforts. The second implementation target's indicator (16.b.1) is also unnecessarily minimalistic. It filters a call to promote and enforce nondiscriminatory laws (16.b) down to an indicator previously articulated under the third target of SDG 10 (10.3). Bringing an end to instances of personal discrimination or harassment will bolster inclusion and promote justice. But doing so without equal attentiveness to party affiliation, political factions, loyalty, and the intersection of business with politics is a recipe for failure.

Taken together, the vast disconnect between SDG 16's encompassing vision and politically myopic and narrow measures of progress is disturbing. The goal is overly reliant on states themselves to deliver good governance (McDermott et al. 2019). And it erases power relations to the extent that it is oblivious to systemic phenomena that prominently promote conflict, pervert justice, and undermine institutions. The contemporary form of political corruption known as state capture, for instance, might persist even as governments that are captured by private sector interests achieve technical progress on SDG 16. Consequently, this goal is not fit for purpose.

The UN secretary general's review at the SDG midpoint was unambiguous about the ways that new conflicts had obstructed the achievement of SDG 16 (UNSG 2023). While the secretary-general's report also called for concerted action to restore trust in political institutions, its presentation was less than direct about its own political assumptions. As detailed above, this goal for peace, justice, and strong institutions is in fact imbued with an excessively liberal idealism. That said, the goal's idealistic ambitions are anything but universal. Some state-based, nationalist, and local capitalist interests reject the notion that governments need global guidance in many of the areas covered by this goal. Social progressives and greens frame the targets and indicators associated with this goal as meek, timid, and unassertive, *and* they also fight nationalist and capitalist interests that use the cover of sovereignty to oppress or exploit people. From a progressive and green standpoint, SDG 16's weak-kneed liberal intentions will not transform the relations, practices, and crises that have stoked the decline of trust in public institutions and political authority in many countries.

References

Burgis, T. 2020. *Kleptopia: How Dirty Money Is Conquering the World*. London: William Collins.

Cobham, A., and P. Jansky. 2020. *Estimating Illicit Financial Flows: A Critical Guide to the Data, Methodologies, and Findings*. Oxford: Oxford University Press.

Engels, B. 2022. "Transition Now? Another *coup d'état* in Burkina Faso." *Review of African Political Economy* 49, 172.

Hsu, J., H. Barroy, R. Allen, and F.S. Rahim. 2022. "Extra-Budgetary Funds for COVID-19: Evidence from Two Years of Implementation." *IMF Blog*, November 9. blog-pfm.imf.org/en/pfmblog/2022/11/extra-budgetary-funds-for-COVID-19-evidence-from-two-years-of-implementation.

McDermott, C.L., E. Acheampong, A. Jonsson, et al. 2019. "SDG 16: Peace, Justice and Strong Institutions — A Political Ecology Perspective." In *Sustainable Development Goals: Their Impacts on Forests and People*, edited by P. Katila, C.J.P. Colfer, W. de Jong, et al. Cambridge: Cambridge University Press.

Transparency International UK. 2022. "US Private Military and Security Companies Fuel Corruption and Conflict Risk." Press release, August 9. transparency.org.uk/us-private-military-and-security-companies-fuel-corruption-and-conflict-risk.

UN (United Nations). 2020. *Peace, Justice and Strong Institutions: Why It Matters*.

———. 2022. *The Sustainable Development Goals Report 2022*. New York: UN.

———. 2023. "Goal 16: Promote Just, Peaceful and Inclusive Societies." un.org/sustainabledevelopment/peace-justice.

UNSG (United Nations Secretary-General). 2023. *Progress towards the Sustainable Development Goals: Towards a Rescue Plan for People and Planet. Report of the Secretary-General (Special Edition)*. New York: United Nations General Assembly and Economic and Social Council.

Goal 17
Partnerships for the Goals

What They Tell Us

> **Mission statement:** Strengthen the means of implementation and revitalize the global partnership for sustainable development.

The 2030 Agenda is universal, and all countries must act to ensure that no one is left behind (UN 2020). Success will require more than the steady yet fragile government support for implementing the Global Goals that we have seen to date. Specifically, strong partnerships between governments, the private sector, and civil society are an absolute must (UN 2023). Multistakeholder partnerships can help us overcome persistent challenges, including scarce financial resources, trade tensions, and lack of crucial data. They can also help us leverage interlinkages between the goals and accelerate overall progress. Only by working effectively and collaboratively can we realize the promise of the 2030 Agenda. Building back better from the pandemic and rescuing the SDGs will necessitate a full-scale transformation of the global economy. International cooperation must be urgently scaled up (UN 2022, 60). Stronger partnerships at all levels can help put us back on track. Individuals should join or create groups in their local communities that seek to mobilize action on the implementation of the Global Goals. They should also encourage their governments to partner with business, and engage with the SDG Partnership Platform to inform, educate, network, and be inspired. The High-Level Political Forum on Sustainable Development continues to take stock of gaps and emerging issues and to make recommendations on corrective actions. Without stronger partnerships, our efforts will assuredly fall short (UN 2020).

Partnership Targets	Indicators
Finance	
17.1 Strengthen domestic resource mobilization, including through international support to developing countries, to improve domestic capacity for tax and other revenue collection	17.1.1 Total government revenue as a proportion of GDP, by source 17.1.2 Proportion of domestic budget funded by domestic taxes
17.2 Developed countries to implement fully their official development assistance commitments, including the commitment by many developed countries to achieve the target of 0.7 per cent of ODA/GNI to developing countries and 0.15 to 0.20 per cent of ODA/GNI to least developed countries; ODA providers are encouraged to consider setting a target to provide at least 0.20 per cent of ODA/GNI to least developed countries	17.2.1 Net official development assistance, total and to least developed countries, as a proportion of the Organization for Economic Cooperation and Development (OECD) Development Assistance Committee donors' gross national income (GNI)
17.3 Mobilize additional financial resources for developing countries from multiple sources	17.3.1 Additional financial resources mobilized for developing countries from multiple sources 17.3.2 Volume of remittances (in United States dollars) as a proportion of total GDP
17.4 Assist developing countries in attaining long-term debt sustainability through coordinated policies aimed at fostering debt financing, debt relief and debt restructuring, as appropriate, and address the external debt of highly indebted poor countries to reduce debt distress	17.4.1 Debt service as a proportion of exports of goods and services
17.5 Adopt and implement investment promotion regimes for least developed countries	17.5.1 Number of countries that adopt and implement investment promotion regimes for developing countries, including the least developed countries
Technology	
17.6 Enhance North-South, South-South, and triangular regional and international cooperation on and access to science, technology, and innovation and enhance knowledge-sharing on mutually agreed terms, including through improved coordination among existing mechanisms, in particular at the United Nations level, and through a global technology facilitation mechanism	17.6.1 Fixed Internet broadband subscriptions per 100 inhabitants, by speed
17.7 Promote the development, transfer, dissemination, and diffusion of environmentally sound technologies to developing countries on favourable terms, including on concessional and preferential terms, as mutually agreed	17.7.1 Total amount of funding for developing countries to promote the development, transfer, dissemination, and diffusion of environmentally sound technologies

Partnership Targets	Indicators
17.8 Fully operationalize the technology bank and science, technology, and innovation capacity-building mechanism for least developed countries by 2017 and enhance the use of enabling technology, in particular information and communications technology	17.8.1 Proportion of individuals using the Internet
Capacity-building	
17.9 Enhance international support for implementing effective and targeted capacity-building in developing countries to support national plans to implement all the Sustainable Development Goals, including through North-South, South-South, and triangular cooperation	17.9.1 Dollar value of financial and technical assistance (including through North-South, South-South, and triangular cooperation) committed to developing countries
Trade	
17.10 Promote a universal, rules-based, open, non-discriminatory, and equitable multilateral trading system under the World Trade Organization, including through the conclusion of negotiations under its Doha Development Agenda	17.10.1 Worldwide weighted tariff-average
17.11 Significantly increase the exports of developing countries, in particular with a view to doubling the least developed countries' share of global exports by 2020	17.11.1 Developing countries' and least developed countries' share of global exports
17.12 Realize timely implementation of duty-free and quota-free market access on a lasting basis for all least developed countries, consistent with World Trade Organization decisions, including by ensuring that preferential rules of origin applicable to imports from least developed countries are transparent and simple, and contribute to facilitating market access	17.12.1 Weighted average tariffs faced by developing countries, least developed countries and small island developing States
Systemic Issues	
Policy and institutional coherence	
17.13 Enhance global macroeconomic stability, including through policy coordination and policy coherence	17.13.1 Macroeconomic Dashboard
17.14 Enhance policy coherence for sustainable development	17.14.1 Number of countries with mechanisms in place to enhance policy coherence of sustainable development
17.15 Respect each country's policy space and leadership to establish and implement policies for poverty eradication and sustainable development	17.15.1 Extent of use of country-owned results frameworks and planning tools by providers of development cooperation

Partnership Targets	Indicators
Multi-stakeholder partnerships	
17.16 Enhance the Global Partnership for Sustainable Development, complemented by multi-stakeholder partnerships that mobilize and share knowledge, expertise, technology, and financial resources, to support the achievement of the Sustainable Development Goals in all countries, in particular developing countries	17.16.1 Number of countries reporting progress in multi-stakeholder development effectiveness monitoring frameworks that support the achievement of the Sustainable Development Goals
17.17 Encourage and promote effective public, public-private, and civil society partnerships, building on the experience and resourcing strategies of partnerships	17.17.1 Amount in United States dollars committed to public-private partnerships for infrastructure
Data, monitoring, and accountability	
17.18 By 2020, enhance capacity-building support to developing countries, including for least developed countries and small island developing States, to increase significantly the availability of high-quality, timely, and reliable data disaggregated by income, gender, age, race, ethnicity, migratory status, disability, geographic location, and other characteristics relevant in national contexts	17.18.1 Statistical capacity indicator for Sustainable Development Goal monitoring 17.18.2 Number of countries that have national statistical legislation that complies with the Fundamental Principles of Official Statistics 17.18.3 Number of countries with a national statistical plan that is fully funded and under implementation, by source of funding
17.19 By 2030, build on existing initiatives to develop measurements of progress on sustainable development that complement gross domestic product, and support statistical capacity-building in developing countries	17.19.1 Dollar value of all resources made available to strengthen statistical capacity in developing countries 17.19.2 Proportion of countries that (a) have conducted at least one population and housing census in the last 10 years; and (b) have achieved 100 per cent birth registration and 80 per cent death registration

The Hidden Politics

Multistakeholder partnerships in support of the 2030 Agenda can be defined as voluntary, collaborative, and institutionalized relationships in which participants interact to achieve common ends (Beisheim and Simon 2018). SDG 17 links the attainment of the Global Goals directly to a global drive to expand multistakeholder partnerships. Consequently, it seeks to normalize the idea that responsibility for progress on the Global Goals is broadly shared (Sondermann and Ulbert 2021). Within the UN system, this perspective has become the new conventional wisdom (Galbraith 1958). According to this political viewpoint, states and the interstate, international system do not command the power necessary to achieve the 2030 Agenda on their own. Many development practitioners find this position acceptable and convenient. It implicitly recognizes the rise of transborder networks of development expertise and advocacy in global governance. Moreover, it acknowledges the fact that states and international organizations have ceded some rule-making authority and governance functions to multistakeholder partnerships. The consistent invocation of the need for partnerships to support the goals has created a new development orthodoxy. SDG 17 has entrenched this position in the development landscape.

Efforts to unpack the politics of partnerships and redress their asymmetries face serious obstacles. Many who work on the SDGs have vested interests in the success of various partnerships that intersect with their areas of responsibility, expertise, or practice. Unselfish work that aims to advance the SDG targets does not exist independently of the reality that partnerships can also directly benefit individual participants. They can create opportunities for further employment, consultancies, board positions, junkets, or other material and reputational privileges that accrue to insiders. Affiliates and collaborators in particular networks might therefore have direct stakes in advancing specific partnerships. And there is no necessary connection between the prominent, well-resourced partnerships that benefit well-heeled cliques and the partnerships that are the most inclusive or effective in relation to the SDG targets.

The heart of the matter is that responsibility for progress on the 2030 Agenda is effectively outsourced to many varieties of multistakeholder partnerships. SDG 17 empowers these initiatives but includes no mechanisms to account for the ways that partnerships can compete with or overrun each other. Research suggests that the effectiveness of partnerships working on the same topics can widely diverge (Sneyd 2011). They can be driven by different assessments of the underlying problem and advance contradictory strategies. Correspondingly, well-resourced partnerships with more minimalist ambitions can exist alongside underfunded but more comprehensive and potentially impactful partnerships. In other words, empowered partnerships can create path dependencies and underperform. They can also overwhelm approaches that might more readily expedite progress towards the goals. Sadly, targets under SDG 17 are not associated with any indicators that assess the impact of power imbalances between or within partnerships.

This omission is exceptionally glaring considering the widespread failure of a range of multistakeholder partnerships to perform as initially planned (Beisheim and Simon 2018). Many partnerships in support of the goals have not been driven by bottom-up participation and inclusion and have not developed strong links to local communities or civil society organizations (Ansell et al. 2022). Multilevel partnerships might facilitate the implementation of strategies to address the interrelated, multifaceted, and hypercomplex challenges identified in the 2030 Agenda (Duane et al. 2022). Yet evidence from a study of the over 4,500 partnerships registered on the UN's SDG Partnership Platform suggests that these partnerships may also perpetuate power asymmetries (Blicharska et al. 2021). Specifically, the disproportionate participation of individuals from high-income countries in partnerships might not be advancing the needs or priorities of countries in the Global South. According to Blicharska et al. (2021), developed countries have dominated the largest SDG partnerships and tended to prioritize economic growth under SDG 8 and other growth-related SDG targets. The unequal global distribution of participation in partnerships exacerbates preexisting power imbalances in the international political economy. Where or when partnerships do not elevate less powerful voices or fail to respect local preferences for actions that decentre growth, old development divides can readily be recreated. Additional research on partnerships confirms the need for all SDG stakeholders to be more attentive to relations of empowerment and disempowerment (Scheyvens and Cheer 2022).

It is consequently noteworthy that the finance-related targets under SDG 17 do not explicitly prioritize global partnerships and exude a dated top-down approach to development finance. The first target's (17.1) call to strengthen domestic resource mobilization, for instance, underscores a need for developed countries to provide capacity-building support to bolster tax and revenue collection in developing countries. This framing imposes a domestic orientation on a transnational challenge that requires local capacity *and* global solutions. No additional language was included in the target on the need for donor governments to empower global partnerships that aim to stop tax avoidance. Partnerships that seek to rein in corporate practices including profit shifting, transfer pricing, and the use of shell corporations, trusts, and offshore tax havens could clearly have a big impact on domestic resource mobilization. Until these partnerships gain traction, capacity-building support will have limited impacts on rates of domestic taxation or government revenues as a proportion of GDP in many developing countries. The second target's (17.2) plea for developed countries to fully implement their official development assistance commitments is similarly constrained. It includes no language on the global partnerships that aim to strengthen the effectiveness of foreign aid, or on the rise of new financial partnerships that might supplant foreign aid. This framing weds the target to the old development assistance architecture and problematically assumes that higher aid flows will necessarily advance all aspects of the 2030 Agenda fully and equally. To say the least, the notion that more aid can advance sustainable development is highly contested (Riddell 2014).

The third target's (17.3) push to mobilize additional financial resources from multiple sources for developing countries similarly fails to consider power asymmetries. This target seemingly encourages developing countries to rely increasingly on debt-based infrastructure development partnerships and on seasonal migration for overseas employment. Its indicators are attentive only to net flows of financial resources and foreign direct investment (17.3.1) and to the volume of remittances (17.3.2). As such, the target simply assumes that more financial resources and more remittances are desirable. It disappears the ways that creditors can benefit from providing development finance to their clients and erases the reality that indebted states can become beholden to the interests of foreign creditors. The target includes no language whatsoever related to other potential downsides or risks of a big push for additional financial resources, such as capital flight or perpetual indebtedness. This framing also ignores the political reality that greater reliance on state-based and private sector creditors might not expedite progress on all other SDGs equally, or even at all. Here, the reality that creditors or development "partners" can use the power of the purse to influence policy has been entirely disregarded.

The unrealistic assumption that all creditors are beneficent and equally committed to assisting developing countries infuses the subsequent target's (17.4) emphasis on debt sustainability. Its sole indicator focuses only on debt service payments as a proportion of exports (17.4.1). Data on interest and principal payments in relation to foreign exchange earnings can certainly showcase instances where development finance has become overly reliant on debt. But this sliver of information only scratches the surface of the relevant power relations. Creditors can have direct stakes in perpetuating excessive indebtedness, especially when their investment partnership agreements stipulate terms that favour their interests in the event of credit defaults. Moreover, so-called vulture funds and other bottom feeders that invest in distressed debt products have interests that run counter to debt sustainability and to the realization of the 2030 Agenda. Yet this target includes no indicators related to their avaricious activities or to the ways that debt-based investment partnerships can entrench asymmetries.

The fifth finance-related target (17.5) exudes unrealistic faith in the potential for investment promotion partnerships to advance the Global Goals. Its indicator (17.5.1) is attentive only to the number of countries that adopt and implement such regimes in developing and least developed countries. Bilateral investment treaties between developed and developing countries can promote investments in the latter when they include investment guarantees and offer financial support or other incentives for outward investments (Our World in Data team 2023). That said, developed countries often have stronger negotiating capacities and can leverage the power imbalance to yield partnership agreements with terms more favourable to their interests (Vis-Dunbar and Nikiema 2009). These treaties also do not exist independently of investment promotion agencies in developing and least developed countries. Investment promotion agencies exist solely to entice foreign investors, and many countries that rely on these agencies also offer prospective investors tax holidays, water and electricity rebates, and other concessions to facilitate foreign direct investment. Thus, it is striking that this target does not include any indicators related to the broader dimensions of investment promotion and partnerships in developing countries. The incentives that poorer countries offer foreign investors can have considerable ramifications for state capacity and for the realization of the SDGs.

The three technology-related partnership targets also suffer from weak indicators and a lack of political realism. The sixth target's (17.6) aim to enhance international cooperation on access to science, technology, and innovation on mutually agreed terms is commendable. Mechanisms to facilitate global flows of technology nonetheless remain subject to deadly serious national and private sector interests and to patents, licences, and other forms of monopoly power. Consequently, the associated indicator's (17.6.1) sole focus on fixed broadband subscriptions per 100 inhabitants by speed is at best troubling. This narrow metric is a woefully inadequate measure of the success of development partnerships in this area. Reflecting the overly individualist lens of the 2030 Agenda, it has skewed data collection efforts away from other relevant barriers to international cooperation. For example, data are not collected on the transfer from developed to developing countries of proprietary technologies that are essential to the production of capital goods. Statistics on this politically sensitive topic would offer a much more robust barometer of global scientific and technological partnerships for development.

The subsequent technology target's (17.7) concern with promoting the development, transfer, dissemination, and diffusion of environmentally sound technologies to developing countries on favourable terms is also admirable. But it too suffers from an indicator that is only weakly connected to these laudable aims (Our World in Data team 2023). At present, data under this target only showcase trends in the value of exports and imports of environmentally sound technologies (17.7.1). They do not speak to the transfer, dissemination, and diffusion of these technologies on favourable, concessional, or preferential terms. Furthermore, data on the dumping of antiquated and environmentally unsound technologies on developing countries are not collected. The final technology-related partnership target (17.8) is similarly deficient. It reiterates commitments that development partners have made to operationalizing a technology bank and a capacity-building mechanism for the least developed countries. But the sole indicator of progress on these worthy partnerships is baffling: the proportion of individuals using the Internet (17.8.1). To address the ongoing climate emergency, science, technology, and innovation partnerships for development must inevitably be about much more than Internet connectivity.

The partnership goal's ninth target (17.9), focused on capacity building, advances a dated view of development partnerships and is also inattentive to the power and interests of donor governments. Its call for greater international support for developing countries to implement the SDGs is nonetheless warranted. Efforts to scale up the provision of financial and technical assistance to developing countries could contribute to building the capacity necessary to implement their national plans. That said, technical cooperation disbursements can be prone to the same kinds of top-down dynamics that undermine the effectiveness of foreign aid. When governments disburse official funds for the further education and training of foreign officials, for example, donor priorities do not magically disappear. The training and programs that beneficiaries participate in or are subjected to do not necessarily align with national priorities and can readily reflect donor interests. The associated indicator (17.9.1) fails to heed these political realities and power dynamics. It simply encourages efforts to track the value of financial and technical assistance disbursements. Moreover, this limited metric advances an out-of-date view of partnerships. Official technical cooperation is not the sole path to building capacity to achieve the SDGs. Many private sector, philanthropic, and multistakeholder partnerships for the Global Goals make serious contributions to the development of local capacity. Here, again, is a striking mismatch between the target's ambitions and the underlying indicator.

The three trade-related partnership goals suffer similar shortcomings. They reiterate long-standing minimalist priorities related to trade liberalization and the greater inclusion of developing countries in the world trading system (17.11 and 17.12). As such, they are infused with liberal ideas about the need for more trade and for global trade governance that is rules-based, open, nondiscriminatory, and equitable (17.10). Remarkably, these ambitions are not associated with any indicators related to the climate footprint of global trade. Likewise, the targets and indicators do not acknowledge the deleterious impacts that trade in certain goods and services can have on life on land or life under water. The underlying political perspective is consequently crystal clear. These targets problematically assume that trade will drive economic growth and thus advance the 2030 Agenda. However, even if this assumption is taken as given, the indicators associated with the trade-related partnership targets are lamentably inadequate. They overemphasize the importance of tariff reduction for developing countries (17.10.1 and 17.12.1) and underplay the need for developed countries to reduce nontariff barriers to trade. They also inflate the relevance of efforts to increase the proportion of exports from the least developed countries in world trade (17.11.1) and obscure the significance of what those countries sell to the world. Many developing countries continue to depend inordinately on the export of raw commodities (Sneyd 2011). Selling more raw materials in a world of reduced tariffs might advance their SDG aspirations to a limited extent. But that eventuality would not end their impoverishing dependence on commodity exports or address any of the social and environmental externalities linked to this status. Trade partnerships that enable the least developed countries to export cleaner and more remunerative value-added products would make more robust contributions to the Global Goals. However, SDG 17 includes no language on that broader, more consequential ambition.

The next three partnership targets related to policy and institutional coherence also radiate exceedingly minimalist aspirations and obscure consequential power dynamics and trade-offs with other SDGs. For example, the target related to efforts to enhance macroeconomic stability (17.13) simply encourages governments to focus on the standard range of macroeconomic performance indicators. Among others, these include inflation, trade, the balance of payments, public sector indebtedness, GDP, and unemployment. This emphasis on old-fashioned understandings of macroeconomic stability is at the very least distressing. It conceals the political reality that the pursuit of macroeconomic stability is now associated with the amplification of the global climate emergency and the entrenchment of greater inequality. By encouraging governments to focus on traditional understandings of stability, and not on new indicators of economic performance that are better attuned to the footprint of "stable" economies, this target is a recipe for the underperformance of other SDGs. Had a new suite of indicators for sustainable and inclusive economic performance been included with this target, it could have also contributed to the subsequent target's aim to enhance policy coherence for sustainable development.

The objective of ensuring that government commitments, initiatives, and practices do not serve contrary purposes in relation to sustainable development (17.14) is as necessary as it is elusive. As is evident above, many of the SDG 17 targets include language that masks instances of policy incoherence. The policies that many powerful development "partners" pursue and worked to build into the 2030 Agenda may not be coherent with the achievement of sustainable development in many developing countries. Yet this target does not focus on the evident incoherence between what more powerful partners would like to see and the policies necessary to achieve the SDGs in particular countries. It focuses solely on the domestic level of analysis and on the mechanisms that individual countries have in place to enhance the coherence of their own policies (17.14.1). This orientation leaves some of the biggest contradictions and trade-offs at the heart of the 2030 Agenda untouched, and masks international and global sources of contradictory policies related to growth, inequality, and the climate emergency.

The final target (17.15) related to policy and institutional coherence encourages governments to respect the leadership of other countries over their own sustainable development policies. In the aftermath of the repeated failure of top-down boilerplate development policies, the notion that developing and least developed countries should enjoy greater autonomy over their policy choices has entered the mainstream. Even so, the indicator (17.15.1) associated with this target exudes a dated view of development partnerships. It is concerned only with the extent to which donors make use of results frameworks and planning tools that recipients have developed autonomously. This narrow take on policy space and local leadership detracts attention from the ways that broader economic partnerships and agreements can diminish the capacity of states to make autonomous decisions. Partnerships for infrastructure and other investment agreements, for instance, can include clauses that reduce the space that governments have to pursue their own sustainable development policies. In some cases, these might rule out the introduction of "buy local" provisions or other measures that could be linked with the realization of social or environmental objectives contained in the SDGs. Where or when preexisting economic agreements constrain the capacity of governments to independently pursue their own sustainable development policies, policy incoherence can flourish. Thus, this target's engagement with the policy space and local leadership challenge is at best superficial. The target focuses exclusively on these imperatives in relation to the old development assistance architecture. Furthermore, it does not acknowledge that past agreements create path dependencies that can readily constrain the autonomous pursuit of sustainable development in the present. This target's failure to offer any guidance whatsoever related to the power that past decisions and commitments can exercise over the capacity of states to develop autonomous policies for the Global Goals is disquieting. On a topic of such importance and consequence, national and international officials could reasonably be expected to devote much more thought and attention to this challenge.

The sixteenth target (17.16) suffers similar shortcomings. It explicitly encourages the development of multistakeholder partnerships that mobilize knowledge, expertise, technology, and financial resources to support the Global Goals. As such, this target encapsulates the new development orthodoxy that animates SDG 17. Its language empowers individuals and organizations that have the means necessary to collaborate across borders, sectors, and disciplines to advance the goals (Murphy and Stott 2021). This viewpoint is woefully inattentive to the range of power asymmetries associated with partnerships discussed above (Blicharska et al. 2021). The sole indicator (17.16.1) associated with this target further obscures relations of empowerment and disempowerment within and between partnerships and between their participants and nonparticipants. It simply urges governments to report on their progress in creating frameworks to monitor development effectiveness that involve the participation of multiple types of stakeholders. At first glance, encouraging states to work with other stakeholders to monitor the effectiveness of collaborative initiatives in support of national SDG plans might seem promising. But this orientation assumes away the political interests that stakeholders often have in prioritizing particular goals or specific courses of action that advance their own individual or organizational objectives. It also fails to acknowledge the fact that different partnerships — even those that nominally support the same goal — can pursue contrary objectives and generate political conflict. Moreover, multistakeholder partnerships that do not explicitly focus on the SDGs exude similar dynamics that could have considerable consequences for the 2030 Agenda (Sneyd 2011). This target's failure to include an indicator that mandates the independent monitoring and evaluation of power asymmetries and political conflicts associated with all types of multistakeholder development partnerships is revealing. It showcases just how entrenched unsubstantiated belief in the benevolence of nonstate actors has become within the UN system.

To those ends, the goal's seventeenth target (17.17) seeks to encourage and promote public, public-private, and civil society partnerships. Despite this seemingly encompassing language, the target is forthright about the UN's increasing orientation towards the private sector (Hustad 2022). Its only indicator (17.17.1) encourages governments to track the value of funds committed to the development of public-private partnerships for infrastructure. As detailed above under SDG 9 and elsewhere in this book, infrastructure development partnerships tend to pose stark environmental challenges, generate inequality, and exacerbate the climate emergency (Bebbington et al. 2018). Consequently, this target underscores the massive contradiction at the core of the 2030 Agenda that stems from its animating commitment to the pursuit of economic growth.

The final two targets under SDG 17 aim to build partnerships that will bolster statistical capacity in developing countries. The former (17.18) calls for capacity building to support the production of high-quality, timely, and reliable data. In so doing, this target accentuates another political priority at the centre of efforts to realize the 2030 Agenda. International and national officials consider indicators of progress towards the SDGs to be of paramount political importance. Despite the serious limitations and shortcomings of each individual indicator detailed above, in official development circles, the belief persists that SDG actions must be "data-driven." This conviction is so powerful that the target was associated with three distinct progress indicators. The first (17.18.1) draws attention to a range of subindicators of national statistical capacity to monitor the SDGs. In other words, it calls for more effective global oversight of national statistical capacity. To those ends, the second indicator (17.18.2) spotlights the number of countries with national legislation that complies with the fundamental principles of official statistics. The final indicator (17.18.3) underlines the funding status of national statistics plans, by the source of funds. Even if each of these indicators were taken seriously enough to generate meaningful progress, there are few reasons to believe that this eventuality would expedite progress towards many of the other Global Goals. *Official statistical indicators that purport to showcase SDG progress do not necessarily have any connection to veritable progress on the 2030 Agenda's targets and goals.* In many cases, much more can be learned about advances on the goals, or the lack thereof, from what the official indicators do not specify. Given the analyses presented in each chapter of this book, this target can fairly and appropriately be described as fundamentally political. Its developers may have had noble intentions, but in relation to the 2030 Agenda, this target encapsulates the triumph of belief in statistics over the fact that the underlying metrics are not fit for purpose. In this light, the final target's (17.19) call for more resources to strengthen statistical capacity to measure progress on sustainable development is necessary but not sufficient.

The UN secretary-general's review at the SDG midpoint noted that progress on this goal was at best mixed. The secretary-general's report highlighted some successes related to development assistance and remittances, and explicitly called out shortcomings in international cooperation that it linked to a rise of geopolitical tensions and nationalism (UNSG 2023). As such, the report implied that nationalism had become a problem for the development of viable global partnerships. This admission was unsurprising. As shown above, SDG 17 advances the new liberal orthodoxy that wide-ranging multistakeholder partnerships are needed to ensure the resilience of the international economic order. It exudes an idealistic faith in the power of partnerships within the current growth-driven and profit-oriented order to deliver on the 2030 Agenda. This political orientation is certainly not unopposed. Despite the inclusion of language that notably endorses national autonomy in SDG 17, right-wing populists and nationalists have baselessly characterized many of this goal's components as international and global overreach. Social progressives and greens challenge the goal's liberal confidence in international cooperation *and* resist the power and interests that nativist, populist, and nationalist politicians reliably advance. Greens and progressives ultimately aim to transform the narratives and practices that animate global partnerships to empower previously marginalized peoples and make peace with the nonhuman world.

References

Ansell, C., E. Sørensen, and J. Torfing. 2022. *Co-Creation for Sustainability: The UN SDGs and The Power of Local Partnerships*. Bingley, UK: Emerald Publishing.

Bebbington, A.J., D.H. Bebbington, L.A. Sauls, et al. 2018. "Resource Extraction and Infrastructure Threaten Forest Cover and Community Rights." *PNAS* 115, 52.

Beisheim, M., and N. Simon. 2018. "Multistakeholder Partnerships and the SDGs: Actors' Views on Metagovernance." *Global Governance* 24, 4.

Blicharska, M, C. Teutschbein, and R.J. Smithers. 2021. "SDG Partnerships May Perpetuate the Global North-South Divide." *Nature: Scientific Reports* 11.

Duane, S., C. Domegan, and B. Bunting. 2022. "Partnering for UN SDG #17: A Social Marketing Partnership Model to Scale Up and Accelerate Change." *Journal of Social Marketing* 12, 1.

Galbraith, J.K. 1958. *The Affluent Society*. Boston: Houghton Mifflin.

Hustad, O. 2021. "From Global Goal to Local Development Policy: How Partnerships as a Policy Idea Changes Through Policy Translation." *Development Policy Review* 41, 2.

Murphy, D.F., and L. Stott. 2021. "Partnerships for the Sustainable Development Goals (SDGs)." *Sustainability* 13, 2.

Our World in Data team. 2023. "Revitalize the Global Partnership for Sustainable Development." ourworldindata.org/sdgs/global-partnerships.

Riddell, R. 2014. *Does Foreign Aid Really Work?* Development Policy Centre Discussion Paper No. 33. Oxford: Oxford Policy Management.

Scheyvens, R., and J.M. Cheer. 2022. "Tourism, the SDGs and Partnerships." *Journal of Sustainable Tourism* 30, 10.

Sneyd, A. 2011. *Governing Cotton: Globalization and Poverty in Africa*. Basingstoke, UK: Palgrave Macmillan.

Sondermann, E., and C. Ulbert. 2021. "Transformation Through 'Meaningful' Partnership? SDG 17 as Metagovernance Norm and Its Global Health Implementation." *Politics and Governance* 9, 1.

UN (United Nations). 2020. *Partnerships: Why It Matters*. un.org/sustainabledevelopment/wp-content/uploads/2019/07/17_Why-It-Matters-2020.pdf.

————. 2022. *The Sustainable Development Goals Report 2022*. New York: UN.

————. 2023. "Goal 17: Revitalize the Global Partnership for Sustainable Development." un.org/sustainabledevelopment/globalpartnerships.

UNSG (United Nations Secretary-General). 2023. *Progress towards the Sustainable Development Goals: Towards a Rescue Plan for People and Planet. Report of the Secretary-General (Special Edition)*. New York: United Nations General Assembly and Economic and Social Council.

Vis-Dunbar, D., and H.S. Nikiema. 2009. "Do Bilateral Investment Treaties Lead to More Foreign Investment?" *International Institute for Sustainable Development*, April 30. iisd.org/itn/en/2009/04/30/do-bilateral-investment-treaties-lead-to-more-foreign-investment.

Conclusions

This book presents an original critique of the SDGs. To do so, I employed a strategy first utilized by Ha-Joon Chang and Ilene Grabel (2004) to juxtapose mainstream viewpoints with a scholarly analysis. Each chapter includes a section — "What They Tell Us" — that presents the goal, mission statement, targets, indicators, and relevant UN progress assessments. This approach to stringing together the pertinent official phrasing enables the SDGs to be read for what they are: nonbinding proclamations with universal pretensions. This technique also spotlights the overarching importance of language, discourse, and persuasion to the 2030 Agenda. After all, the SDGs are not associated with any enforcement mechanisms or legal arrangements, and ultimately rely on national-level political engagement and uptake (Dalby et al. 2019).

The subsequent section in each chapter — "The Hidden Politics" — offers a critical analysis that sharply contrasts with the idealistic and supposedly robust approaches that the UN tells us about. These analytical sections are driven by this book's primary research question. By asking in what ways, if any, the goals, targets, and indicators are inattentive to political factors, ideas, conflicts, and power relations, these sections showcase the hidden politics of the SDGs. Taken together, they expose a yawning gap between the 2030 Agenda's idealistic intentions and the SDG indicators of progress. Moreover, these analyses contradict and challenge the veracity of the powerful narrative that the goals are a "data-driven" exercise. Indicator by indicator, the political economy analyses presented in this book document statistical inadequacies and gaps in the data that purport to indicate progress towards the SDGs. In many cases, the indicators are at best indifferent to political factors, ideas, conflicts, and power relations that could have consequential impacts on the success of the SDG project. Thus, the content of these sections challenges scholars, policy- and decision-makers, corporations, nongovernmental organizations, global citizens, and other development stakeholders to think more critically about how progress on the 2030 Agenda is measured.

My effort in this book to identify the limitations of the SDG project and reveal the political deficiencies of its indicators is itself subject to political interpretation and potential misreading. Like all scholarship on political problems, this effort to stand back from politics in order analyze it does not exist in a political vacuum. The perspective offered in this book may be critical and analytical, but powerful people who are not politically disinterested have big stakes in its content. Viewpoints on the world order have not remained static since the goals were agreed upon in 2015 at the highwater mark of Obama-era idealism. The SDGs are imbued with universal, global, and liberal affectations that today are less broadly shared than they once were. Liberal visions that aim to maintain or modestly reform the global order now contend with vociferous nationalist and populist views that oppose any initiative that can be portrayed as too "globalist" or "elitist" in origin or orientation. In this starkly divided political context, progressives and ecologists who push for transformative change must now wage peace and social and environmental justice on two difficult fronts. They must challenge the forces that have aligned in support of system maintenance, and they must also confront the emerging agents of reaction. The rise of new, assertive, and radically different viewpoints on ordering the world has subjected the content of the SDGs to greater political contestation. Consequently, this book does not simply assume away emerging political conflicts over the goals. It offers its readers entry points to think more deeply about the politics that shapes and constrains efforts to build a more inclusive and genuinely sustainable future.

The concluding paragraphs of each chapter above reiterate the UN's sombre progress assessments and elaborate contrasting interpretations of the liberal content of each goal. They also accentuate the political challenges that the 2030 Agenda *and* the rise of populism and nationalism pose for progressive and ecological points of view. It is now abundantly clear that the big push for the SDGs to shape the limits of what is politically possible or desirable in the current world order no longer stands above domestic politics. Reforms that intend to bolster the liberal international economic order are now fiercely contested in many countries. In some cases, this politicization has become so strident that nationalists, in their rush to critique so-called globalist ideas, have overlooked the true nature of the 2030 Agenda (Worthington 2018). As this book has shown, the Global Goals are embedded with liberal orthodoxies related to the maximization of individual rights and freedoms and the pursuit of economic growth. Consequently, the goals are aligned with greater reliance on global finance, freer world trade, and higher flows of foreign direct investment and development assistance. They also stress the new orthodoxy that governments must partner with corporate actors to deliver on this global agenda. These pro-capitalist components of the SDG project offer direct evidence that refutes the spurious idea that the goals radiate an encompassing left-wing agenda. In the post-Brexit and post-Trump era, even idealistic initiatives that aim to entrench capital accumulation now must contend with incendiary and often wrongheaded populist critiques (Drache and Froese 2022).

Green and progressive voices increasingly challenge the liberalism of the SDGs *and* the right-wing populist surge. Their viewpoints on the failure of the goals to advance a transformative vision for a more equal world economy cannot merely be dismissed as pie in the sky. The issues that progressive and green intellectuals and change-makers give voice to draw our attention to a yawning gap between the purported ends of the SDG project and the means that governments and international organizations are employing to achieve the goals. A diverse range of progressive and green intellectuals, politicians, organizations, movements, and activists now call for the transformation of the 2030 Agenda. In the wake of the problematic 2023 UN Climate Change Conference — an event that welcomed 2,456 industry-affiliated fossil fuel lobbyists directly into the negotiations venue — the views of greens and ecologists must also be taken much more seriously (Lakhani 2023). Many scientific and research-based perspectives on the goals that are cited in this book conclude that the SDGs are not aligned with the rapid achievement of more robust ecosystem health and the prevention of planetary collapse. SDG supporters might argue that their critics on the left are striving for perfection and risk becoming enemies of a project that seeks to do "good." But that hypothetical knee-jerk defence of the SDGs is about as political as it can get.

Simply put, if we desire a fairer and greener world, more attention must be paid to the politics that now envelops the 2030 Agenda. A collaborative and transnational effort to analyze the political perspectives that compete to shape the world order is called for. What regular people can reasonably expect from their governments, the global economy, and the world order is arguably more hotly contested today than at any time since Robert W. Cox (1979) applied his analytical lens to situate and re-present the politics of global ordering in the 1970s. In this book, I primarily analyze the politics of the 2030 Agenda on its own terms. But I also show how a range of perspectives on global ordering and governance have informed and challenged the limits of this political project. There is now a clear need for new tools that enable us to better comprehend political divides and alignments related to global governance, sustainability, and development. Such analyses could be used to identify the perspectives that are holding back the realization of a more inclusive and greener world order.

This book's political economy analysis of the goals, targets, and indicators, and of the broader politics that animates and holds back the SDGs, makes several contributions to the critical development studies literature. It provides concrete, goal-by-goal evidence to support Clive Gabay and Suzan Ilcan's (2017) claim that the SDGs treat political problems as technical matters. This technocratic orientation obscures the political factors, ideas, conflicts, and power relations that can advance the goals or hold them back. As such, the 2030 Agenda is not well tuned for the present moment of enhanced political conflict over the future direction of the global order. This finding also counters Lars Niklasson's (2019) view that the SDGs can be best characterized as a collaborative effort in global learning, or a policy of continuous improvement. The SDG project's overarching aversion to engaging with or even acknowledging the scale of the relevant political challenges does not reflect a desire to "learn" or to "continuously improve." Rather, this reluctance demonstrates just how thoroughgoing the liberal and technocratic assumptions of its most stringent backers have been. If learning had been front and centre over the past years, global conversations about the politics of the first principles or basic propositions associated with the means and ends of the goals would have been much more robust. The goals now face political headwinds that many of its politically inattentive advocates failed to anticipate.

This book also adds to the rigorous work that Magdalena Bexell and Kristina Jönsson (2021) have done to assess the politics of the SDGs. Bexell and Jönsson understand the SDGs to be political insofar as they are the result of political negotiations and can be realized only through the actions of political institutions. Their comprehensive approach emphasizes numerous political challenges associated with implementing the goals. Specifically, they home in on concerns related to legitimacy in the translation of the goals from the global level to national contexts. They also spotlight questions of responsibility and accountability in relation to local and global implementation efforts. As such, Bexell and Jönsson offer a conceptually driven account of the political problems that work against the realization of the 2030 Agenda on its own terms. Their diligent and meticulous treatment of these dimensions of politics should be commended. That said, their research to date has not engaged with the underlying "hidden" politics of the goals, targets, and indicators. Their analysis also did not foreground the rise of political perspectives that challenge the international order that the SDG project seeks to consolidate. As such, the analysis of the SDGs presented in this book starts where the detailed empirical efforts of Bexell and Jönsson left off. It reveals the political limitations of each target and the associated indicators and speaks directly to emerging political conflicts beyond SDG-related implementation processes.

The analysis presented above also challenges left-leaning and reform-oriented scholars and practitioners to attend more closely to politics and power relations at the international and global levels. Over the past years, researchers and practitioners have articulated many new prescriptions for institutional reform to address the challenges that the new global political climate poses for international cooperation. Of these, Kevin P. Gallagher and Richard Kozul-Wright's (2022) *The Case for a New Bretton Woods* stands out. In it, the authors comprehensively sketch an alternative future that they claim would advance long-standing aspirations for economic development and expedite the reform of global institutions. They seek to improve the international monetary and financial system, reform the global trade and investment regime, and catalyze development finance. Despite the evident strengths of their program, Gallagher and Kozul-Wright present it without substantively engaging with the political perspectives that now compete to order the world. They articulate their agenda for reform without due consideration of nationalist forces that believe global governance to be an abomination. The authors also largely disregard the perspectives of those who seek to truly transform the world order to advance equality and avert planetary crises. When experts do not fully consider the politics that intersects with their own analyses or prescriptions for change, they can inadvertently contribute to amplifying political problems. And when they are indirect about the political interests their analyses can serve, or when they fail to be forthright about their political assumptions, they can become political in ways that they do not necessarily intend.

I have attempted to avoid such pitfalls in this book. Standing back from a powerful political agenda to assess it directly and situate it in relation to contemporary global politics is never an apolitical exercise (Sneyd 2019). Recognizing that reality, I have endeavoured to be as analytical as possible in my assessment of the politics of the SDG targets and indicators. I have also tried to include the full range of political perspectives that now contest the SDGs. That said, as a political analyst, I can never fully escape my own assumptions and convictions. And if these are not already crystal clear, I should note that the analysis above strongly suggests that progressive and green critics of the SDGs have a point. In my estimation, they are on the right side of history.

The political myopia of the 2030 Agenda, and the political inadequacies of the targets and indicators that have been associated with its goals, require a course correction. Governments around the world have devoted consider-able resources to developing their own SDG governance frameworks and implementation strategies. The hard work that civil servants, corporate employees, and representatives of nongovernmental and charitable organizations have done to support the Global Goals has also not been misguided. But these new governance approaches and public engagements have been saturated with political perspectives that have skewed priorities. Even in the highly unlikely scenario that many goals were achieved by 2030, it is doubtful that this improbable result would advance the Brundtland Commission's original understanding of sustainable development. Whether or not the goals are achieved, unsustainable consumption will continue to compromise the ability of future generations to meet their own needs. Consequently, this book concludes that it is time for a fundamental rethink of the 2030 Agenda. The SDGs have not been properly calibrated for the critical juncture we now face in the global order and will require a full overhaul — not a simple tune-up.

Without the necessary redesign, moving forward, the SDG project could itself become a political liability. Those that support the Global Goals now must contend with the reality that their ambitions are not universally shared. Nationalist voices in many countries are making concerted attempts to reduce the domestic impact of global ideas related to sustainable develop-ment and disempower international institutions. SDG supporters also face a growing backlash among progressives and environmentalists who aim to transform the world order. As these reactions intensify, it is by no means clear that those that promote the goals command the power or political willingness necessary to achieve them. Rethinking the SDGs will require simultaneous attention to accommodating demands for a new global order. In the aftermath of the August 2023 BRICS Summit held in Johannesburg, there is no doubt that increasing numbers of developing countries are committed to resetting international cooperation and global institutions. Progressive activism in support of renewing the NIEO, or New International Economic Order, and building a movement that unifies nations and global citizens in a drive for global justice is also gaining traction. So too are global movements for climate action and planetary justice.

The UN platform for the follow-up and review of the 2030 Agenda cannot dismiss or ignore the extent of the challenges that these trends pose. The High-Level Political Forum on Sustainable Development now presides over woefully deficient SDG implementation architecture, but faces an unprecedented opportunity to renew the relevance of sustainable development. It could exercise its leadership and facilitate new conversations that aim to correct the deficiencies of SDG indicators, eliminate political contradictions between SDG targets, and revamp the content of the goals to better align them with the new political climate.

The High-Level Political Forum could also encourage governments to engage in the stakeholder consultations necessary to ensure that the overhaul does not simply replicate past political problems. But I'm not holding my breath. The forum has become a vehicle for the dissemination of SDG-related propaganda that aims to consolidate the legitimacy of the project. I, for one, would like to think that a so-called political forum worthy of the name would at least make space for critical conversations about its own politics. For now, however, shortcomings and possible course corrections do not appear in the political declarations that the High-Level Political Forum adopts annually. Until that day comes, Sustainable Development Reports that purport to assess global progress towards the goals (see Sachs et al. 2022) will continue to reflect all the inadequacies and disorder detailed above.

That said, I see at least one reason to be hopeful that the triumph of flash and dazzle over the substance of sustainable development could be fleeting. A powerful constellation of forces now seeks to inject the 2030 Agenda with a dose of political reality. While this amalgamation is replete with contradictions and potential threats, hope can be found in its potential to stimulate critical dialogue on the governance innovations necessary to expedite development that is truly sustainable. To get there, as this book strongly suggests, empowered and privileged sustainable development practitioners must become more politically attentive, engaged, and accommodating. They must rethink the wrongheaded notion that indicator-driven SDG implementation is apolitical and somehow stands above political contestation. And they must recognize and act to redress the political orientation and limitations of the SDGs themselves. Hopefully this book can contribute in its own small way to the needed reset as the global movement for social and environmental justice continues to challenge the UN to deliver more for people and the planet.

References

Bexell, M., and K. Jönsson. 2021. *The Politics of the Sustainable Development Goals: Legitimacy, Responsibility, and Accountability*. London: Routledge.

Chang, H.-J., and I. Grabel. 2004. *Reclaiming Development: An Alternative Economic Policy Manual*. London: Zed Books.

Cox, R.W. 1979. "Ideologies and the New International Economic Order: Reflections on Some Recent Literature." *International Organization* 33, 2.

Dalby, S., S. Horton, and R. Mahon. 2019. "Global Governance Challenges in Achieving the Sustainable Development Goals." In *Achieving the Sustainable Development Goals: Global Governance Challenges*, edited by S. Dalby, S. Horton, R. Mahon, and Diana Thomaz. London: Routledge.

Drache, D., and M. Froese. 2022. *Has Populism Won? The War on Liberal Democracy*. Toronto: ECW Press.

Gabay, C., and S. Ilcan (2017). "Leaving No-One Behind? The Politics of Destination in the 2030 Sustainable Development Goals." In *The Politics of Destination in the 2030 Sustainable Development Goals: Leaving No-One Behind?*, edited by C. Gabay and S. Ilcan. London: Routledge.

Gallagher, K.P., and R. Kozul-Wright. 2022. *The Case for a New Bretton Woods*. Cambridge: Polity Press.

Lakhani, N. 2023. "Record Number of Fossil Fuel Activists Get Access to COP28 Climate Talks." *The Guardian*, December 5. theguardian.com/environment/2023/dec/05/record-number-of-fossil-fuel-lobbyists-get-access-to-cop28-climate-talks.

Niklasson, L. 2019. *Improving the Sustainable Development Goals: Strategies and the Governance Challenge*. London: Routledge.

Sachs, J.D., G. Lafortune, C. Kroll, et al. 2022. *Sustainable Development Report 2022; From Crisis to Sustainable Development: The SDGs as Roadmap to 2030 and Beyond*. Cambridge: Cambridge University Press.

Sneyd, A. 2019. *Politics Rules: Power, Globalization, and Development*. Black Point, NS: Fernwood Publishing and Practical Action.

Worthington, S. 2018. "Populist Nationalism Threatens Progress on the Sustainable Development Goals." *InterAction*, September 18. interaction.org/blog/populist-nationalism-threatens-progress-on-sustainable-development-goals-but-ngo-community-can-be-the-difference.

Acknowledgements

Dr. Lauren Sneyd lived and breathed the political shortcomings of the SDGs with me as I endeavoured to piece together this analysis. Her perseverance and efforts to keep me fuelled and fired up made this book possible. So too did Errol Sharpe and the Fernwood team. Errol's faith in this project and his consistent engagement with me about my orientation sharpened the analysis and refined the presentation significantly. All errors are of course mine and mine alone, but without Errol's guidance, this book would not have held together. To those ends, award-winning copy editor Erin Seatter used her eagle eyes to magically rework the text, and she also made the editorial process lively and fun. At Fernwood, Lauren Jeanneau and Anu Gokhale were an absolute joy to work with. John van der Woude's amazing cover image is an interpretation of the SDG wheel logo with a crystal-clear message: "In case of emergency, break glass." I also feel blessed that James Schneider found the time to pen the foreword for this book around his serious responsibilities and skyrocketing career at the Progressive International. James can communicate in very few words what it can take mealy-mouthed academics like me pages (or even books!) to articulate. Colleagues in Canada and around the world also gave me some great feedback on specific chapters and on the overall analysis. I would particularly like to thank the two anonymous reviewers who took the time to engage with earlier drafts of the manuscript. Many friends within and beyond political science and development studies also offered encouraging words on this project. Their encouragement provided comfort and kept me going as I encountered and engaged with all the political problems detailed above.

Index

A

absolute deprivation, 13, 17
accountability, 61
action plans, 114, *See also* national
  planning
adaptation, 120, 121
affordability, 57, 65
agenda-setting, 95–96
agricultural research, 25
agroecology, 25
Aid for Trade, 78–79
Anthropocene, 119
antidiscrimination
  limits of, 49–50
antioppression, 50
anticorruption, 148–149
asterisk, 118
ATMs, 78
austerity, 94
authoritarian regimes, 15

B

bad indicators, 165
bezzle, 36
biodiversity loss, 86, 125, 134, 137, 139
blue economy, 131
boomers, 95
brain drain, 44–45, 86
Bretton Woods Institutions, 95
bribery, 148–149
Brundtland Commission, 75, 110

C

Canada, 121
capacity-building, 122, 123, 161
capacity development, 61

carbon dioxide, 1
carbon emissions, 128
carbon intensity, 85
Chang, Ha-Joon, 9, 168
chemical waste, 112
China, 69
circular economy, 108
civil society, 111
clean energy, 64, 68–69
climate action, 119
climate change, 3, 59
climate emergency, 18
climate footprint of trade, 162
coffee, 114
commodity markets, 26– 27
commodity dependence, 162
communicable diseases, 32–33
communities, 99
conflict-related deaths, 146
conservation, 129–130, 134, 136, 139
constitutions, 121, 150
consumption, 7, 75, 110
conventional wisdom, 156
cooking, 67
COVID-19 pandemic, 1, 31
corporate interests, 70
corporate lobbying, 35, 60
corporate power, 62
corruption, 148–149
counterpower, 4
countervail, 5
course instructors, 10
Cox, Robert W., 6, 170
creditors, 159
crises, 1, 2–4

critical thinking, 43–44, 114–115
critical juncture, 173
cronies, 102
cultural heritage, 103

D

data, 24–25, 34–35, 165, 168
debt, 78, 101, 159
decent work, 72, 76
decentralization, 57, 141
decision-making, 149–150
decolonization, 103, 136
deficient definitions, 83
desertification, 138
devolution, 121
disasters, 16, 103–104, 120
discrimination, 42, 49, 93
disempowerment, 17
disruption, 3, 42
Dubai, 119
dynamism, 23

E

economic diversification, 88
economic enclaves, 131
economic stability, 162
ecological footprint, 104–105, 112
ecosystem health, 24, 60, 119, 125, 128, 132, 136, 170
education, 38, 122
electricity, 64
emergency food provision, 22
empowered women, 52
energy efficiency, 68
enforcement, 138
entitlement, 52
environmental regulations, 35
equity-seeking groups, 94
European Union, 138
exclusive economic zones, 128
extrabudgetary allocations, 149
extrajudicial killings, 150

F

fair-trade, 114
fair washing, 113
false equivalencies, 58
fatal attacks, 143
federated states, 121
financial services, 16

financial mobilization, 25, 122
financialization, 94
fiscal policy, 94–95
fishing, 125, 128–129, *See also* subsidies and sustainable fisheries
flag-waving jingoists, 43
food system, 22–23, 105
food waste, 112
forced labour, 77
foreign direct investment, 70
forests, 136, *See also* sustainable forest management
Forest Stewardship Council, 138
forever chemicals, 112–113
for-profit education, 40
fossil fuels, 68, 70, 115
fraud, 36
freedom, 7
freshwater withdrawals, 59
functionalist, 42

G

gender equality, 43, 47
gentrification, 103
gig economy, 77
global citizens, 43–44, 122
global elite, 9
global food crisis, 20
global ordering 5
good governance, 145
Grabel, Ilene, 9, 168
Gramsci, Antonio, 2
green cement, 83
Green Climate Fund, 122
green growth, 75, 77
green space, 105
greenhouse gas, 117, 121
greenwashing, 113
growth ideology, 72, 74, 76, 115, 158

H

harmful practices, 50–51
hazardous chemicals, 35, 112
health systems, 29, 34
high-income earners, 92
Holocene, 1
human trafficking, 77, 146
hunger, 20
hydropower, 67–68, 69

I

ideologies, 9
illegal logging, 137
illegal wildlife trade, 140
illicit arms, 148
illicit financial flows, 148
implementation, 132
impoverishment, 17
inclusion, 84
income-centric, 14
incomes, 23
independent human rights institutions, 151
independent verification, 137–138
Indigenous Peoples, 43, 57, 93, 103, 140
Indonesia, 138
industry, 81
inequalities, 57, 90
infrastructure, 81, 83, 159, 165
informal settlements, 15
informal work, 77
ICT skills, 42
innovation, 81
institutions, 26, 149
investment promotion, 160

J

K

L

land
    access, 83
    intensification, 85, 102, 103
    rights, 15, 84
landlords, 101
learning, 171
legitimacy, 5
liberalism, 5, 19, 169
liberal international
    economic order, 6, 170
lifestyles, 110, 122
lobbying, 60

M

malnutrition, 22–23
marine pollution, 127
material footprint, 75, 111
maternal mortality, 32

megaprojects, 87
metals boom, 122–123
migration, 86, 96
military contractors, 146
minimalist, 5
mobile money, 78
modern energy, 66
modern slavery, 77
monitoring, 57
mortality, 33–34
motorcycle taxis, 102
multidimensional approach, 22
multistakeholder partnerships, 156–158

N

national appropriateness, 15, 51, 123
national planning, 111, 120
nationalist thinking, 87, 169
natural resources, 111
New Deal, 76
New International Economic Order, 3–4, 6–7, 173
net zero, 117
Nile Basin, 60
nonformal further training, 41
nonhuman species, 86

O

ocean acidification, 128
ocean-based extraction, 127
Official Development Assistance, 26, 61, 87, 97, 158, 161
offsets, 115
offshore tax havens, 158
oil, 69
oil-producing regions, 121
organic cotton, 24
organic standards, 114
organized crime, 147
orthodoxy, 164, *See also* conventional wisdom
outlier target, 130
overclaiming, 130, *See also* WTO

P

Paris Agreement, 122
partnerships, 153, *See also* multistakeholder partnerships
party affiliation, 149–150, 151
patents, 35, 87

path dependencies, 163
Plumpy'Nut peanut paste, 22
police, 146, 147
policy coherence, 162–163
policy failure, 15
policy shrinkage, 53, 130–131, 136
policy space, 163
political prisoners, 147
political will, 16
pollution, 64
poorly defined terminology, 65
populism, 169–170
poverty, 12
    dimensions of, 14
power imbalances, 96, 150, 157–158
power relations, 146
pre-primary education, 41
privatization, 61
privilege, 52
process and production methods, 86
productivity, 12, 17–18, 23
Progressive International, 7, 176
propaganda, 51
pro-poor spending, 16–17
protected areas, 129, 139
protection rents, 101
public education, 40
public procurement, 114
public relations, 51, 111, 113
public safety, 146

 Q

 R

racialized people, 93
rare earth elements, 122–123
raw materials, 162
rebrand, 67
recycling, 113
redesign, 10
redistribution, 92, 94, 97
reef blasting, 86
regulation, 115, See also
reliability, 66
renewables, 66–67
representation, 95
reproductive rights, 52–53
resilience, 16, 24, 117, 120

resource efficiency, 75
resource extraction, 85
responsibility, 110, 111, 118
rethink, 10, 173
right-wing populism, 9
rule of law, 147
rural roads, 83

 S

Saito, Kohei, 8
sanitation, 58
scholarships, 44
school feeding, 44
scientific research, 86
short-termism, 120
slum upgrades, 101
small-scale farming, 24
social policy, 76
socialist, 7
sovereignty, 15
stakeholders, 83, 111, 123, 145
standards, 24, 66, See also independent
    verification
state capture, 151
statistics, 165, See also SDG indicators
Stockholm Convention, 112
subsidies, 130
success stories, 17
sustainable agriculture, 24–25
sustainable food systems, 110
sustainable forest management, 136–138
sustainable fisheries, 131
sustainable tourism, 77–78, 110
sustainability reports, 113–114
SDG indicators, 165, See also bad
    indicators
SDG project, 7, 164, 172
sweatshops, 84
system maintenance bias, 97–98

T

tariff reduction, 96–97, 162
taxation, 92, 94
tax avoidance, 158
technical cooperation, 161
technologies, 25, 53, 68, 75, 86, 131, 160–161
technologist viewpoint, 110
temperatures, 1
terminology, 22

Theranos, 36
topsoil degradation, 120, 139
torture, 150
trade, 26
traditional economies, 17
traditional knowledge 131
transboundary cooperation, 59
transformative, 5, 7

 U

ultra-processed foods, 23
unbanked, 17
union-busting, 77
unitary states, 121
unpaid work, 51–52
unsustainable practices, 113
UN-ese, 69
UNFCCC, 118–119
UN Secretary-General, 9, 18, 27, 36, 45,
    53–54, 70, 88, 97, 106, 115, 123, 132, 141,
    151, 165
United States, 69
urban development, 99
urban planning, 99
user fees, 57

V

vaccine apartheid, 32
value, 51–52
value addition, 88
value chains, 85
violence against children, 146
violence against women, 50
voluntary national reviews, 51
voting shares, 95
vulnerability, 16

W

waste management, 104, 108
wasteful consumption, 115
Waring, Marilyn, 51
watch dogs, 51
water access, 15, 55, 56
water quality, 59
wealth inequality, 92–93
whistleblowers, 51
women's empowerment, 52
workplace sustainability, 74
World Central Kitchen, 104
world ordering, 8

World Trade Organization, 79, 130, 161 *See also* overclaiming
world system, 2–3

 X

 Y

youth, 76

 Z